GOOD GUYS, BAD GUYS

GOOD GUYS, BAD GUYS

Violent Crime and Psychiatry's Dilemma

MARTIN LUBIN, M.D.
as told to PHYLLIS COE

McGRAW-HILL BOOK COMPANY

New York   St. Louis   San Francisco
Toronto   Hamburg   Mexico

1 2 3 4 5 6 7 8 9 D O D O 8 7 6 5 4 3 2 1

ISBN 0-07-038913-6

LIBRARY OF CONGRESS CATALOGING IN PUBLICATION DATA

Lubin, Martin.
Good guys, bad guys.
Includes index.
1. Insanity—Jurisprudence—United States.
2. Insane, Criminal and dangerous—United States.
3. Forensic psychiatry—United States.   I. Coe,
Phyllis.   II. Title.
KF9242.L8   345.73'04   81-12329
ISBN 0-07-038913-6   347.3054   AACR2

Book design by Roberta Rezk.

*Persons associated with each of the cases discussed in this book
have been generally given pseudonyms to disguise their identities.
Locations and times and circumstances have also been changed
to mask the individuals involved in these matters.*

Contents

Prologue

In 1977, I was a consultant on the Son of Sam case, first for the police and later as a psychiatrist for the defense. My years in forensic psychiatry had given me extensive exposure to the criminally insane and their crimes, but I had not seen a more dramatic example of how vulnerable the public was to a madman with a plan. Never was there such an extreme confusion of good and bad in one psychotic. The court's handling of his case reflected it.

On the one hand, there were indications that David Berkowitz, the so-called Son of Sam, had been insane when he killed his victims and was entitled to defend himself by claiming insanity at his trial. On the other, he was so willful, vicious and organized in his murders that our criminal justice system could not bring itself to allow a conventional application of the law. An incompetent, delusional defendant wanted to go to prison to preach and the court accommodated him. The case exposed the weaknesses of the experts, institutions and laws we depend on to protect us from dangerous men.

GOOD GUYS, BAD GUYS

Son of Sam made me feel that I must write the book I had determined to do when a friend of mine disappeared fourteen years ago. I will tell Dr. Holden's story, for I can date my uneasy discovery of the illusions we have about order and safety in our lives from that time.

Al Holden was co-chief with me on the Psychiatric Prison Ward, N,O-2, at Bellevue Hospital. Our function there was a typical one in forensic psychiatry. This specialty has to do with situations in which psychiatric and legal considerations merge. It has applications in civil law, generally around the issue of someone's capacity to care for himself or his property. In criminal law, it deals mainly with two questions—whether a defendant was sane (criminally responsible) at the time that a crime was committed and, more frequently, whether he is competent to stand trial. On N,O-2, our job, Holden's and mine, was to evaluate prisoners solely for the latter issue of competency— could a man understand what was happening, assist his attorney and adequately take part in his own defense?

The laws governing competency for trial were designed to help the good guys. By good guys, I mean those with significant mental illness—or sometimes retardation—who were inadvertently involved in crimes because of their impaired judgment. Our aim was to cull these deserving individuals from the rest and divert them from jail to be treated in a hospital. In many instances, but not in all, the charges against them were terminated with their mental hospital commitment.

If the good guys went to the hospital, then the opportunists, bad guys, would try to do the same, to get there by faking mental illness and avoiding their criminal charges. We tried to stop them. The decisions we made were uncomfortable and dangerous because the prisoners saw us as judges of their fate. Threats against our lives seemed to go with the job.

Psychiatrists don't usually make judgments about good and bad, but it became a frame of reference for me then and later. When I refer to good guys and bad guys throughout this book, it is in the sense of my work on N,O-2. (If the reader finds his own good or bad guys in the story of disillusion with the system, I am not averse to that.)

At that stage of my professional life, on the prison ward, I dealt with competency for trial. Later, as an expert forensic witness testifying in the courts, I would be dealing for the most part with the issue of criminal responsibility which involves the insanity defense.

The much-misunderstood insanity defense operates according to a formula. Its essentials are that the mentally ill person did not know what he was doing or could not tell the rightness or the wrongness of his act. If a jury finds that he was not criminally responsible, then the violent act is not considered a crime. He is found "not guilty by reason of insanity" (NGRI) and usually is sent to a mental hospital, to be released when he is well.

After leaving the prison ward, at the end of the sixties, I was able to observe crime and criminal justice from other perspectives. Working in community psychiatry, and as a consultant to a major welfare center, I saw helpless ex-mental patients dumped in the city and forced to live with predators, addicts and ex-cons, in the notorious single room occupancy (SRO) hotels. This particular substrate grew into a frightening environment. A decade later, Mayor Koch of New York would refer to it as "a climate of fear."

In another way, I witnessed the breakdown of the criminal justice system in the courts during all the years I testified as an expert. The courts were packed, detention centers overflowed, and the misuse of the new "due process" protections delayed cases and forced plea bargains. People didn't serve time: crime after crime was committed with relative impunity. In 1981, the situation is worse than ever. Daily headlines shock us: "Ninety Percent of Felony Arrests Do Not Lead to State Prison" or "Mayor Says Criminal Justice Stinks!" The Mayor of the City of New York actually went on TV to warn people not to wear their jewelry outside their homes. Unarmed teenagers who call themselves Guardian Angels patrol the subways and are welcomed as protectors by commuters. Everywhere, crime has constricted our lives.

This city is only one example. Violence has reached out from large cities to small ones and to rural areas that once seemed safe. Crime is escalating across the country and the most disturbing phenomenon is the appearance of a new kind of criminal, the random killer, whose wantonly brutal crimes have no conventional motive. On the highways, there are drivers who pull alongside another car and blast away at any occupant. In the cities, policemen are shot for asking pedestrians to turn down a radio or put out a cigarette in a no smoking area. Strangers slash at people walking down the street. Subway riders stand well back from the edge of the platform in fear of the random hand in the crowd that will reach out and push them over.

There is no defense against this kind of crime. The killers must be vicious or insane or both.

To most people, these acts suggest that there are more and more psychotically violent individuals among us. Mental health professionals had long rejected the idea that the mentally ill committed more crimes than the average person. They are less sure today because there are so many confusing aspects to the problem. A liberal legal and treatment philosophy has released many former mental patients in the community. They are too visible on the streets, with too much publicity about their frequent need for police assistance. Their involvement with random crimes is rarely provable because such crimes often go unsolved, but the phrase "ex-mental patient" appears with ominous regularity in newspaper reports of criminal acts. We still don't know if, as a group, they have become more criminal or violent.

I have a particular concern with the growth of violence in the mentally ill. Son of Sam was obsessed with the news media, and I have seen more and more individuals who perverted material from television and movies to construct the pattern and rationale for their bizarre crimes. These observations raise a new question that goes beyond the conventional debate about whether violence on TV breeds violence in Americans. We may now have to go further and focus on whether and *how* TV violence impels mentally unstable individuals to commit crimes. Does it make some mad people mad and bad?

In the past, not enough was done to alert the public to the peril of publicized violence. My consciousness of such violence and the insights from early years of work in prisons, welfare hotels and criminal courts would be reason enough to write. Yet the precipitant was Alan Holden and the final catalyst was Son of Sam. One was a victim, I believe, and the other a killer typical of this new kind of criminal. Both images intrude on our consciousness today. As the space between a sudden killer and ourselves as victims narrows, we feel more at risk.

My book deals with cases and situations I encountered. The results of what I saw then affect us all now because we are living with past mistakes. I do see a hope of change as we grow more knowledgeable and less accepting of plans and policies made without public safety as a factor.

POLICE DEPARTMENT
City of New York

ALAN HOLDEN

Missing from his residence
1199 Park Avenue, New York, N.Y.
since 7:00 A.M., July 3, 1967.

Description: W-M-36-6'3",
180 lbs., slim build, sallow complexion,
brown hair and eyes, clothing unknown.

Subject reported missing in 23d Precinct.
Any information please call the Missing Persons
Unit, Canal 6-2000, or notify nearest police officer.

1 | The Ghost of Alan Holden

Alan Holden may be dead or alive, but he is certainly missing. This man, whose desk was inches from mine in our office and with whom I shared a boat and a summer cottage, has not been seen or heard from in fourteen years. In 1979, *The New York Times* published its last article still wondering, "Whatever Happened to Dr. Holden?"

I was vacationing in Florida on July 6, 1967, when I received a long-distance call. The chairman of the department of psychiatry at Bellevue Hospital, my boss, asked me, "Where is Holden?" As co-chief of the prison ward, Al was in charge during my absence. "We can't find him. He didn't come in to work after July 3."

If a workaholic like Al hadn't come in, something serious had happened to him.

I asked about the police and was told that the detectives of the Twenty-third Precinct, in which Al lived, were investigating his disappearance. They had been through his apartment, cleaned everything out and returned all his effects to his family. Missing Persons was circulating the description

1

of Al used in this chapter. It was standard operating procedure all the way—but nothing was happening.

On the flight back to New York, I thought about Al's recent behavior. Reliable, yes, and conscientious, but for the past few months, not at his best. Considering our kind of treadmill, he was entitled to a little goofing off and I hadn't thought that he might be in trouble.

There was one immediate answer to his disappearance and some part of me believed it. We were always aware of the possibility that one of us might die (or disappear) because we were threatened by resistant men we sent to jail or to state hospitals. When I thought of appeals, indeterminate sentences in jail and the lack of security in the hospitals we supplied, I knew that sooner rather than later, angry men we sent away would be out on the street again. I remembered awkward moments when I sensed danger while interviewing prisoners. Al in particular had a cool, imperious manner that could send out challenging messages to disturbed men. He made them uneasy and skittish; the stiff way he sat in his chair (because of a chronic back condition) made him look judgmental.

Back in New York, I found that there were no new facts. The police search of Al's apartment had provided evidence only of an interrupted life: food in the refrigerator, dishes in the sink, an untouched newspaper for the day he disappeared. They found a bankbook and small change in his bedroom, sports clothes and luggage in his closet. Al could have gone out on an errand, but his tan car was still parked around the corner. Was he forced out? Or did someone get him on the street?

A social worker on the ward put our thoughts into words when she said, "You remember the thing about the doctor who was killed in his own apartment by a hospital patient? Al talked about that a lot."

I didn't have to be reminded. Al's disappearance was the climax of a long series of violent crimes at Bellevue. First there was a rash of burglaries and robberies that began with the high admission rates for addicts. Then nurses were raped near the hospital and several psychiatrists assaulted on the wards. My

2

friend Jerry, an OB-GYN resident, was shot on duty in the general hospital. In another case, a surgical resident was stabbed. A terrifying incident began right in the Psychiatric Admitting Office. (The office was an old problem and when I did night duty there as a resident I had protested futilely to the Hospital Director that patients came in armed with sticks, knives and lengths of pipe.) On this particular night, a popular senior resident went off duty and was followed out of the hospital by the paranoid patient he had just interviewed. The man stabbed him repeatedly.

Psychiatrists know that their profession can be dangerous, but it's not gut knowledge until a friend gets hurt. In this case, the resident did not die and I had the odd experience of professionally evaluating the man who had stabbed him. I also see my gynecologist friend and he looks none the worse, these years later, for the bullets he took. Only Holden remained a question mark, and the dead-or-alive uncertainty frightened other doctors so much that applicants would not take the open positions on the prison ward. Finally the hospital administration had to draft doctors from their jobs on other wards, assigning them periods of time they had to serve with us.

After a few weeks without results, I began to ask questions of the police. They had not followed the obvious leads. They were less than impressed when I told them about the threats we had received from violent patients, stressing that they had no evidence to suspect homicide, no bloodstained carpet or spent cartridges. It was almost as if we were talking about a missing car.

I asked a sympathetic judge I knew to build a fire under the police. (Judges feel vulnerable too.) He made a few strategic calls that prompted some cooperation. But police interest in Al's case faded rapidly and the riots that broke out in East Harlem that summer forced any detectives who might have kept the case alive into duty in that uptown combat zone.

Though I regularly called the police with new leads and they accepted them, it was clear that no one was actively working on Al's case. If there was going to be any further investigation, I'd have to do it myself.

I couldn't rule out any possibility; he might have been killed, killed himself, been abducted or just walked away. I wanted to think that it was the last possibility and so did the prison staff. We made a case for a deliberate disappearance: Al was in love with Europe, he spoke competent French and German and his camera work was good enough to let him make a living as a photographer. We got some nervous, hopeful laughter out of the idea of Al, a beach nut who could fry for hours, finally getting tan enough on Mediterranean sands, sustained by the money he'd made on stock and silver speculation and his rumored Swiss bank account. Of all the doctors I knew, he was clever enough to do it. His safe deposit box did prove to be empty when his lawyer got the family's permission to open it, and the passport I knew he had was never found. But—there were several serious "buts" to consider. If Al took his money to start a new life, why were months of uncashed paychecks for his work at Bellevue found in his apartment? If he never intended to come back, why didn't he sell his car? And why did someone as nearsighted as Al Holden leave all his eyeglasses behind?

Al's parents had nothing to add. I'd been calling them in a supportive way with suggestions like "Go over his canceled checks," but it was clear that I knew more about his current life than they did.

Okay. There were several directions I could take. He was a bit of a loner and had been gloomy for months. Psychiatrists do get depressed and kill themselves; in fact, we have the highest rate of suicide among physicians. But as I debated the pros and cons with myself, they simply didn't add up to suicide.

He could have been kidnapped. It wasn't so farfetched in that era of routine hijacking and general terrorism. No ransom had been demanded—maybe he was in the hands of a psychotic. I didn't want to think about that one. It seemed easier to go the next step and figure out who might have killed him. Patients had threatened him on the ward and in Commitment Court. Some were in institutions, some were released and it would be a big job to track them down. I kept daily notes, made lists of what I planned to do. As I read those slightly yellowed papers of 1967, scrawled with abrupt notations, most of it comes back to me:

Get list of recently contested commitment hearings involving Al's testimony. I wrote to the directors of the state hospitals, inquiring about specific patients, and built up a file of replies. A few men had been sent away kicking and screaming, but reports from Kings Park and Matteawan State Hospital proved that they were still there. There was a strong possibility from Creedmoor. The man I was asking about had escaped on July 1 with several other patients, overpowering two attendants and taking the keys. He was still at large. I called his description in to the police—July 1, and Al had disappeared on the third! I called in more leads as Manhattan State, Bronx and Rockland sent me information about our ex-patients who were discharged shortly before that July weekend. I had no confidence that these leads would be followed, but what else could I do but inform the police?

List all returned cases from Matteawan Hospital. At the time, Matteawan (for the Criminally Insane) was the only maximum security correctional hospital we used. I wanted a list of the most dangerous men we had sent them.

Rikers Island. List disruptive men who faked mental illness and were transferred to a specific unpleasant place there.

Supreme Court Forensic Clinic. I wanted them to go back to the year before, when Al had worked there. Did anyone remember threats against Holden?

Check with all attorneys. That meant the lawyers who came to our ward, especially Legal Aid.

So-called Muslims. I have three names listed here with the notation *good bets.* That meant they were bad guys and actually not real Muslims. Those we saw at Bellevue were rarely authentic. The real Black Muslims, who might be equally militant against white authority, were disciplined people committed to the abstinent and religious way of life. The others tried to look the part, with shaved heads, skullcaps and single earrings, but they were either psychotic or going along for the ride because of all the Muslim publicity at the time. They were bad news to interview, suddenly blowing up and shouting "Racist!" or threatening. Next, I see a

5

reference, "Call Captain Lynch, mention you know Judge G." That was still the Muslim angle; Lynch must have been a member of the special section set up by the police as a liaison to the Muslim movement. If Al had been "taken out" by a pseudomember of the Brotherhood, then the special section grapevine could have heard something.

At the bottom of that page, I had written another note to myself: "Is it possible to get a list of all the guys released on murder charges, either acquitted or postsentence for the past few months?" I was looking for criminal felony-murder types, but I couldn't get that information.

Next, I followed the jailhouse grapevine on to Ward N,O-2, asking help from the prisoners, taking aside a tough Hispanic for a private conversation.

I said, "Hector, you remember the tall blond doctor, Holden? You know he's not around. Did anybody get to him outside the hospital? Can you find out?"

It was a wild thing to do—and it didn't work out. All the long shots, all the people in distant hospitals who were said to resemble Al—I had sent out fliers with his picture—all the sure-thing hot tips about who did him in came down to nothing.

I knew that I'd have to go into Al's private life. I argued with myself about invading it and searching for a man, who, if he was still alive, might not want to be found. But I had to go on. We who worked with Al cared about his loss but also feared for ourselves! The police were not interested in the case and neither was the hospital. The one thing that was clear in the Holden affair was that we had operated with a false notion of security because we worked for a big, prestigious organization. We realized now that the service we thought so important was not that valued. Nor were we. Because of this belated realization, we *needed* to know what had happened to Al Holden. Again from my yellowing pages, I note these reminders:

Did Al have specific plans for the weekend of July 4?
Call his psychiatrist.
Go over his list of private patients.

I discovered that Al had had a date in the Hamptons on the weekend of July 4. The story was that he wanted to go to bed with some woman but he hadn't made it and a friend added that he had lost out to a smooth internist driving a foreign sports car. No one else had reported seeing Al after that date. Could anger and jealousy have triggered an impulsive act in a man who was already depressed?

Psychiatrists may have their own psychiatrists. I questioned Al's, but he might well have held the analyst off at arm's length just as he had the rest of us, and there was no evidence for suicide or fear of homicide from that source.

Using his diary, I began to make inquiries about his private patients. Al's practice was different from mine. I had a part-time practice in a Park Avenue office where, as a counterpoint to the psychotics on the ward, I saw average urbanites whose problems related to their jobs, marriages or midlife crises. Al's patients were more diverse and difficult. I found that he accommodated those who couldn't pay the usual fees by the conventional method of charging less, but he worked out "deals" with others. The widow of a very famous painter was supposed to have paid for her treatment with one of her husband's pictures. This became part of the Holden mystery because the picture would have been instantly recognizable if found in his apartment. It wasn't there, and the widow had suddenly moved to South America. She seemed typical of the patients who asked for a lot of his time and got it. He had more empathy with difficult people than I would have thought from his generally abrupt, even flinty manner.

Some of his patients were more than difficult. I was able to establish that he'd actually spoken to the police about two different women in the months prior to his disappearance. Both of them had threatened his life and he had recorded one of the threats on tape! Al's office was in his apartment, always a touchy situation. Some years ago, another Bellevue prison ward psychiatrist had avoided death—but not tragedy—in *his* apartment-office. An angry patient seeking him mistakenly killed the psychiatrist's wife instead.

The police had the name of one of the women who had threatened Al. They said they had investigated her. By then we had an idea of what that meant. The general opinion on N,O-2 was that the police had once asked the lady if she had killed Dr. Holden. Years later, when I researched this chapter, Al's sister produced the original tape with its repeated threats and said she didn't think the police had ever listened to it. That seems possible.

The other vengeful female was a very difficult patient who had created such a scene in Al's office that he'd had to call the police to get her out. This incident had occurred only a few months before, in the spring. I checked further and found that she was a woman who had been admitted to Bellevue some years earlier after a spectacular suicide attempt. She'd gone from Bellevue on transfer to more plush surroundings as a patient in a psychiatric facility uptown. Her record told me something else: she liked to threaten psychiatrists.

Call her Laura Delkan. She came onto Bellevue's Ward N-7 (female disturbed) screaming and cursing, immobilized in a wheelchair with arm restraints. With her came a letter of committal from the private psychiatrist who had been treating her for months. He stated that she needed observation and care after an attempt to overdose herself with barbiturates, and that the hospital where she'd been couldn't handle her. Restraints were necessary on admission for this typical N-7 "management problem," who was dirty, disheveled and covered with bruises from her battles.

Two days later, the straps were gone. Laura sat washed, combed, clean and attractive, waiting for the psychiatric evaluation to begin. The woman who emerged when the tranquilizers took hold was a Phi Beta Kappa graduate who had studied in Europe on a scholarship, a tall, lean redhead who worked as a model and was seen in the flashy Broadway mix of show business and mobsters.

The tests Laura took revealed a chaotic background and a superior IQ of 128 which she had not used to attract superior men. For four years, she had been involved with a jealous man who humiliated her. "He had other women. He didn't want me even though I had an abortion for him, even though I tried to be like him and take his personality into myself."

8

I looked over the Bellevue resident's notes. In conversations, he had observed a "constant hysterical tension" and the tests had shown "unfocused hostility directed at herself and the environment." Suspicious and wary, Laura "saw danger everywhere and felt that safety could only be achieved by retaining full control."

After several weeks in Bellevue, she was taken out by her psychiatrist and re-admitted as a patient in the private hospital uptown. She surfaced later, before Al Holden took her on, as the would-be patient of a woman psychiatrist. I contacted that doctor. Her report described their single encounter. It may have begun a few days before Laura's scheduled appointment when someone entered the doctor's office and "rummaged" around. But nothing was taken.

Laura had the last appointment of the day. She was alone in the waiting room for quite a while and was highly nervous when she went in to the doctor, demanding to be taken on as a patient.

"She kept one hand in her purse, as if she had a weapon there," the doctor wrote. "She told me she knew my family, knew where we lived and what we did. She knew my office!"

When the doctor wouldn't accept her as a patient, Laura threatened retaliation against the family.

"I couldn't get her to go," the doctor continued. "I finally made a gesture to go out the door and that broke up the paranoid thing. She began to scream hysterically. 'I won't hurt you! Take me on as a patient!' I said I couldn't. I maneuvered her outside the door and locked it. Outside, she began to pound on it and scream, 'I'll get you if it's the last thing I do!' The pounding finally stopped. But five minutes later, the phone rang. It was Laura, sounding more subdued, and saying, 'You think I'm crazy like all the rest?' "

This woman psychiatrist, who still maintains an office on the Upper East Side of New York, made a sensible effort to avoid a person who was not readily treatable in a private practice situation. Why then did Holden take her on? Two possibilities: she might have presented herself to him as a calm, pretty, intelligent woman. Or, maybe some of the turmoil showed through and he was accepting a challenge. Whatever persona she brought to him was transient. Laura's relations with psychiatrists were apparently violently ambivalent. She sought them out and then attempted to threaten and dominate. The first thing recorded about her when she'd arrived on the disturbed ward several years before was her screaming of "I've been raped by a psychiatrist because I loved another man!"

Of all the leads I found, Laura was the most likely suspect. She could have done it. Al might not have paid much attention to just another threat, but he wasn't on the barred ward at Bellevue. This time he was facing a very disturbed patient in his own home. When he called the police to eject her, she could have repeated the threat she had made to the other psychiatrist: "I'll get you if it's the last thing I do!"

By learning his routine and stalking him, patiently watching his apartment until the right moment came, she could carry out her threat.

Yet she would have needed help to dispose of his body. According to her Bellevue records, Laura was a tall, willowy hundred and ten pounds. Al was six foot three.

I half-remembered a remark he'd made to me about models and mobsters, and thought of Laura's jealous boyfriend. From some other sources, I got an impression that he was Mafia-connected. Could Laura have goaded him into taking care of Al? Disposal of the body, properly weighted, in some lonely upstate lake, would be just another business proceeding.

When I looked for Laura, I didn't find her. One model agency I phoned finally reported that she had gone to Paris on a job—shortly after that July Fourth weekend! Unbelievable. There my luck ran out: no Paris trail, no further connection with the model agency. Laura had vanished.

There are two cryptic notes in my records: "Called Interpol" and "Called French Consulate." Was it about Laura or about Al? I don't remember. One day, when I was very tired of the search, I invented a scenario that Al had run away to Paris and run into Laura there—or even that they'd run away together! For a few moments I thought that was hilarious.

One last flare of excitement came on the morning I looked down a list of men remanded to Rikers Island and saw the name John Delkan. How many Delkans do you know? I've never met any. I was optimistic that this was someone in Laura's family, a relative she might have enlisted to help her dispose of Al.

From Riker's Island, John Delkan had been committed to the mental hospital at Creedmoor. I called and discovered that he was still there, had incontrovertibly been there when Al disappeared.

That was it. I could not say that Laura Delkan had killed Al. I had nothing to support it. And she was certainly out of reach.

More notes, this time for disappearance:

1. He intentionally disturbed his apartment. The money and checks were deliberately left there.

2. No communication with friends, also intentional.

3. When Al's safe deposit box was finally opened, it was empty. Only he could have done that, but when? It might have been done years ago.

4. Where was that damn passport of his? [The Passport Division had been no help.]

A wild card, Al's famous Swiss bank account, did in fact exist. His family finally got some mail addressed to Al from Switzerland and readdressed to them by the post office. They discovered that there was money in the account, presumably from his market speculation, but so little that it was hardly worth the trouble of keeping it there. Had he taken out the rest—if there ever was more?

I was dead tired of so much equivocal "evidence" from all sides and made one definite gesture. For months, as a private ritual, I had been starting Al's dusty car in the Bellevue garage. Now I stopped.

I had lost hope, and something else with it.

Not long after Holden disappeared, I was testifying before Judge M. in the contested commitment of a man I'll call James Clause. Clause began to talk to me, not scream, talk. He looked right at me and calmly told me he was going to get me. I suddenly decided that he might be the one who could do it.

I asked the court stenographer for a copy of the transcript, at least for the pages in which Clause said, "Lubin, you're doing a good job, baby," and "I'm going to get you, I'm going to get you." I sent a copy of the transcript to a friend in the Manhattan DA's office and asked him to hold it, just in case.

My feelings of immortality were in shreds. I was punchy enough to give my boss my resignation. It took a year for Bellevue to find my replacement. That next year was 1968, when all of the prison ward's problems were aggravated. The work was harder than ever but that wasn't the reason for my determination to leave.

Al's case had shown us our vulnerability. We needed a certainty of outcome about him, but never got it. Holden haunts us still.

2 | Bellevue: Prison Ward

A heavy steel door with a small barred grid was the only entrance to Ward N,O-2 from the outside world. It wasn't easy to get on the ward even if you worked there. Every morning, I'd lean close to the grid, shout "On the gate!" and wait for admission. I knew it was noisy inside but Corrections guards were within earshot of the entrance. I'd wait, but in all my years on N,O-2, I never got used to the delay.

To get to my job, I walked across the entrance hall of Bellevue Psychiatric Hospital, then up the main staircase with its grand curve of marble steps that divided and turned again toward the central administrative offices on the second floor. Just in front of the offices a corridor branched right and left. To the right was P,Q-2, the female "quiet" ward that received the ladies from female "disturbed" after they'd been treated with Thorazine. My way, to the left, led down a long stretch of dingy corridor to N,O-2's steel door. You could also reach it by a slow-moving elevator I rarely used. An adjacent elevator opening on the ward itself carried food carts up from the hospital kitchen. One man had made a successful escape by hiding in an empty cart that was being taken down. The Corrections men who patrolled the ward never forgot that escape.

Eventually, they opened the door and I walked into the mid-corridor of the ward. To the right and left were barred steel gates, and just ahead, the blue-uniformed Corrections sergeant at his desk. It was the end of the outside world, the last moment of feeling entirely comfortable, and at the same time, the beginning of my working day. Seeing patients in the doctors' office beyond the O corridor gate on my right would immediately end the nervousness I felt on entering the building. That nervousness had come after Al Holden disappeared.

Ward N,O-2 was really "wards," and its overall shape was a giant U. The two wards where the prisoners were kept, N and O, ran parallel and formed the long sides of the U. The corridor which connected them contained all the staff offices. There were three gates in midcorridor, and two others, one at the entrance to N and one at O. The constant clanging and clashing heard all day long came from the three midcorridor gates. Like canal locks, they moved the traffic from one compartment to another. Any staff member on an interoffice errand was bracketed between gates until the Corrections guard on duty recognized him, opened his gates in proper sequence for the traffic at that moment and let him pass. A patient in transit took precedence over everybody else and we waited until he was safely past the single exit to the outside world. All gates had to be closed immediately after anyone passed through; no two gates could be open at the same time. You might joke about the security—and we did, or we tried to— but we were all in prison on that ward.

The nurses' and the staff psychologist's offices were on the N side of the corridor. On the O side were the doctors and the social workers. Beyond the central reception area was the office where Corrections Warden Koson presided over the homemade "daggers" he had found on his periodic shakedowns of the ward. They were sharpened wood or shards of formica stripped from tables and countertops, effective in the sudden fights that erupted

14

or when hallucinations or despair made men on the wards slash themselves.

The social workers' room represented a loss for Corrections officers versus the psychiatric staff. When the hospital hired three new female social workers who needed an office, the only available space was the Corrections locker room and bathroom. So the women got it, while the daytime shifts of Corrections men had to make do elsewhere. Each night, the guards reclaimed their old room and left enough of a mess so that the daytime users would get their message.

A total of forty New York City Corrections officers were then deployed at Bellevue Hospital. Ward N,O-2 had twenty-five of them, working three eight-hour shifts on rotation. A man who came on duty stowed his gun in his locker—according to regulations. Minutes later, he'd be in among fifty patients on N or O. The unpredictable men could curse him, or suddenly punch him in the stomach as they milled about. At any sign of real trouble, the guard would throw the ward keys through the barred entrance, sliding them fifty feet to the safety of midcorridor. No matter what happened to him, he couldn't now be forced to open the gate and let the patients pour out into the corridor. You'd hear the orchestrations of trouble as you worked in the doctors' office: sudden screaming, the clash of the thrown keys, the sound of running as Corrections men converged on the trouble and the gradual fading of noise that meant it was being handled. (I remember reading a leaflet from the Mental Health Information Service—MHIS—that described prison ward duty as "not dangerous.")

Overcrowding and danger made increasingly good reasons for the psychiatrists to stay in the main office and stop making rounds, but four or five times a day the nurse went on the wards. She—a woman with a fullback's build—would plant herself solidly among the patients with a tray of medications.

"Come and get it!"

She was dispensing the tranquilizers that doctors had ordered for the patients they interviewed. Patients? Our men were also

15

criminal detainees awaiting assignment: unsegregated boys and men, homosexuals and straights, crushed together regardless of the type of crime or degree of explosiveness. It was an all-male holding action where the tranquilizers prescribed to help the sick also helped keep the peace.

Our nurse was more "macho" than the doctors and enjoyed more popularity. Generally, agitated men took such injections as were needed without complaint. Only the most uncomprehending, resistant psychotics were wrestled to the ground by two male attendants who accompanied the nurse when they were needed.

Perhaps her visits represented entertainment. The men had little else. There was no frequent or easy visitation as on the civil wards nor any place they could be turned out to exercise. Each of the wards was crowded with beds, even into the wide central hall. At one end, the hall widened into what was called a day room, furnished with rickety tables and chairs. The men ate at a common mess and used a common latrine. Everything was out in the open except for a few isolation cells holding men who would attack others, or those whose confusion made them prey. The men stood in groups, or sat solitary in corners, blanket-wrapped, sometimes nodding and mumbling. Of course there was no telephone and the television sometimes worked. When men paced the long hall fights could erupt without warning and mattresses fly. After fighting, the most popular diversion—documented in an MHIS report—was "trapping and torturing the rats that infest the hospital."

It was onto these wards that the social work supervisor sent three young girls wearing their sixties miniskirts: Elyse, Connie and Carol, our brand new caseworkers. Initially, they would go out onto the wards from time to time, quickly on, quickly off, followed by the Corrections guards. Their supervisor, however, decided that she wanted to institute a program of games therapy. Who the hell would send pretty young girls with their panties showing to play volleyball on those wards?

This happened once, twice, three times until the jiggling little innocents sensed the thick quality of silence in the men who

16

watched them turning and twisting at the net. And they saw the beds shuddering as other men, cloaked in blankets, masturbated frantically. Anything could have happened in there with only a couple of Corrections guards against so many men! But nothing actually did happen except that everyone waiting outside sweated through those volleyball games until they heard the sullen clank of the ward gate closing and saw the girls reappear, untouched. Our felons, rapists and murderers had been—comparatively—gentlemen.

I first came to the ward in 1965. In 1967, I became co-chief with Al Holden, and after his disappearance, psychiatrist in charge. Every year the overcrowding grew worse. In 1968, the year of the great census, we had more than a hundred patients in an accommodation that was designed for fifty. And what patients! I reviewed random case reports from those times. Here are excerpts:

1. *Charge: Felonious Assault* He says he is God and Jesus Christ and that he communicates with the Virgin Mary by means of signs which he sees when he closes his eyes. But voices call him bad names and that "shouldn't happen to God."

2. *Charge: Homicide* A sullen, very guarded young man says, "Why do you ask these questions? You must be the police. Don't you know that the narcotics law was written just to get me?"

3. *Charge: Assault Third Degree* There are scars on his neck from self-mutilation. His arm is still bandaged from a serious suicide attempt. He is so depressed that he cries as he talks, saying, "I want to go back to jail and I want to kill myself."

4. *Charge: Homicide* He is a youth with an effeminate gait, scarred from prison fights, who answers with grossly inappropriate confidence and laughter when asked how he feels. He says, "Fine, just marvelous!"

5. *Charge: Assault* On present psychiatric examination, the defendant is withdrawn, mute and bewildered. He appears to be responding to auditory and/or visual hallucinations. He does not respond to questions, appears to be tense, frightened and potentially explosive. I would recommend immediate hospitali-

17

zation on the prison ward of Bellevue Hospital. *Diagnosis: Schizophrenia, catatonic type.*

The catatonic defendant was with us for a while until one day he fulfilled the promise of explosion and went berserk. Defendants one, two and three were declared suitable for commitment to a mental hospital. Number four, though he certainly showed signs of mental illness, was declared legally competent and returned to the jurisdiction of the court.

One day, when it was 209 percent over ward capacity, I closed the ward to new admissions and sent them back to wait in jail until we had space for them.

Our men came from Bronx and Manhattan Courts, sent to Bellevue on the motion of the district attorney, the defense attorney or the judge himself. Something about their behavior or crimes suggested psychosis. We had men who had been acting strangely in jail before trial, some defendants who were already on trial but pleading insanity and a good number of Matteawan returns. These were felony-level defendants who had been committed to Matteawan Hospital for the Criminally Insane before their trials and who were now returning, improved, to be reevaluated by us. Usually, they were sent back to detention to continue the judicial process that had been delayed by their Matteawan committal.

Our job in every case was to make a judgment of a man's mental status and establish competency or the lack of it. The conclusion for legal competency was typed on the bottom of each psychiatric evaluation: "We find that the defendant is/is not in such a state of idiocy, imbecility or insanity as to be incapable of understanding the charge, proceedings or making his own defense."

A man found competent by this conclusion was called "fit to proceed" and sent back to the old White Street Detention Center, better known as the Tombs. A man found to be incapable of understanding his situation was designated as not competent; that would usually get him a place on N or O until his case could be presented in Bellevue's Commitment Court. If he didn't object to a committal, he could be processed straight through to a hospital. But it was almost a rule that the sicker a man was, the less he wanted to go to the hospital. He would then contest his case in that same court and might remain on our ward for months.

Each incoming man was processed: first given a brief physical, then a preliminary interview with a social worker and finally a psychiatric evaluation during which he would see two different doctors at different times. The information would finally be pooled in an official report to the judge signed by two qualified psychiatrists, or QPs.

This two-tiered system served us well. Before the heavy census of 1967–68, we had only one full-time social worker to take the preliminary histories. Then, just in time, the three new women were hired. In their office, which still contained the guards' big white toilet, they gathered necessary information: circumstances of arrest, reason for referral, screening reports from the referring court's clinic, probation records, previous time spent in mental hospitals and all they could coax from the patient about his personal and family history. Occasionally, a patient would tell them something he wouldn't tell a doctor, or he'd present an entirely different story each time around.

Armed with their information, under the pressure of time, I could cut off a patient when he attempted certain detours around revealing facts:

> PSYCHIATRIST: I noticed something in your record about your having a hospitalization in the state of Maryland just before you were arrested in the bus terminal last week. You hadn't mentioned it to me.
> PATIENT: I didn't want you to think I was crazy.

This patient had walked away from that mental institution and come to New York. It seemed likely that his arrest for indecent exposure while urinating near the bus terminal had to do with his mental condition and was not associated with an intent to expose himself.

We were short of typewriters and secretaries, yet everything we did centered on paperwork. Men charged with homicides required verbatim transcripts of interviews. We had to document any extra tests done by the ward psychologists because the judges and lawyers knew the names—if not the purposes—of the tests and asked for them:

"Did this man have a Rorschach? An IQ test? Have you given him a Bender? Has everything been done for this man?"

In the crowded doctors' office, three doctors worked almost knee to knee, interviewing patients while a secretary took dictation and another typed reports. What space was left between the desks was often packed with students who were auditing the procedures. There were medical students on electives as well as those from a law and psychiatry course in which I was a participating lecturer. It was important for these future doctors and lawyers to witness interviews, to hear and recognize the patients' answers expressing psychosis or plain bad judgment.

Lawyers were very much a part of N,O-2 since the due process reforms of the Supreme Court brought them into the mental hospitals. Brand new law school graduates interviewed clients on the big bench in the corridor outside the doctors' office. Too often they were young Turks, out to do their bit for the oppressed patients in the hands of the Establishment.

Before work in the mornings, the room smelled of fresh coffee and food. There was the paté and croissants our psychologist, Dr. Jim Cravens, brought in for his breakfast and the giant doughnuts favored by Mike, the big roaring man whose title was chief administrative assistant.

Mike had a hard time getting used to what he called "the college kids"—by which he meant our staff, newly in the pay of the NYU Medical School instead of the city's civil service. He was an old Bellevue hand who knew all the rules and advised the patients. Mike had covered well for notoriously flaky prison doctors in the past and was pretty used to running things his way. The new young social workers unnerved him, and when he had to share a desk with Betty, the equally dazzling secretary I had coaxed from the head of the department, he retaliated by ignoring her. (Bellevue had allowed us the new secretary, but not the desk and typewriter she would need to do her work.)

Mike's job might have grown too big for one man, even one good man, but he had staked out his territory and defended it from invasion by what seemed to be planned chaos. Only he knew the recondite names of all the legal forms needed in the processing of patients and only he knew where they were in the towering piles of paper on his desk. We weren't learning what we needed to know because Mike wasn't teaching. In an all-out effort to achieve some order, I put up a big blackboard on the wall near his desk. On it we listed the name of each new patient and marked him through the stages of evaluation and processing until his name surfaced in the "Incomplete" column for lack of a document or signature, or, if he was committed to a hospital, under "Scheduled to Be Committed" and then "Waiting for Transfer." It had taken me six months to get that blackboard from the hospital and I was pleased with it. But I wasn't pleased, many mornings, to discover that the names of new cases had been erased. Total confusion. We were back to square one.

I think the stalemate was broken when I found a small desk and typewriter for Betty in the catacombs of the Bellevue cellars and Mike no longer had to share with her. In time he was generally mollified, especially since a very determined Connie rechalked the names on the blackboard just as diligently as they had been mysteriously erased.

Mike came over to our side after six months. He has retired from Bellevue now, but when I speak to anyone who was on the ward in 1968, his name still brings a smile: he is both "most unforgettable character" and "best liked."

None of us smile when the conversation inevitably turns to Al Holden. In a curious way, he is still a phantom presence on N,O-2. He affected its operation directly because after he disappeared we could no longer get doctors to volunteer for service. Open positions had no takers. I was there as senior qualified psychiatrist and there were two other regularly assigned doctors: Charley Smith, who replaced Al, and Tom Powers. Other psychiatrists came and went, literally drafted by the hospital administration for periods of service on N,O-2. They were more than wary; they were scared of the ward. Al's problematic fate left a

21

legacy of fear which has endured. Recently, I called N,O-2 to speak to the sweet, rather chirpy woman who was a ward clerk in 1968 and is still on the job. When I told her that I wanted to use her name in this chapter she was immediately alarmed:

"Oh no, Doctor, not unless you call me Operator Two. I can only be known as Operator Two."

I asked about the other secretary on the unit.

"You can't use her name either, unless it's her code name. That's what she wants."

"What is her code name?"

"Miss Anonymous."

Miss Anonymous! She was dead serious. That tells me something about today's conditions on N,O-2. When I recently spoke to the head of a busy Criminal Courts unit which also evaluates prisoners, he admitted that he was nervous. His private office had been bombed.

Nothing much seems to have changed.

In those days, I would start each morning by piling new charts on my desk. Each patient's chart included his basic medical record, the social worker's history and the copy of the criminal indictment with the judge's referral (court order) clipped to it. I'd pick out a group of easier cases first. They might be men who were obviously psychotic, and patently so ill that their cases presented no problems in deciding about disposition. Our secretaries could get to work on commitment papers for them while I went on to more complex cases.

Felonies presented problems of extra time and paperwork. These men were facing longer sentences in state prison. I needed all the information I could get, including the yellow police "rap sheet" of prior arrests and convictions. It saved a lot of time when a man went into the circumstances of his arrest:

> PATIENT: Gee Doc, I don't know why those people were so surprised when I took the gun I'd found outside the liquor store inside to show them.

PSYCHIATRIST: Well, I see that you have three prior arrests
   for armed robbery. Didn't you use a gun in those?

This was not confrontation. But if he knew that I knew, he
might decide to give a more cogent explanation. Commonly,
these fellows who repeated preposterous alibis would be sent to
us at the suggestion of their own lawyers, who reasoned, "Who
else but a psycho would stick to such a story?"

We used to be amused by the many men who offered similar
stories based on a most exquisite sense of legal propriety. For
example, the arrest was unfair because the officer found the
packet of heroin lying at their feet instead of on their person.
They were only passengers in the cars they were caught running
away from and they didn't know the cars were stolen. The gun
found in their hand was just picked out of a garbage can and of
course they were about to bring it into the precinct house. All
of them, always, were unfairly arrested. The fact of their crimes
and of their guilt was of small magnitude compared to the violation
of technicalities. Even the dullest could persuade themselves that
they'd been had by the system. Men who saw themselves as
victims under all circumstances made the likelihood of rehabilitation
a joke.

My evaluation would begin as the man walked toward me
from the other side of the room. I'd watch the way he moved
and his coordination. At close range, I'd know if he bothered to
wash himself, or if he used one of the hacked-off toothbrushes
it had taken me a year to get for the patients on the ward.
Toothbrushes were banned as potential weapons when I first
came here, but after persistent nudging, the administration agreed
that I might cut off the handles and issue the bristled stumps.

A man's body language could tell you if and how to proceed.
Sometimes just a glance at him would direct me to the right area.
If I got an impression of limited intellect, I could ease into the
evaluation with some simple addition and subtraction. But I
knew that the mere mention of arithmetic could make some men
so nervous that they looked ready to bolt. So I would automatically

build my questions into such facts as the size of his family and his place in its sibling order.

> PSYCHIATRIST: You say your brother Robert is thirty-seven? You're what . . . twenty-five? That's a lot younger. How many years younger are you than Robert?

If we didn't test on arithmetic, we would find out how they read or spelled. But mainly, intelligence could be gauged by how they talked and the skills they had. One thing I knew in advance: if I was alerted that a man sounded significantly dull, the answer to my question, "How did you do in school?" was going to be "average." He wasn't going to help me assess his inadequacy, and I'd have to be tactful and persistent till I had the proof of it.

He could be dull; he also may have been a behavioral problem. When I evaluated someone "average" who told me that he had graduated at the age of sixteen from the eighth grade in New York City, I might learn that he had been a student at one of the city's special "600" schools for problem children and was "average" there. And I could reasonably expect to turn up a corresponding history of juvenile trouble with the law.

Key questions in every category, often simple, opened the path an evaluator could follow to a correct diagnosis. We saw men who would stubbornly deny the facts on their arrest sheets. If I asked, "Why are you here?" such a man would answer, "I don't know." I'd look at the charge against him and say, "Why did you undress the little girl?" He'd answer, "I wasn't there. She was my friend." At such an answer, I knew I could be dealing with a borderline defective.

Typically, he'd be unelaborative, monosyllabic in his answers. He'd have a poor fund of information and perhaps a primitive speech pattern. We saw many of them at Bellevue: arrested for a variety of crimes and often showing the concurrent emotional disorders that had prevented them from learning.

One of our new social workers once startled me by objecting to my questions about geography and current events. She took the obvious position that a man from the inner-city ghetto might not have the information that Washington was his country's capital or that California was on the Pacific Coast. She really wanted to protect her patient, but to me hers was a condescending attitude. No matter how narrow a man's turf, he should know at minimum something about the world that exists outside it. If he doesn't, maybe he isn't competent.

Generally, the borderline men knew they were dull and they would try to shield themselves from exposure as they had from childhood. You had to coax them out, show that you were easily pleased with the right answer to a simple question, the proverbial 2×2. If they realized that it was okay not to be good at something, not to be bright, then they might admit their vulnerability and discuss the crimes they'd committed, instead of stubbornly, self-destructively denying the facts.

We had thus made them competent.

Such defectives might become psychotic under pressure, but that did not necessarily make them legally incompetent, unable to cooperate with their lawyers. These men could be returned to the jurisdiction of the court.

If a man seated beside my desk avoided eye contact, looked preoccupied or afraid, he might be hallucinating. His lips might move, head tip to one side, eyes darting in the same direction. Or he'd suddenly turn and search the empty air behind him for the source of his "voices." If he admitted hearing them, I'd ask him what they said and whether they told him to do good or bad things. One such staring, preoccupied patient described his voices' change of attitude: "At first, they would tell me to do constructive things. Then they got negative, like they would say that I wasn't going to do anything so I should throw myself in front of a truck."

The watching law students, there by his permission, would be stunned. It sounded to them as if I was interviewing his hallucination. But a good, content-laden answer from its owner could explain his motive for the crime. Our report was often the first and only explanation the man's lawyer would ever get.

GOOD GUYS, BAD GUYS

I'd continue to draw him out beyond the voices, perhaps concentrating on the goodness or badness of his behavior because that could be extremely important.

It just came naturally to us to think "good" or "bad" in spite of our training, which suggested that patients were the sum of their experiences and simply did what they did. Morality was irrelevant and we were not supposed to judge. But we had to judge. It wasn't only because our legal system demanded that men be considered as exerting free will when they committed crimes, but also, in our efforts to get necessary information that would help them, we were constantly thinking about their criminal intent and/or feelings of guilt.

Sometimes a psychotic man was guilt-ridden and covering up facts that could be helpful in his case. Other men who talked of their "voices" were too fluent in describing their experiences. Over-fluency is not characteristic of a true hallucinatory state, but it's on the mark for a Bellevue repeater who knows the procedure and is generally trying too hard to be found incompetent.

I had to have a question or a reservation if a man piled on symptoms that didn't match his other complaints. These would-be "crazies" followed similar patterns: staring, incoherent talk, "Why am I here, God?" and "There must be something wrong with my mind but it doesn't matter now because I want to die!" The pretenders often overdid it because they didn't know how crazy was crazy enough to influence the doctors. And if histrionics didn't work, they might try menace, shouting and threatening. Then I might think of pressing the concealed alarm button newly installed at knee level on each doctor's desk. The Corrections guards would come running in and take the ham actor back to the ward. (We had to be careful of those buttons. We had finally wrested them from a reluctant hospital administration, but now we discovered how easily a shaky knee could set them off. I know the Corrections Department resented the false alarms.)

Nearly all the people who pretended insanity, the ones who would scream all night in the Tombs prison or repeatedly attempt suicide, were intent on taking advantage of the "termination of charges" feature that went along with commitment to a mental

26

hospital. For the successful manipulator, that law in the penal code was a revolving door which put a man who had committed a crime back on the street without a penalty.

Let us say a man—arrested on a misdemeanor charge such as breaking and entering—does something so bizarre while awaiting trial that the judge sends him to the psychiatric prison ward to determine his competency. He succeeds in hoodwinking the psychiatrists, is found mentally incompetent, and in the process, crosses over from the Department of Corrections' criminal jurisdiction to that of the Department of Mental Hygiene. At the precise time that he is committed to a state hospital, Section 730 of the Code of Criminal Procedure specifies that the criminal misdemeanor charges against him are terminated. He becomes a civil commitment. Now all he has to do is escape from the hospital, an easy job for a sane or insane man, and he's completely free. No one is looking for him: not the police because the charge against him has been terminated, and not the Department of Mental Hygiene. Until 1979, there was not even a regulation that required the department to report such civil commitment escapes! A man didn't have to wait until he reached the hospital. He could do it by simply walking off the bus that was taking him there.

Back on the streets, he could next be arrested for a bigger crime such as armed robbery and pull the same stunt, pressuring his way back to the Bellevue Psychiatric Prison Ward. But now a new element of jeopardy enters his scheme because the robbery makes him a felony-level defendant who is not entitled to have his charges automatically terminated. He would normally be sent to a secure hospital because he must appear for trial after the term of his commitment. But what if the man has been committed before the glacial bureaucratic processes of justice send down his felony indictment? I don't know how it happened, but I saw men who had actually been released or who had escaped from the hospitals to which they were sent, thus gaining freedom and avoiding prosecution for the felony. The man who once learned how to beat the misdemeanor might beat the felony too. So why not try to get to Bellevue at all costs?

I remember one such man who was able to repeatedly commit armed robbery and rape in the area of New York Hospital and Rockefeller Institute. He would find a late-working woman employee, rob and rape her, and if arrested, manage to get back to Ward N,O-2. How could he *not* remember that several times before, the Bellevue Commitment Court had relieved him of the charge against him and literally delivered him back to the Manhattan State Hospital with its convenient footbridge to the city's East Side!

The men we saw at Bellevue who tried to take advantage of the revolving door of terminating charges called it "bugging out." A dedicated bug-out knew our procedure, knew how to get to N,O-2 and keep returning. If he was uncovered in a psychiatric exam and anointed fit to proceed, he could still "win" later through his other manipulations. Simulating epilepsy was popular: a convincing fit with plenty of thrashing and convulsions would get him first medical attention at the jail and then a referral right back to us so that we could establish whether the epilepsy was contrived, a psychotic pseudoseizure or the real thing. One man on a show-off trip actually demonstrated how he feigned convulsions in jail. While we watched, he went through perfect tonic and clonic movements, turned blue and rolled up his eyes. He admitted it wasn't a hundred percent performance, apologizing for not losing his urine in what, after all, was only an exhibition.

They weren't all that good. Another man's best efforts could only bring restraints or a straitjacket after he'd battered everything within reach. But even that could be a "win" because the bigger the apparent seizure, the better the chances that the Corrections guards would be afraid to take off the restraints unless he was in a hospital. They were reluctant to transport him to any jail because he could stage his big performance in the Detention Center in the middle of the night. If some foreign or naïve doctors apt to misunderstand the situation were covering at the jail, he could be ordered back to N,O-2 in the morning. The Corrections men knew these patients and wanted to avoid the trips.

Every time a man suspected of faking a mental disorder came back to N,O-2, it meant more observation, probably another psychiatric evaluation and, of course, another chance to be committed. We all knew that a bug-out who wanted to get to the hospital would get there sooner or later while a man who belonged there would usually refuse help and have to be put away by a doctor's testimony in a battle over commitment in Bellevue's little courtroom.

I saw a lot of malingerers. If I became suspicious during an evaluation, I could confront such a man with his discrepancies or show by my expression that I knew I was listening to drivel. When he ran out of unlikely answers I might even remark, "It must be tough to keep up a pose of insanity."

Men I had sent back to jail would keep returning. There were several so brazenly confident that they'd tell me there was nothing I could do to stop them from coming back to Bellevue like a yo-yo. But I had one surprise in store for such repeaters. I would pick up the phone and call the social worker in charge of the Mental Observation (MO) unit on Rikers Island. He understood the problem very well. Ward N,O-2 was a scary place, but in those days the isolated unit on Rikers was immediately recognizable as a dead end, a collection of cold, bare, stinking cagelike cells ranking even higher on the fright scale. If I could arrange a transfer to the Rikers MO unit for the challenger, he would usually find that he was "cured" in the morning and could be sent back for trial. The problem was that I couldn't make this informal transfer arrangement as often as it was needed.

I've included below some excerpts from a typical report I wrote on a man who didn't fight me all the way to Rikers.

Presiding Justice
Bronx Supreme Court
851 Grand Concourse
Bronx, New York   Re:_____

Honorable Sir,

The above named, charged with manslaughter in the second degree, had been committed to this hospital for examination as to his mental condition.

HISTORY: Patient was referred to state hospitals for behavioral problems as a child, the last time at the age of thirteen. He has lived with his mother, states that he attended school until he was seventeen and subsequently worked until his arrest. He gives his history of being attacked by the alleged victim and finding himself involved in the trial that led to his conviction. Through his contact with another inmate, he was made to believe that it would be profitable for him to pretend to be insane. He describes his statements to a court psychiatrist that led to this evaluation at Bellevue.

PSYCHIATRIC
EXAMINATION: Patient is a twenty-year-old male who responds directly to questions and offers a history of his having attempted to "bug out." He has changed his mind and wants to clarify that his descriptions of hallucinations were fictitious. He says that he is bitter that he must face a prison sentence for attempting to defend himself against an attacker in his building and feels that he will be vindicated at a later date when he succeeds in having his case appealed.

DIAGNOSTIC
IMPRESSION: Without psychosis

We find that the defendant is not in such a state of idiocy, imbecility or insanity as to be incapable of understanding the charge, proceedings or making his own defense.

What if a man like this hadn't been found out, had stuck to his original story and succeeded in making an end run around the psychiatrists? As a felony conviction, he would have been certified for commitment and transferred to Matteawan Hospital for the Criminally Insane, a high-security facility and ultimate scary place in Beacon, New York. After a period of improvement, or convincing the Matteawan doctors that he had improved, he would have returned to serve his sentence and immediately appealed his case. This particular man—I recall him as fairly pleasant—was not alert to the way that he could use a Matteawan commitment as a lever for later plea bargaining. Wily defendants knew that a Matteawan return label had a wonderful advantage attached to it. One could be presumed insane at the time of a crime if shortly thereafter he had to be committed to that facility. Returning to Bellevue for reevaluation and from there back to detention, he would have the groundwork for an NGRI (not guilty by reason of insanity) defense against the original charge of manslaughter. Percentages would be in his favor: the high probability that the district attorney's office involved would lose against an NGRI defense, the paperwork involved, the fact that the man had already been in Matteawan—all factors combining to make the DA "flexible." There would be no insanity defense trial. The DA's office would provide a much easier plea bargain and in a short time the man would be back on the streets. I coined a name for this procedure that stuck: the "Matteawan Plea."

I never felt that it was the DA's problem as much as it was ours because we were charged with the weeding out of malingerers before they got as far as Matteawan. But that didn't stop me from making sure that they knew about the situation.

In 1968, I wrote to an assistant DA who was in charge of administrative matters in Manhattan District Attorney Frank Hogan's office. (See Appendix A.) I outlined the problems of the revolving-door patients and explained that as often as we'd tried, we couldn't keep these competent but unstable men in jail. They knew how to manipulate the system and would use any tactic to get back to us in an effort to obtain hospital commitment and the termination of charges. It was the first description of the problem I'd made to a DA. Incredibly, I found myself doing it again in 1980, in connection with preventive legislation. The problem had never ceased.

It became my cause to keep these invulnerable criminals from walking in and out of hospitals at will. But it also became harder and harder to see that every suspicious case was thoroughly investigated when overcrowding accelerated on our ward. The previous year's figures showed 1,749 admissions and the 1968 statistics would top that. As patients poured in, the worst defendants lingered on the ward. One became quite an old resident:

GOOD GUYS, BAD GUYS

Charge: Fugitive
The patient has beaten his mother, father, wife and strangers. He gives a history of having anonymously arranged to have his father's arm smashed, of forcing his wife to have an abortion, striking her with a pistol butt, having sex with other women in her presence and pistol-whipping his business partner. He details most of his history in a matter-of-fact, affectless manner. It is his claim that he has taken as much as one hundred milligrams of amphetamines a day.

This man's case was complicated by his fugitive charge. He was with us long enough to become one of the kings of his ward.

Not everybody who sat down beside my desk was such a heavy. Some were basically good guys who'd committed one fluky, not-to-be-repeated crime or had an attitude which got them into trouble. It was easy to find out if a man knew what a trial was, what the function of a DA was and why the judge was needed. If he answered my standard opening, "Why are you here?" with "Some honky sent me," it described the function and the power of the court adequately for competence, but I knew that we must explain to him how the chip on his shoulder would affect his ability to defend himself. When we took a fuller history, he'd recognize our effort and believe us when we said that his attitude would get him a tougher plea and a longer sentence.

Another kind of man might not have a police record, but I'd find evidence that he had been hanging out with friends who did. Many suggestible men gravitate to a tough crowd and are moved into crime by someone brighter than they are. We began to call such men's families to ask more definitive questions about them, and to have social workers corroborate details of their case histories. I think it was a "first" for the prison ward and it brought in results. We all succumbed to "good deeds" fever.

I'd try to help dissimulators who had no records. Dissimulators are people who for their own notions of self-respect will deny that they are mentally ill. They are the opposite of malingerers, but equally capable of fooling judges and psychiatrists. I remember Carlos, a proud and dignified man, who sat silent through our first interview because to speak at all would mean that he was cooperating with a premise that he might be insane. He was a Hispanic who had been exploited and evicted by slum landlords during his youth and who had saved money for years to buy a rundown apartment house that he might transform into a model dwelling for poor tenants. But he found that his tenants did not love him—they were tearing his place apart, negating the reasons for the scrimping and self-denial of so many years. Carlos developed delusions, well concealed, but during a bout of mounting paranoia he shot and killed a teenager who he thought was breaking into his home. Here was a man who could be reclaimed and returned to society, but he wouldn't admit that he needed hospital treatment. He'd accept the punishment but not the cure; he fought to go to jail because jail had no stigma of insanity. I managed to have Carlos committed to Matteawan, saw him again when he came back, improved, and saw him after his shortened term in jail. He was the best kind of candidate for an NGRI defense in that he was a good man, inadvertently involved through his illness, and after being helped, would continue to help himself. He had indeed had a paranoid psychosis, but if one could judge at all, I'd say this man would not be likely to repeat criminal behavior.

We turned out a new kind of report to the judge when I was at Bellevue. Previously, reports from referral centers like Bellevue or Kings County had been defensively short, because anything a psychiatrist volunteered beyond fit to proceed or not competent could be "used against him" in cross-examination at the upcoming commitment or sanity hearing. Sometimes the sequelae of good works came much later: I've been subpoenaed by lawyers on cases I had evaluated five or six years before. The client, appealing his case and claiming that he hadn't had a proper examination, would require that I be asked to remember the reasons for the conclusion I made in my original evaluation of him. Without a decent report, I can only say that I don't remember the case, and at the worst, someone might criticize me for forgetting. With a comprehensive report, there are plenty of items on which the defense attorney can aggressively cross-question me, but the amount of detail also helps *me* remember. If my memory is

33

jogged, I may be able to list the ways in which he'd tried to malinger. The convict, in these appeals, never failed to be angry with me.

Somewhere along the line we stopped being defensive about future subpoenas. In selected cases, we began writing what Mike, who typed the reports, called "goddamn novels." Our reports included complete histories, diagnoses and, often, recommendations for the legal disposition of cases. Cautious at first, we grew bolder with time and could suggest that a judge in a clear-cut case ask for a conference of opposing lawyers with the new information we provided. And the judges made use of our recommendations. One day, a judge I had never met stopped me outside the Bellevue courtroom and asked to shake my hand.

The realization that just a few more pertinent facts about the crime or the defendant could alter lives and serve justice was pretty heady stuff. This sense of power and worth was welcome to professionals in a frustrating system, when traditional authorities like psychiatrists had begun to lose credibility.

The police, especially, suffered from the anti-Establishment sixties. Police officers were called "pigs." They reacted massively when the times cast them as villains. Some stopped making arrests; others went further. Rogue cops shook down drug dealers and skimmed off gambling operations. But I remember one who was different. He was on our ward for months, paranoid when I first saw him, and later recovered. He had been a member of the safe and lofts squad (burglary). But when he saw corruption in his superiors and their arbitrary handling of him, he reacted by becoming a burglar himself. He told me he more or less did it to "get even," but it was also self-punishment, not uncommon for a moral overreacher who lets himself question whether morality is its own reward. Most such people simply get depressed. But this fellow took action on his bitterness. When I first saw him he was thin and gloomy-looking, trying to regain the use of a left arm that had been shattered by a gunshot wound suffered during his brief stint in a life of crime.

The sixties made many casualties in authority professions. We saw doctors, lawyers, even clergymen on the ward. Everyone's gods seemed to be failing. And if God was dying for some believers, so were certain generalities.

What a look there was on a Jewish social worker's face when she interviewed her first Jewish madman! This mild fellow had killed his next-door neighbor because "she was a prostitute who kept making dirty remarks" to him. Pure delusion. After her initiation with him, the social worker was braced for the eighty-year-old doctor who killed his wife because he thought her unfaithful. Later came the student charged with sodomy, robbery, sexual assault, menacing, possession of a deadly weapon. He hunted women on the subway and committed sadistic acts. Her cultural assumption that "Jews don't" died hard—but it died.

Every year, one man who was especially frightening would appear on the ward. I can still be unnerved by the memory of one particular prisoner. He embodied all the suppressed violence on N,O-2. The pressure of that place was usually relieved by sporadic patient outbursts. Corrections guards too could lose control and slap a patient, an explosive reaction after years of containing their natural fear of being unexpectedly struck themselves. This one man was untouched by any of the ward's tension because he helped create it. He was like the "cold spot" in a haunted house that refuses to grow warm; inexplicably eerie.

The man was an American Indian, thirty-one years old and captured on a fugitive warrant in New York City. He had a long legal history complicated by problems concerning his competency for extradition to the Western state where he was serving a life sentence for murder. He had also murdered in escaping twice from a high security prison, committed another murder, been transferred to a mental hospital, threatened suicide and escaped from there. On his first admission to Bellevue, he was found incompetent, sent to Matteawan, and returned to Bellevue on a technicality, dropping into a kind of legal limbo on our ward. He had been there for nearly a year.

This was no tattooed, growling brute, but an unremarkable, middle-sized man whose unusual light green eyes looked through yours. He could slowly recite the details of his known killings— he mentioned others too—with smiling calm. He often smiled, though of course he hadn't the slightest sense of humor. That smile and a certain way of cocking his head quizzically and staring meant that he was concentrating on you, bringing you into his personal focus of interest. And it wasn't for effect.

There was the chilling part. He took a personal interest in you. I know of no other patient so wise as to how the ward was run, no one else so interested in the staff. Only he could have been the one clever enough to collect bits of information about us from the office wastebaskets. He even had the self-assurance to come to the Corrections guard on his ward and tell him to watch a certain man because he "was getting suicidal." He was right, but what prompted him to do it? It wasn't concern for the suicide, and he didn't look as if he wanted to impress anyone. The only thing clear to me was that this enigmatic, determined, ward-wise murderer had decided to make N,O-2 his permanent home. The law required him extradited, but he had decided to stay and was pitting his will against the move. For obvious reasons, his Legal Aid lawyer was terrified and took care always to agree with him. The tough black militant Five Percenters and so-called Muslims who threatened judges and assaulted Corrections guards left this soft-spoken loner to himself. He had all the space he wanted. They knew he was made of some alien stuff.

I had already made up my mind that the legal knot had to be untangled and that he must be dislodged. I stepped up my efforts when he seemed to be focusing in on Connie. She had just gotten married and her nervous husband asked her not to tell anyone on the ward her new name. She was careful. But when she came back from her honeymoon, the Indian, with his odd smile, offered her congratulations, using her new married name. I don't know how he found out, but the fact that he could, and the sight of her face, made me try harder. We knew there could be no safeguards for us. A single error in the arrest procedure could free a man we had just sent back to the court. Anyone with a grievance could scout us on First Avenue after work, and follow us home. Holden could have been killed that way; it was so easy. I didn't want to think Connie could be victim of someone's homicidal focus without my doing everything I could to prevent it. The administration of the hospital was finally bothered into making the concentrated effort to bring this eerie defendant's case to life, and he was finally extradited.

If fear was always there in 1968, so was another current. The ward had a high sexual charge: some gay men, now more assertive and fearless of the guards, did their thing in the open. Straight patients just up from the Tombs couldn't help reacting to the unexpected presence of young women. Straight out of school, our social workers were idealistic and would do more than they were asked. No one told them that it was all right to be afraid, and from the first day they felt they had to be good soldiers.

Connie, Elyse and Carol, not knowing what to expect, tried extra hard to look imperturbably professional. Connie's first interview on the job was with a young Black Muslim involved in the murder of a shopkeeper in the Bronx. They were almost of an age, twenty-one interviewing eighteen, and they were both frightened, which made it easier for Connie. Carol had her moments of sudden panic. She remembers an early interview with a cigar-smoking homicide defendant when she was sure that the man sitting next to her desk was about to reach over and put his hands around her throat. He made a sudden movement. She was up and running for the door before control reasserted itself, before she could turn, see his startled face, walk back, sit down and take charge. Elyse remembers that she was both frightened and incredulous when she realized that a man she was interviewing was masturbating as she talked. She struggled for the proper reprimand, then blurted, "If you don't stop that, I'll send you back with the guard."

He looked up, surprised. He had wide, staring eyes. "Stop what?"

N,O-2 was a long way from home for this college graduate.

They brightened our gloomy office. It was a little easier for any of us to stay late dictating or typing the reports. The girls brought in plants—which died—put up posters and finally banished the original paint under a layer of Age of Aquarius purple.

Our weekly routine posited the heaviest work load on Monday when we began to process the men who had come in over the weekend and those who arrived on that day. Tuesday was Commitment Court. On Wednesday, Dr. Morris Herman came down. He was chairman of the department of psychiatry of the NYU Medical School and supervisor of the prison ward. It was he who had given me my original assignment there. He came for two hours of patient interviews and discussion of cases, a good professional experience that took us off the midweek treadmill. But by Thursday, we were beginning to falter again from the weight of the place. We looked for things to make us laugh. There were unintentional absurdities like the good-will donations our social workers coaxed out of the public relations departments of big companies. The PR men sent us what they thought we could use—one day Revlon sent us sequinned eyelashes. Elyse— we'd named her "Cupcake"—handed them out to the homosexuals on the ward. Revlon was right. They *were* grateful!

More men came in on Friday but by afternoon the schedule was loosening and the doctors and social workers would send out for hero sandwiches from Trinacria's, the legendary deli that had served Bellevue for a generation. Then "Operator Two" would put a red sweater on her lap and read the tarot cards, or Mike would bring in cheese and tell us stories about the old days. He swore that until we came nothing had changed on the ward for twenty years. I liked it when he buttered us up, but we weren't the catalyst of change. It was the sixties, the decade of revolution and reform.

There was no question that the ward looked better to me on Fridays, but that was not enough to keep me there. The effect of the Bellevue years had been cumulative. I had never asked my boss to return the resignation I'd submitted after Al Holden vanished, and Holden's specter still troubled me. The anxiety I now felt about going to the job each morning troubled me more; if I couldn't lick it, I felt I ought to leave. I was fond of my coworkers and knew I would miss them. It might be a long time until I saw such a number of interesting cases or held a job with that much challenge. One thing I would not miss was the downer of my weekly appearance in Commitment Court. That alone might have forced me to resign eventually. For every pleasant Friday afternoon, there was a Tuesday morning in the court.

3 | Bellevue: Commitment Court

Tuesday was always bad news. I knew that the judge would be late again and I'd spend what seemed to be hours waiting and wondering where N,O-2 was on the docket. I'd go back and forth from the ward to the court. If His Honor had come, the sounds from the courtroom told me that the doctors from the other wards were already in combat with the patients'-rights lawyers. I'd do my best to catch the attention of the hospital's chief commitment clerk, signaling her that my prisoners were ready to come up and could we be next.

So many things could go wrong on a Tuesday. The evidence of what had gone wrong for N,O-2 was there on the big blackboard in the doctors' office. In one column were the names of men becalmed in the commitment process for weeks by repeated adjournment of their cases in that once-weekly court. The stationary names meant that the treadmill operation of N,O-2 came to a frustrating pileup because we were now expected to process at least thirty men a week. The men who lingered with us did not go to a hospital or to jail, but did take up bed space. That, and the crush of each day's new arrivals, made me fume.

When the clerk finally said, "Dr. Lubin, you're on next," I'd call down to N,O-2 and the Corrections guards would bring our men up in arm restraints. The men scheduled for hearings were those whose psychiatric evaluations had shown them to be "suitable for commitment to a mental hospital," but who had contested that finding. Bellevue filed an application for each commitment proceeding: if a man contested his case, he was entitled to a full-dress hearing in the court; if he did not contest, he could be processed through as an involuntary civil patient to any of the hospitals we regularly supplied with misdemeanants. Our hospital roster was Bronx State, Brooklyn State, Rockland State, Creedmoor, Pilgrim State and Central Islip. There was an apportionment, or "address factor," at work in the assignment of hospitals; consequently most of our traffic was concentrated at Pilgrim, Central Islip, and Rockland State Hospitals (now called Psychiatric Centers).

As far back as 1965, I visited several of these hospitals to have a firsthand look at them. They were not snake pits. I did find little in the way of treatment and extremely boring environments. Nevertheless, they served three square meals a day, were protective, and offered some drug therapy to alleviate the anxieties and psychotic thoughts which made our patients a danger to themselves and others. If the judiciary was a little naïve about what could be accomplished here ("Give this man care and treatment!" the judges would say as they signed commitment orders), then at least they were right in assuming that it was better for incompetent men who were prey for others to be out of a prison environment and off the streets. I have never apologized for sending men to these hospitals.

The bureaucratic aspect of commitment was a stately pavane of paperwork, advancing through a maze of forms from the original psychiatric evaluation with its attached Designations of Psychiatrists and Oath, in which the doctors swear to "fairly determine . . . and make a just and true report." Six copies of the evaluation were needed: to the commissioner of the Department of Mental Hygiene, to the district attorney's office (Burton Roberts in the Bronx, Frank Hogan for New York County at that time), to the Bellevue commitment office and, of course, to the patient's family and to his defense attorney.

There had to be a Notice of Application for Commitment (six copies to all of the above persons) and an Affidavit of Service (four copies) that it had been delivered to the patient and his family. The affidavit proved that the application was sent out at least five working days before the Commitment Court's regular session.

If, after the hearing, the patient was found to be legally incompetent by reason of mental illness and in need of hospitalization, the Court signed the Order of Commitment and the papers were held until the agents from the state hospital designated by the Commissioner of the Department of Mental Hygiene could take custody of the patient. If mental deficiency, rather than mental illness, was the cause of the incompetence, a little different procedure was followed and the Bellevue Prison Ward forwarded the necessary papers to Albany.

If a man was found competent to go back to jail and on to trial for his crime, the papers he needed canceled each other: the remand order to the criminal process went with him when he left the prison ward while the Order of Commitment ready and waiting for him was carefully marked "Void."

The civil wards had to demonstrate to the Commitment Court judge that their patients needed hospitalization because they were dangerous to themselves and others. Our job encompassed that assumption, but went further; specifically, we had to demonstrate how and why our patient could not defend himself in the legal system, how the workings of his psychosis contributed to that incompetence. It's not an easy job: competency is a very relative state.

A mentally deficient person is still legally competent to contribute to his defense if he can follow the processes of his trial and put the procedures into a frame of reality. A very bright person who sees everything through a distorting prism of delusion is not competent, no matter how high his IQ, because he can misunderstand everything he hears.

41

GOOD GUYS, BAD GUYS

Within the legal definition, a man may be mentally ill yet competent. Everything depends on the nature of his thought disturbance: whether, and how, it is confined, or whether his delusional material is so general that he is completely out of touch with reality.

The possible decisions that may be handed down at the termination of a commitment hearing reflect this: a man "not mentally ill" is remanded to the custody of the Commissioner of Corrections, to detention and the criminal law process. A man not competent "by reason of insanity" is committed to the custody of the Commissioner of Mental Hygiene and sent to an appropriate hospital. If a man is "mentally ill, yet competent," the court may either determine that he is fit for trial or issue a Civil Commitment Order for thirty days' observation and further disposition afterwards.

If they were misdemeanants, our patients had their charges terminated on committal to the *civil* state hospitals. They became not criminal, but civil commitments. By specific legal design, the felons—the "bad" guys who were charged with murder, rape, robbery—did not have charges terminated. They were civilly committed to a *correctional* hospital, the tough and secure Matteawan Hospital for the Criminally Insane in Beacon, New York. Their lawyers would immediately protest this "discrimination"; they worked up a fair head of steam about the "illegality" of the automatic Matteawan commitment for their incompetent clients.

What they meant was that their clients, even if caught in the criminal act and indicted, were still "presumably" innocent because they had not yet gone to trial. They should thus have been sent to the state hospitals with the misdemeanants and not to hospitals run by the prison service. Perhaps this extra security was unfair to the rare innocent detainee, but whoever designed that jag in the law was doing the general public a service.

The state hospitals did not have enough security personnel to keep a bad guy from walking off the grounds. A Matteawan commitment guaranteed that the felon would stay there until he later reappeared at Bellevue for evaluation of his recovery before going to trial. One-day "cures" could occur after exposure to violent and genuine psychotics. Or we might see them processed back after several months. Only the most persistent bug-outs would stick it out at Matteawan; continuing to act crazy so that they could use the time for later plea bargaining.

The Commitment Court on the seventh floor of the Psychiatric Hospital, five floors above N,O-2, was perhaps the size of a large classroom. It boasted unexpectedly handsome oak paneling, and it came complete with a black-robed Supreme Court judge, a court reporter, clerk of the court, bailiff, American flag, witness stand, alert professional audience of doctors and lawyers—but hardly ever a district attorney. This was due to circumstance. The commitment actions were tremendously important to the newly employed young lawyers who worked in the hospital, trying out their skills and fervent with sixties patients' rights enthusiasm. However, they were penny-ante stuff to the staffs of the prosecutors' offices, who were bogged down in the Criminal Courts. We couldn't get a district attorney to send a prosecutor to the courtroom, and this role was unwillingly assumed by the doctors. Somewhere between the spectators and the witness stand, the patient became a defendant, and the doctor, whose professional duty made it sometimes necessary to send people to hospitals who didn't want to go, was cast as both witness and prosecutor.

Nobody wanted that job.

If a doctor testified too energetically, the judge could accuse him of acting like a prosecutor. If he was reluctant to embarrass the listening patient by reciting his clinical symptoms in court, then the judge could complain that he was intentionally obscure. The best of the judges understood the testifying doctor's dilemma and tactfully sought information without abusing the doctor as a witness or the patient as a defendant. The court needed the doctor's advice because the defendants were often much sicker than they sounded.

A judge, listening to a defendant give some lucid answers about himself or his crime, might falsely conclude that he is legally competent if the testifying doctor doesn't clearly explain the otherwise trammeling role that the psychosis would play in his ability to cooperate at trial. And a lawyer, listening to his client repeat, "I'm okay, I don't feel like killing myself any more," will fight for his right to return to jail to face his charges. But back in jail, without the security of regularly prescribed medication, this psychotic client might revert to his predisposition towards suicide. He could then exercise his free will about whether to cut his throat, or "hang up."

As the only full-time senior psychiatrist on Ward N,O-2 in 1968, I did a lot of testifying. My colleagues Charley Smith and Tom Powers were juniors and did not testify. Al Holden had appeared in Commitment Court fairly often; I can remember him on the stand: tall, precise, impatient, even intolerant, yet he presented cases effectively. But Al was gone now and the QPs from other wards who had to be drafted into service on N,O-2 were scared by Al's case and disinclined to take on the battles in Commitment Court. I was the main man in the box for N,O-2. I'd look out over the faces, noting the familiar ones that belonged to the students from my law and psychiatry course, and wonder if they too thought of me as a prosecutor.

I had in fact studied law, until sudden family illness made me decide to change my goals in midtraining. Twenty-seven was late for medical beginnings, in those days, but I went through medical school and was delighted to get a psychiatric residency at the NYU–Bellevue Medical Center.

There was an endless variety of cases in the great receiving hospital and I wanted to stay there. Three years later, a job appeared that seemed hand-tailored for me. Dr. Herman told me that he would create a job as forensic fellow on the psychiatric prison ward. It was a melding of my past and present interests, law and psychiatry. During my training, I had done an elective stint on the prison ward. Yes, the staff had a reputation for eccentricity, but perhaps working conditions had a lot to do with it. Tuesday mornings didn't help.

I could never consider Special Term Part Two as a real courtroom. I felt it was pseudolegal, partly theater. Bizarre events were common. The doctors, lawyers, students and patients' families in the audience never knew when a defendant might flip out; it could happen as I was giving his history. He'd leap up, shouting, angry at what I was saying, threatening me or someone else who was present. The judge might try to gavel down the interruption, then realize that you couldn't expect a mental patient to observe the decorum of the court. But it was unnerving, and His Honor, a different Supreme Court judge each week, was always out of his element and never knew quite how to act.

Even the walk into court was traumatic. To reach his sanctuary in the courtroom, the judge would get off at the front elevator on the seventh floor. Standing in the elevator foyer area, he'd be in earshot of the male and female disturbed wards. There would be plenty of noise. Even on a Tuesday morning, with the weekend admissions now relatively tranquilized, there were enough sudden howls and weird sounds to make an elderly judge acutely conscious that his court was in a loony bin. He'd be nervous. At the end of a case hearing, with full judicial gravity, he'd often announce "Decision reserved." This gave the impression that His Honor would come up with a decision after further study. In fact, he had already made up his mind. "Decision reserved" was evasive action to prevent the defendant from making an outburst in court if he didn't like the verdict.

Another reason that "Special Two" seemed so unreal was that all the basic relationships were askew. Lawyers played down any evidence of mental illness, while defendants who had yet to be proved capable of giving rational aid to their counsel suddenly supplied all the evidence for their cases against commitment. Often, as I testified, I'd see the defendant and counsel in hurried conversation and then the lawyer would leap up and shout "Hearsay!" trying to discredit the medical history I'd invariably gotten from the defendant himself. At times, judges and lawyers seemed to take the defendant's version of his case verbatim, yet at other times, they'd argue over the man's past and future as if he weren't there. The word that comes to mind is "absurd."

The late sixties was an era of rights representation and mental patients were one of the latest persecuted minorities to be discovered. Real advances such as the Gideon case had made it possible for mental patients to have lawyers at commitment hearings. In 1967, the court-created Mental Health Information Service had begun to work in all the hospitals in New York City to protect patients' rights, and such assignments were usually filled by recent law graduates. In the sixties that meant civil libertarians caught up in "due process" safeguards. Their attitudes were preset against us. We were lumped together as authority figures who carried out Establishment policy by railroading patients into mental hospitals and warehousing them there. So the young legal eagles set out to strike a blow for liberty by confounding us. They got satisfaction in court by loudly challenging doctors' clinical opinions and even suggesting personal sadistic motivation.

In those angry days, I once cut loose at a young attorney who was pushing his suicidal client's demands to go back to the Detention Center. My notion of free will didn't extend that far and my job was to keep the man from harming himself against the better day when he wouldn't want to.

I said, "What's more important, his rights or his life? It's easy to let him go back, Counselor, but when this man tries to kill himself and makes it, it will be on your head!" At once, I thought it was cruel of me, but there wasn't a flicker from the lawyer. Then I saw him smile. He'd gotten the prison ward psychiatrist angry—it was all a game to this kid.

In the sixties, we were suffering from the popularity of a book called *The Myth of Mental Illness* by Thomas Szasz. All the lawyers at Bellevue had read it. Szasz saw greater harm in hospitalizing a man against his will than in letting him go free even if the risk of suicide was great. Some lawyers delighted in the view that there was no mental illness, only a situation in a place like Bellevue where doctors conspired and were intent on depriving patients of their liberty. I'd finish my testimony on a particular case; then the lawyer would get up and present a case for the defense by citing civil liberties denied and never even mention the issue of mental illness. This, at a medical hearing! I was to be cast as the heavy who would railroad the client into a hospital. And I was handicapped in the anomalous position of witness-prosecutor. I couldn't argue over the patient's condition in front of him, object to his lawyer's comments or take issue with the judge's decision.

There was another long-range bad effect of the legal rhetoric. To a man just holding his mental processes together, "Special Two" looked like a courtroom, sounded like a courtroom and therefore he must be on trial. He had a lawyer who was helping him, but there on the stand was a doctor telling lies about him, sending him someplace he didn't want to go. How could a sick man avoid transferring the hostility he felt for the doctor in the courtroom to any doctor he met in the state hospitals and doctors in general?

Some lawyers went to extraordinary lengths to play hero to the doctor's villain because it was an effective way of gaining the defendant's cooperation. Asking for an adjournment was the usual tactic. It was cool to do that, it meant that your lawyer was somehow fighting for you. (Didn't the doctor look angry at the mention of adjournment?)

Judges, too, might decide to adjourn a case without good reason, not realizing the hardships caused by overpopulation on the prison ward; lawyers came up with some very creative reasons for it. I remember one attorney who felt it incumbent on him to study the original minutes of his client's original Grand Jury indictment; it developed into a two-month project. There was another lawyer who had a technique of impeding where he could not win. He advised psychotic men not to speak in court, not to answer questions such as the name of the mayor or the President unless he coached them first, and he did.

This counselor also demanded that his clients be dressed in civilian clothes instead of the general blue hospital pajamas and robe. That was for "their human dignity." He once loudly abused the mother of a defendant because the unhappy woman had decided to help commit her son. I tried to have this operator removed from our ward by writing to his chief, but this, like many of my other campaigns for improvement, had no results. I was creative: I wrote to the building inspector to see if the overcrowding on the ward might not be against the building code (no reply is recorded), and I wrote to Greyhound Bus Lines to see if we couldn't contract their equipment to transfer men to state hospitals more quickly and thus unload the ward (no reply).

GOOD GUYS, BAD GUYS

The lawyer I thought almost as erratic and unstable as his clients remained assigned to our ward. By unfortunate coincidence, he was appointed Legal Aid counsel for that particularly eerie murderer and fugitive who had focused in on Connie. He didn't get a chance to do his worst for this client only because the push to extradite that man from the ward had started and was destined to be successful when it finally reached the state attorney general's office.

Equally frustrating to me was the fact that some men couldn't be helped. Certain mentally ill men do not benefit from any medical-legal procedure designed for them: they fall through the cracks in our system and can't be contained anywhere. I am thinking of one in particular who came three times to Bellevue and appeared seven times in Commitment Court. I'll call him Juan Ignoto—"unknown John" in my homemade Spanish approximation of John Doe—knowing that Betty, our secretary, will laugh when she reads this. She was my Spanish interpreter during evaluation interviews. She sat next to my desk, taking dictation and warning me that my attempts to speak reassuringly in Spanish translated into oddities like "Have a pity on my head, Señor." Betty would also be called into Commitment Court from time to time as an interpreter: incredibly, there was no regular interpreter for the many Hispanic defendants.

She became enough of a regular in court to be threatened. A defendant charged her with being "a member of Nelson Rockefeller's family" and warned her that she would pay for the Rockefeller crimes. Betty will recognize the basic history of Juan Ignoto because she typed some of the evaluation reports on his three trips to Bellevue. He was a cipher to himself, without apparent direction or purpose until the brief period during which he worked for the City of New York as a youth adviser for two hundred dollars a week. This gave him a persona and a cause.

I first saw Juan in 1967, but I was handed a record that went back to 1955. He was eleven when he first came to Bellevue: small for his age, aggressive as a short boy had to be in a fighting gang in the Bronx. He was arrested for juvenile delinquency, throwing rocks at a rabbi's house, and during that Bellevue examination it was concluded that he was defective in intelligence and was emotionally immature. Luckily, he lived at home with his mother and other religious relatives in New York who apparently provided enough stability for him to remain in a public school until the age of fifteen.

As a delinquent child in 1955, Juan was placed on probation by Children's Court. The records show a violation of it in 1956, and an appearance before Magistrates Court in the Bronx on a disorderly conduct charge that was subsequently dismissed. He was arrested again in 1957 and sent to a state training school. He may have learned some trade, but he never worked at it; there is a positive record of only a few days of work exposure at a wholesale market in the Bronx. In his own words, regular work was "not for him." But he had an expressed ambition to be a gangster and it seemed that he worked at that.

By 1961, Juan was just old enough to be sent to Dannemora Prison, a correctional facility for felony offenders. The sentence was five years; the charge, aggravated felonious assault. He had shot a man with a rifle during a street argument.

Juan deteriorated rapidly in prison, complaining of "tape recorders playing back at night everything I say all day." He was transferred to the prison hospital, where he ran his head into a stone wall, cutting it severely. He was then placed on the usual drug therapy—Thorazine, Stelazine—but the only thing that improved was the scope of his paranoid beliefs. Now he was "attacked by the Mafia in jail because I was a Hispanic fighter."

On December 14, 1966, Juan was discharged from the prison under corrections law which allowed transfer of a sick man who had served enough time, and he was accordingly transferred to Rochester State Hospital. There he remained under the jurisdiction of the Board of Parole until the maximum date of his sentence, April 11, 1967. He was discharged from Rochester State with a bleak prognosis for the future: *Psychotic with psychopathic personality.* Condition on discharge: unimproved.

August to October of 1967 were his days of glory. He was hired by the Youth Board as an adviser on Puerto Rican activities for two hundred dollars a week. He was at that time very intense, voluble about the rights of black and Puerto Rican minorities, and comparatively well spoken. He grew a mustache, continued to live at home with his mother and says that he contributed to her support during this period. He liked to watch baseball and "read history."

In September of 1967, he was arrested for felonious assault and possession of a deadly weapon. His victim was a Youth Board supervisor who disagreed with Juan on policy. The complaint states that Juan Ignoto "did point a revolver at the deponent's head and chest, did spin the cylinder of the said weapon, exposing bullets therein to the view of the deponent. While engaged in these acts, the defendant did state to the deponent, 'You are no exception to be killed.' "

Juan's case was heard in Bronx Criminal Court. It was the *prosecution* that raised the sanity issue, and Judge G. sent Juan to Bellevue for psychiatric evaluation for the second time in his life. It happened in November of 1967 and I admitted him to N,O-2.

At twenty-four, Juan was still below average height and his teeth protruded as they had in childhood. But he was now stocky and powerful-looking. His physical examination revealed an old bullet wound in the right leg and a long scar in his side; a serious operation, the removal of one kidney had resulted from another wound. Juan did not remember that operation or did not choose to talk about it because it was in his past. He wouldn't answer questions about the past. He said, "The past is past. It doesn't matter now. It shouldn't be used against you!"

But he did want to explain why he had threatened to kill his Youth Board supervisor. It was because the man "was not honest, and his friends were trying to betray the organization." Juan claimed to have been very active in Puerto Rican rights in the half year since his release from Dannemora and Rochester State. He said he had frequent association with New York political figures because of his plan "to control riots in the city."

Juan began to grow angry with the questions and he could no longer sit still. He rocked back and forth in his chair, looking around the room in a distracted manner, showing distinct paranoid trends in discussing his present difficulties. He alternated between anger and inappropriate smiles or bursts of laughter.

I noted, "His sensorium is clear. His judgment and insight are severely defective and he appears unable to cooperate meaningfully in his own defense." My diagnostic impression at the end of my report was "schizophrenic reaction, chronic, undifferentiated." I found him a "suitable case for commitment to a mental hospital." The other examining psychiatrist concurred in the opinion.

Juan challenged it, demanding a competency hearing. He would not accept a Legal Aid lawyer because he felt that he could be represented only by a man dedicated to civil rights. It sounded all right in the sixties, but the fact was it reflected his preoccupation with victimization and a limited ability to cooperate with the law.

In Special Part Two, Judge M. sitting, Juan was committed to Bronx State Hospital for observation and treatment for six weeks. At the end of that time, he was discharged. No further recommendation was made by Bronx State. Juan went home.

Three and a half months later (it was now April 1968) Juan was again sent to Bellevue for examination because of a disturbance he caused during a demonstration for minority rights at City Hall. He was also arrested on a warrant for the previous unterminated felony charge of attempted assault. This was not at all uncommon; coordination was so slipshod between departments in the system that warrants pursued many men whose cases continued unresolved. Juan certainly should not have been sent home from Bronx State; if their diagnosis was "without psychosis," then he belonged in jail.

This time at Bellevue, there was a new, much more hostile Juan. The entries on his medication record show that he refused it three times in six days. During his preliminary workup, Connie tried to coax him to talk and he answered, "I been here three times. You have my records. I don't have to talk."

But he finally did, for Connie. She wrote: "He asked me many times just to get him through so that he could go back to court. He says he is now a civil-rights leader and has become a

51

Muslim Five Percenter. He laughs continually throughout the interview, brushing off the charges against him."

I scheduled him for an evaluation. He glared, didn't answer, got up and walked out.

The next day, when I had him in again, he was nursing a badly swollen hand. He did remember punching someone on the ward, but didn't remember why. I told him I would send him to the surgery clinic for X-rays of that hand. We made some progress in the interview, but when I asked him whether he heard the tape recorder voices any more he exploded:

"You people think I'm a fool. You keep calling me in and asking me things, the same things. If you keep on calling me in, I'll do something."

One of the things he had in mind to do was sue the hospital and the state for persecuting him. He now believed that all those in positions of authority in American society were against the Hispanic organization he identified with so closely. He had "become" that organization.

Essentially, Juan had not changed since his last admission three and a half months before, and I said that in my report. I could only recommend hospital commitment again, but this time I wrote to Dannemora Prison and to Bronx State Hospital to corroborate the details of his history in those places. The Bronx State records did not arrive, but that was typical.

In Commitment Court on April 30, 1968, Juan was represented by a private attorney from the Bronx. I gave my testimony. The attorney asked for more time to study the case and it was adjourned.

On May 4, the next hearing, the case was adjourned at the attorney's request.

Juan returned to N,O-2.

At the May 21 hearing, I testified and Judge L. granted the attorney's request for adjournment.

Juan continued on the ward.

At the May 30 hearing, I testified. Juan's attorney asked for an adjournment to search for the records from Bronx State. Judge W. granted it.

Juan returned to N,O-2.

At the June 4 hearing, I testified, and Juan's attorney asked for an examination by a private psychiatrist. The court appointed one and Judge M. granted the adjournment.

Juan saw the psychiatrist on the ward.

At the June 25 hearing, the psychiatrist made his report. It was not detailed, only one page long, and it indicated that while Juan was indeed chronically ill, he would probably be able to assist counsel in making a defense. Juan's attorney said that he had made his own personal examination and felt he had enough information to handle the defense. Judge B. granted that week's adjournment.

We were scheduled for a July 9 hearing before a judge whom I knew to be elderly, rather indifferent and not remarkable for his close attention to testimony. So I made a decision, and before the ninth, I wrote a letter to the Presiding Justice of the Bronx Supreme Court. It was labeled a supplemental report; it actually was the white flag of surrender. I withdrew the application for Juan's commitment. I wrote:

> It may be that his hostility to us was not totally inappropriate, possible that he believes we were responsible for the delay in the prompt handling of his processing and that our initial findings were unjustified in view of the fact that Bronx State Hospital recently discharged him and that both his private attorney and psychiatrist consider him competent.
>
> In view of this, we believe that his attorney should be given the opportunity to proceed with the case and therefore we are returning Mr. Ignoto for trial.

Not for a moment did I believe that it was the right thing to do, but I was beaten. And tired. I wondered, why go on opposing the maneuvers in Commitment Court when I really had nothing more remedial to offer? As Juan had pointed out to Connie, it was the third time he'd been on N,O-2; we had his records, we should know the answers to the questions—if there were answers for him.

How long can a man who combines a neurotic need to show off with paranoid aggressions stay out of trouble?

GOOD GUYS, BAD GUYS

I could prophesy for him: he had done time for assault, he would do more. He had been on our prison ward and I'd give any odds he would turn up on another one, though I sincerely hoped that it wouldn't be Bellevue. He had already been committed to a state hospital and discharged. I was only trying to send him to another such place. Now, he would return to trial, and in all probability, a term in jail. He'd been there before, too; he'd serve his time and hit the street and whenever his aggressions exploded, he'd commit another assault with a weapon, or it might well be homicide, if his aim improved.

Then the cycle, which was all society had to offer, would begin again: arraigned, remanded most probably to Bellevue, committed to (most probably) Matteawan, then back for post-commitment evaluation to the psychiatric prison ward, then on to a state hospital as part of a plea bargain—or he'd "walk" because of time served. I had thrown in the towel and called him competent, but given the repetitive nature of mental illness and the psychotic (bad) judgment it involved, my calling him competent now would not inevitably affect things. He'd be back again if somebody didn't kill him in the meantime.

He didn't fit the solutions, and most of us will only go so far in watching over problematic people for whom we will not be held personally accountable. The Legal Aid lawyer can insist that a man be set free, knowing that he himself will not be found wanting whatever that man may subsequently do or whom he may harm. The lawyer's professional function has been exercised: no judge will reproach him with later developments, saying "Why did you argue so hard for that case?" The judge too does his job without asking himself too many questions, as do the professionals in prisons or hospitals where the men are sent. It is possible that an incompetent man could die of starvation at Pilgrim Psychiatric Center, as *The New York Times* recently reported. It was said that no one cared enough to find out why he was starving himself; the reason was that his stomach hurt from undiagnosed ulcers.

With the tools that society provides, we are geared to maintenance or temporary solutions, and not to humane responsibility.

The situation in the Commitment Court finally produced

efforts at improvement in 1968. There were more meetings to discuss streamlining procedures: getting me more QP help, putting the N,O-2 cases on the docket before the civil cases. There were proposals that I arrange precourt consultations about patients with the Legal Aid lawyers. In one letter proposal, I asked that the Mental Health Information Service be formally requested to examine instances of arbitrary adjournments and cumbersome technicalities so that the treatment of patients would not be delayed. At such times, I had in mind Juan Ignoto and others like him—dangerous yet somehow pathetic men. We didn't have the answers for them then. And we still don't.

4 | Tilting at Windmills

In December 1980, New York Mayor Ed Koch said in an interview, "The state policy of releasing deinstitutionalized patients without adequate support has turned the city's neighborhoods into mental wards and the police into hospital orderlies."

In 1969, when I left Bellevue to work in community psychiatry on New York's West Side, this same policy was being touted as a great humane reform, an expression of patients' rights that was long overdue.

Deinstitutionalization swept the state hospitals of New York, California and many other states almost clean of mental patients. They were often relocated in urban areas. The reasoning was that the mentally ill had become so institutionalized in hospitals, or by hospitals, that they had ceased to improve. It was thought that they would do just as well, or better, if they were discharged into the communities with aftercare and medication. The growing network of federally sponsored Mental Health Centers was set up to function with this new emphasis on outpatient care. The particular center I joined was part of the Roosevelt Hospital in Manhattan.

57

GOOD GUYS, BAD GUYS

The Community Psychiatry unit was to act as a kind of early warning system detecting mental illness before it became chronic. That meant quick intervention, treating both patient and family in their own environment.

Statistics tell us that 20 percent of Americans have some form of mental illness that needs intervention. The situation on the West Side was much worse than that. Too many of our local residents could be called patients: not only the crushing load of those recently discharged from the state hospitals but also thousands of old, poor, foreign and otherwise inadequately cared-for people. There is no way to estimate the size of this huge shadow population that we—just the few of us—were supposed to treat.

While I was still at Bellevue, I saw that the state hospitals had begun to turn away new patients. One reason after another was given for keeping people out: too old, insufficiently suicidal, or not enough of a danger to others. At the same time, there was a rush to qualify patients for discharge, with a clear failure in appraising them and deciding who could function outside the hospitals.

The discharged patients were the largest nonfunctioning aggregate of people ever to hit the cities. And the cities were not at all prepared for them; community care was an illusion. If they somehow managed to connect with a place where they could get the antipsychotic drugs they needed, they were not supervised: it was not mandatory that they take the medicine or return for follow-up. The burden was on these people, warehoused and directed for years, to make such decisions and take advantage of the new freedom.

So they didn't get to clinics or take the medicine they needed. They would forget, just as they'd forget to pick up the welfare checks that were their only income or give the money away to whoever asked. They'd forget to eat even if they could pay for food. Wandering, sleeping in the subways if they feared to return to their single room occupancy (SRO) hotel, they lived as dim observers of the life around them, not sure which voices they heard were real and which hallucinatory. Some lived in a drifting fog of angry confusion so that a chance contact—someone passing, accidentally touching, seeming to threaten—could provoke a violent, irrational response.

This was what the public saw on city streets and what made them afraid. What they didn't see, or couldn't distinguish from the wild-looking mental patients, were the real predators who moved among them. The danger came from these parasites on the mentally ill, the ex-cons and junkies who were housed with them, under the welfare umbrella, in the SROs of the inner cities. Part of my function in Community Psychiatry was to act as a consultant to a major welfare center. I saw the mental patients sitting side by side with criminals to register for public assistance. The patients were the easiest kind of prey, so easy that the criminals stuck close to them and the affected neighborhoods where they both lived disintegrated into fearsome places where you couldn't send a child to the store for a bottle of milk or your wife was afraid to push the baby carriage down the street.

Without medication, some patients grew periodically agitated or violent. The psychiatric social workers attached to the Roosevelt Hospital Community Psychiatry unit were supposed to know about the violently psychotic people in our territory and try to deal with their crises. I remember one social worker who took real chances. Gary Walsh now has a psychotherapy practice in San Francisco. When I first met him, he was just where he wanted to be as a member of the Neighborhood Outreach team of the Community Psychiatry effort. The city and its incredible problems had drawn Gary all the way from Sioux City, Iowa. In college he had written his master's thesis on poverty in New York. Gary had been trained and thought he knew what to expect. When I spoke to him recently he immediately dredged up the memory of one patient he would never forget, a man called John T.

John T. followed the usual postdischarge route from a hospital into a welfare office and onto the rolls. Welfare put him in a typical building filled with such placements. It was 807 West 85th Street,* a place not remarkable for its size or appearance

*807 West 85th Street is a fictitious address.

but with a certain definite personality: when Gary was assigned to 807, he was told that twelve people had been murdered there.

The 120 tenants in the building were the usual mix of society's untouchables: deteriorated alcoholics, unemployable ex-cons, unemployable former mental patients, old, disabled or disoriented people who for one reason or another had loosened their grip on life and were waiting to die. Gary, the visiting nurse and the alcoholism counselor were there to do what could be done; they spent several days a week in 807. Much of Gary's time was spent in finding John T. when that became a neighborhood necessity.

As Gary explained to me, "When John T. was on the edge of one of his slides into violent psychosis, he would go through the neighborhood throwing rocks at windows, setting fires in 807, or standing on the roof, waving a machete. He'd threaten anyone going inside, or sometimes he'd cut the electric wires so that it went dark in 807. These were signs that he wanted to go to the hospital for medication."

Gary said that John was always unpredictable. "I remember coming into 807 on a Monday morning and hearing that people had been afraid of John for days. He'd set a fire, but they got to it in time, and then he threw a brick through a bakery window. I knew I'd have to go looking for him."

"Before you called the police, Gary?"

"No. I called the police. But in the meantime, I had to find John. I went around the neighborhood and spotted him at Eighty-sixth Street and Broadway. That was a crosstown-bus street, a subway street, and it was always crowded."

I asked what John was doing.

"He wasn't doing anything," Gary said. "He was just standing in the crowd, watching the people. I went up to him and said what had worked with him before. 'I know about the fire, I know you're not feeling well, I want to go with you to the hospital, the police are coming, but I'll stay with you,' the usual. This time he turned and smashed me in my face."

Gary's voice was professionally neutral, as if he were complaining about his own tactics. "There should have been some way to short-circuit that, so I wouldn't get smashed in the face."

I could only agree. "Did John go to the hospital?"

"Yes, and I went with him in the ambulance. When we passed the place where I was staying, near 807, he pointed to it and said he knew I lived there. He said he would come back and kill me for bothering him."

"And you knew he'd be back."

"Where else would he go, Marty? He lived in 807. Bellevue would usually keep him forty-eight hours, sometimes less. They'd give him his meds and send him out with no follow-up. He'd be back. If he remembered, he'd look for me."

"So you were scared."

"I want to tell you I was scared! I stayed with a friend for four days before I went back to my own place. By that time, it was all right. But you never knew how much the medicine was really doing for John. I was walking with a friend in the neigh-borhood—off duty—and I saw John across the street. He suddenly turned around, grabbed the two people who were walking behind him and began hitting their heads. Maybe he knew them, or maybe they just had the bad luck to be there."

"Gary, did I know about this case? Why the hell didn't someone put John T. back in the state hospital?"

Gary sounded surprised at me. "Nobody would do it. No one wanted to take the responsibility. Don't you remember how it was, Marty? Don't you remember what you had to do about the old lady with the ulcerated leg?"

I did remember. The little old woman Gary mentioned rep-resented a different kind of problem but equally urgent in its way. This emaciated soul would die if she wouldn't let us help her. She had an ulcerated right foot that had developed gangrene, but she lived behind a locked door in 807 and she wouldn't let Gary or the visiting nurse in to treat her. After several days of persuasion, Gary had gotten her to the point where she would open the door—keeping the chain on—and thrust her blackened foot into the hall so that the nurse could work on it. While I was there at Gary's request to see what I could do, she finally decided to open the door all the way.

Hers was a room like so many others I'd seen. The old and

addled made lairs to hide in, dens where the floor was thick with papers and their own droppings. There was eighteen inches of something on this woman's floor; my feet crunched and slipped on the debris. When she saw me, she crawled into a cave of blankets and clothes.

While she watched—suspiciously—I took pictures of her and her room with the Polaroid automatic camera I'd brought for just such a purpose. A woman who could live with a foot blackened by gangrene must be treated medically and ought to be readmitted to a state hospital, though it would be against her will. She looked and sounded totally psychotic, but I'd long since learned that this diagnosis might not be enough to do it. Only a picture of the foot in living color—no way to include the smell of rot— would pressure the receiving hospital where she would be going for treatment. In this case, as in most Manhattan cases, the hospital was Bellevue.

I was angry in advance. I knew Bellevue would say she was too old to get back into a state hospital. They had a policy of turning away people over sixty-five; I had seen the directive excluding senior citizens sent by a deputy commissioner of the state Department of Mental Hygiene while I was still working on Ward N,O-2. But I thought I could use a little leverage with my friend who was now head of the Psychiatric Admitting Office. I gave Gary a note for him, emphasizing the old woman's prior history of psychiatric hospitalizations so that Bellevue couldn't treat her medically and send her home on the pretext that she was only a "confused" old person. The note read, "Tell 'em she's an old schizophrenic and they can't keep her out!" (I'd had several such frustrations on my "house calls" and I was fed up.) If that didn't work, I told Gary to flash the pictures and strongly—very strongly—imply that I was thinking of sending them to the *Times*.

The lady with the foot did get a stay in the hospital and she didn't return to 807. It was some choice. I couldn't guarantee that she would thrive in a state hospital; the mortality rates in the medical-surgical buildings were fantastic. But it wasn't worse than the terror, isolation and starvation she was free to enjoy in her SRO room. I knew that someone would soon be carrying her skinny corpse downstairs from there.

The frustration was that I couldn't make the right things happen, and if her pain had not been so great as to force her to cooperate, I'd never even have gotten her to Bellevue. As a physician in the Community Psychiatry unit I was supposedly dedicated to keeping people out of the hospitals; wouldn't you think I'd have a little leeway the few times when I felt that someone needed recommitment? Theoretically, two categories would be readmitted: the really suicidal and the homicidal. In practice, we would have to prove even those cases. But John T. could definitely get in again after he'd killed someone.

That's how it was. No one wanted to be identified with the results of dumping people on the neighborhoods. Yet the ex-patients, and even the ex-criminals, had a certain economic value. Welfare needed rooms for them and landlords suffering with older buildings in the inner city needed tenants. Everyone got something out of it except the public and the liberal West Siders who had listened in good spirit to those urging them to open their neighborhoods to the disadvantaged. By now they knew how badly they'd been had and would escape by moving away as soon as possible, leaving still more vacancies for welfare tenants.

Ironically, one of the charges against state hospitals was that they "warehoused" patients. What then to call the huge apartment houses and disused hotels where the patients lived unsupervised? They were warehouses and, worse, de facto state hospitals without nurses or medicines or safety. So many "freed" patients huddled in their little spaces, never answering a knock at the door, afraid to go out on the street yet afraid to be there when the drug addicts who burgled so many rooms broke into theirs. I used to marvel at the door frames of those rooms whenever I had reason to visit the SROs. They were chewed and scarred by tire irons— it wouldn't take a minute to get inside.

One of the everyday ironies of Community Psychiatry was that communities, in the sense intended, did not exist. The Roosevelt Hospital was the center of a designated community area and the term made you think of an orderly place with trees and a town square. The reality, the 300-odd blocks that stretched from 30th to 86th streets, was a patchwork of sharply different neighborhoods that survived by not interacting with each other.

At the southern end of our territory were five-floor tenement walk-ups in Chelsea and Clinton. "Hell's Kitchen," which used to be home for Irish stevedores and prizefighters, was now crowded with people who spoke Greek, Italian and all varieties of Caribbean Spanish. Further up, through the sixties, there were Orientals, Indians and out-of-town singles in the buildings that had become boardinghouses. A junkie nation surrounded the drug dealers' territorial capital of Needle Park, a treeless triangle in the middle of Broadway at 72d Street. Going west toward the Hudson River, the remnants of the middle class and that last bastion of refugees from Middle Europe were losing ground to welfare, house by house. To the east, beyond the bodegas selling groceries and the few remaining Irish saloons peddling nostalgia, was a moneyed enclave of big apartments. Beyond Amsterdam and Columbus, a fair number of rich folks held firm right on the edge of Central Park. They rarely walked west.

As Roosevelt Hospital's Community Psychiatry unit picked up staff and momentum, most of its action took place at the Henry Hudson hotel on West 59th Street. The Henry Hudson was exactly the kind of big old barn which sheltered welfare placements, but its location across the street from Roosevelt made it valuable to us. There were some offices on the sixth floor, but the entire eighth floor had been rented and was a warren of Community Psychiatry cubicles and treatment rooms. Tiny hotel rooms became our tinier offices.

Officially, I was the psychiatrist in charge of the Neighborhood Care teams. This was the outreach operation in which people like Gary Walsh were sent to deal with problems on site. Later the teams were separated into northern and southern areas of operation. Northern (above 57th Street) went to Dr. Josephine Martin. I headed the southern team but continued to have overview and act as troubleshooter for both. I was a kind of GHQ man, usually to be found at my duty station in the Henry Hudson. But I'd be called into the field when, for example, my doctor's authority was needed to break into a room in which some frightened ex-mental patient had barricaded himself, refusing to eat. The police came with me on these legal break-ins. We knew everything we had to do except what would happen if the delusional tenant inside had a gun. Several times a month, I made these unrequested "house calls."

At the Henry Hudson offices, our patients were referred to us by many local sources, and after the usual registration, they funneled through to me for diagnosis. I would prescribe emergency intervention by our neighborhood teams, medication, or an appropriate therapy group or social agency. By far the most popular therapy group was family therapy. Meetings were held in rooms with electronic audio systems and two-way mirrors so that Community Psychiatry trainees could observe and hear the family in therapeutic action. In family psychodramas, the participants interacted by yelling, screaming or crying, with the therapists urging them to "let it all come out!"

Most of the staff *loved* family therapy. I got one dissenting opinion from the secretary in charge of the family therapy waiting list, none other than my old friend Betty from Ward N,O-2. She had wanted to leave Bellevue and I'd helped her get a job with the head of outpatient services at Roosevelt Hospital. We had a big reunion.

"Too much family therapy training" was Betty's opinion. "All the people who have emotional problems want to do it. They're giving couples advice while they're being divorced themselves!"

"How do you get along with them?"

"At a distance." Betty was wary of what she called the "wacked-out people" doing family counseling. She described her encounters with them.

"When they haven't seen you for a day or two they'll hug you and kiss you and tell you how good, how *good* it is to see you. They're so into touching and feeling that they can't behave any other way. And if you chance to tell them any little problem you have, they burrow in. They want you to expose your soul."

That was true. The kids who had gotten their professional credentials in the sixties pushed like crazy for all their patients to be loose and uncontained. The cure *and* the treatment had to be a community project. Some therapists seemed to have more interest in the family than the problems of the irrational "index patient." Instead of focusing on him or her, they'd be busily collecting insights from everyone else in the family and urging the kids to describe their *real* feelings about their parents.

You can imagine how that went down with the Hispanic families where there was never any question that father knew best. The Hispanic men we saw had already lost much of their traditional machismo because of working wives whose salaries topped theirs and Americanized, independent children. The therapist threatened to shrink them further. Some families tried interaction once and never came back.

I had an Orthodox Jewish rabbi in the Community Psychiatry program who had trained in pastoral counseling. He had his own problems with the all-out therapy approach and almost gave up his participation.

Rabbi Jerome Fishman asked, "How do you teach a child to be disrespectful of its parents in the name of psychiatric therapy? That's against my own tradition. Suppose parents don't want to be called by their first names, to be diminished in front of their children?"

I too thought there should be limits to the informality. I didn't care to be introduced to patients as "Marty, your doctor," yet that was routine. I'd see the blank incomprehension in the eyes of older, out-of-country people. They were from other cultures, they were struggling to comprehend English, and when some bright kid in turtleneck and jeans introduced them to "Marty," there wasn't a flicker of response. They were looking for the *doctor*. After a while, I introduced myself as Doctor before anybody could call me Marty. I also wore a jacket, shirt and tie.

Enthusiasm and good intentions were there, but general efficiency was very low and the set-up itself encouraged goofs. Rabbi Fishman, who often worked with school groups, found himself addressing a group of parents and children who didn't speak English. (At least the parents didn't.) He called for an interpreter out of our scant supply and made do with a nice

Mexican woman, a community worker whose Spanish was wildly individual and whose English was off the wall. So picture the rabbi, wearing his yarmulke, talking to people who didn't understand him through an interpreter who didn't speak their kind of Spanish, echoed by children translating again for their parents' comprehension. He finally made some sort of common ground by talking about his own parents and the timeless poverty and discrimination they suffered as immigrants in New York at the turn of the century. The group made a nice vignette for a Norman Rockwell painting, but the rabbi had a question about its professional effectiveness.

All around us there was fraud. Too many people were getting money from welfare by claiming not to have a husband in the home or falsifying the number of children in the family by "borrowing" from the neighbors when the caseworker came. They'd even collect money from several agencies at once because they knew it was difficult to check. Finally, to spare costs, caseworkers were told not to bother to check at all.

That suited some but not others. I saw caseworkers who really didn't care where the money went; they were in it for the job or to avoid the Vietnam draft. Others did not want to be part of something rotten and pleaded for a system of accountability.

Our own Community Psychiatry teams could have used it too. Federal seed money had given the Community Mental Health Centers across the country their start, but operational funds were supposed to be matched by the state, city and the hospital in which each center was located. The Roosevelt Hospital would want to know how many Medicaid- and Medicare-reimbursed patients we were seeing, and in the cheerful chaos of our office, I had my doubts about how well those records were kept.

I set out to remind the people around me that we were working for a hospital and instituted the old tradition, medical morning rounds. These were regular morning meetings of my team to discuss the cases that had come up the day before and to plan for the day ahead. They were a discipline for team members; the orderly presentation of cases ensured that patients would be seen and follow-ups done immediately. We also wrestled with continuing problems like the family S., whose members had earnestly asked for help but would not keep appointments for family therapy sessions. At least one of the daughters had turned prostitute to meet family needs and more than one of the sons was involved with drug dealing. We'd managed to get them on welfare—and there were many thanks for that—but there was nobody home for our "home visits." It didn't dawn on me for quite a while that my southern team members were nuisances interfering with a family enterprise. It was Señora S. herself who sent her sons and daughters out to work the streets!

But we had a better record of success than family S. might indicate. Three times a week, I asked for special reports on problem situations and we'd discuss such topics as the heavies in welfare hotels who were assaulting others. We would ask the police precinct for help in controlling these characters, and an officer who was liaison to community groups sometimes came to our meetings. But each problem solved opened the door to others demanding solutions, and that meant more meetings when we already suffered from such a plague of meetings that the part-time staffers had no time to make home visits to patients.

We wouldn't survive if we couldn't get more patient referrals and reimbursible patient-staff contacts from the community. It was that simple. Out in the big informal state hospital in the streets, very few people knew about Roosevelt Hospital's Community Psychiatry unit. And we were stepchildren to the hospital's regular services. If we could have screened some of the miserable many who packed the hospital's emergency room, we'd have been up to our necks in Medicaid-reimbursibles who needed psychiatric help. But that didn't happen. It was hard to make the emergency room cooperative: no big emergency service with lots of trauma cases or heart attacks has time for "psychos." A hallucinating man who stumbled in with alcohol on his breath would as likely as not be labeled AOB (Alcohol on Breath) and sent out as a "simple intoxication." A John T. could easily miss the emergency room psychiatric resident on call if he was sent home as a drunk. Even if there was a consultation, he'd probably find that there were no beds available in Psychiatry. And rarely would an AOB be transferred to another hospital for care.

I had a notion of how to involve the local community in our need for patients which caught on. I called it the "spotters" program. The spotters we asked to help us lived and worked in the neighborhood. We gave them fliers about Community Psychiatry: the barber shop, the laundromat, the restaurants and stores passed out our literature. If Victor Muñoz, a bodega owner on Ninth Avenue, had a customer who couldn't pay for groceries, who seemed depressed and unable to cope, he'd call us and a team of social workers would try to make contact with that person. The super of a rooming house on West 55th Street might hear a child's screams once too often and report his suspicion of child abuse. We'd try to contact the family. Dr. Melendez, a neighborhood physician, would directly refer those of his patients who needed psychiatric help. We had spotters behind the counters in bodegas, over at the Clinton Drug Addiction Center on West 49th Street and above all in the churches. Some very practical help came from the churches, both patient referrals and volunteer workers. We had young seminarians from New Jersey, and nearby St. Paul the Apostle Church sent priests as volunteers. Some spoke Spanish.

We were also successful in involving the clergy from the once-prosperous Protestant churches in our area. They were having identity crises of their own as their former congregations disappeared, and a few of the young ministers really needed something to do. But the troops from the Catholic seminaries were our real assets. They were just good people whose traditional training offered them motivation and protection against the misery they found. They were armored against disgust at the drunks lying in urine and booze, and they were patient with the apathetic, befuddled, pitiable people they escorted to the hospital for much-needed medicine. I remember that a few of these young men left the priesthood, but they didn't go far away. They took jobs helping the needy and got more of the same brand of experience.

The spotters program brought in some results from the regular community people only because we really pursued every lead. It wasn't enough; the outreach teams would now have to spend time in the welfare hotels to reach that large population. The need was there, and the Medicaid too. The big hotels to the north in the seventies and eighties were Medicaid mother lodes.

When the block associations began to make protests about conditions on the streets around those hotels, we saw the complaints as opportunities to visit some of the largest ones and try to shoehorn our teams inside. I would usually approach the manager as advance negotiator.

"Hello, sir. I'm Doctor Lubin from the Roosevelt Hospital Community Psychiatry team."

"A psychiatrist? What are you doing here, Doctor? Did you come to examine my head?"

All the managers seemed to have the same sense of humor.

The particular hotel I'm going to describe was a big one on Broadway in the seventies. The usual tenants were visible on the day I walked in: drug addicts, criminals, weakened, wizened alcoholics and the empty faces from the state hospitals.

Inside, the lobby was covered with the small white tiles often found in the kitchens of old city tenements, here arranged in geometric patterns with a border. Plywood partitions had narrowed a lobby space originally much larger to create the hotel's office and reception space. It was protected by a counter and glass partition.

Two men met me. They were managers or lessees who had probably taken over the building for owners who were intentionally obscure, but they had the power to let our team come in. Both were graduates of concentration camps; it was bizarre that so many guardians of these welfare warehouses had numbers tattooed on their arms! They were old experts in the warehousing of souls, jovial enough, a few inches down, but underneath that, layers of impassivity blanketing whatever was left at the emotional core. They reminded me of *The Pawnbroker*, a movie about a man who worked at avoiding the ordinary emotions of life. Whatever went on in the rooms upstairs would be accepted without surprise, taken patiently until the managers could leave for the night. I felt that they were not ill-disposed to their tenants, not disposed at all, in any way. They had passed beyond that.

One asked me, "Are you here on business, Doctor?"

Yes, I was there on business and I pushed my own case as practically as I could, coming on like one shrewd operator who recognizes that two other shrewd fellows have a good thing going, but can show them that it pays to listen. If the objects of my persuasion thought that I had a deal going and was somehow making something above and beyond my hospital salary by getting a team into their hotel—so be it. It made me less suspect as a do-gooder.

My pitch was that our team would do the hotel no harm and a positive good, since its presence would pacify the block association's complaints. The managers would look benevolent at no cost. All that had to be done was to communicate with us, even minimally, and we'd have an alcoholism counselor on duty as well as psychiatric help. Problems with the tenants' mental health could be referred to us.

That offer in particular clinched the deal.

I asked, as I usually did, for the use of several rooms near the entrance. We needed a few partitions, tables, chairs, some paint, and we were in business.

The team installed in that hotel consisted of two alcoholism counselors, a social worker, a registered nurse and a Spanish-speaking case aide. The alcoholism counselors were both recovered alcoholics themselves and one was an impressive ex-priest.

They needed a miracle to do any lasting good. Remember that the hotel had three hundred and fifteen rooms full of lost souls. But they were available and they did make a difference, especially in one of the managers. They opened a little crack in him, and through it poured enough stored benevolence to make up for his years in limbo. He thawed and came to life again.

The fact is that we were stretched very thin in the outreach operation. The combined strength of the north and south teams, for all their commitment and energy, was still only twenty people. They had to visit so many welfare hotels that it was a triage operation. Triage, certainly, to put two nurses, Lois Dwyer and

Joanne Sweeney, into the Endicott Hotel. The Endicott, on West 81st Street, had gotten heavy publicity in the newspapers as a choice hellhole. You'd cross the street to avoid it for all the usual reasons lounging on the steps, and also because dogs and cats had been known to come hurtling down from the roof to die on the sidewalk. The place also had a reputation for lots of homicides. That's where we stationed two of our senior nurses.

I used to have an occasional Friday night drink with team members. One of them, Joanne, would talk and talk, ridding herself of the weight of the Endicott for a weekend of normal life. It may have been Joanne, or Gary, who told me about one particular Christmas Eve when team members from several welfare hotels decided to meet after hours to celebrate together. They looked around at the neighborhood, thought of what was inside those buildings, and began to cry. All of them stood on the street crying with Christmas Eve guilt for what could not be changed by all their effort. It was a gust of emotion that blew in and blew out; afterward, they went for a drink.

We had the usual human mix of talkers and doers, dreamers and practical people, but some of the best had the worst of jobs. They were fueled by an idealism and a sense of personal responsibility which had brought them into this wretchedness from nice clean places all over America.

Barbara Oliver, a former inpatient nurse at Roosevelt and a member of my southern team, used to accuse herself of ineffectuality each time she went on a home visit with her Spanish-speaking "buddy." (The buddy system was mandatory for protection.) As she climbed still another flight of dark, leaning, disfigured stairs, Barbara would think, "What am I doing here with all my training? How can I help? Any damn thing could happen to me here!"

She'd walk into an apartment and have to choke back the request to ask for a window opened for fear of insulting the family who lived with that smell. Barbara was the professional, the one who knew the right questions to ask, but it was the other woman, the Spanish-speaking, city-bred paraprofessional, who was getting through to the people who had "everything wrong with the way they lived." Barbara didn't like her own reactions; she saw herself as a middle-class tripper down from her home on Cape Cod, not functional in these surroundings.

Bob Clark, also on my team, was a former divinity student from Texas. (Later he married Barbara Oliver and I interviewed them together.) In New York, Bob found that his religion and philosophy courses were supremely irrelevant to the new environment. His first assignment was a call from the Endicott Hotel: a woman had thrown a sink into the street. What was he going to do about it? When he knocked on her door, she opened it a crack, looked at his blond mustache, shouted "Hitler Nazi!" and slammed the door again. Bob hadn't any idea what to do next, except laugh and wonder where she'd found the strength to heave a bathroom sink out the window.

But there was no laughing later when he pulled a young woman who had been dead for two days out of her room. In the weeks and months that followed he had to wait for an immunity to build up before he could laugh freely.

"In my better moments," Bob said, "I saw what I was doing as temporary relief. In my worst, I saw it as trying to change the structure. And that was the worst because as much as I wanted to, I knew I couldn't do it."

Surprisingly, the most valuable people I worked with might be politically conservative with a strong religious background. They understood morality and compassion in a basic way and I saw them empathize with patients when the articulate types with the too-skilled psychiatric patter couldn't make the contact. People who knew too much about the politics of health care delivery or talked too much about "caring" didn't seem to be around for the dirty work. On the other hand, I did have one caring radical on my team at Roosevelt, a very pretty young Puerto Rican woman. She joined the Puerto Rican FALN or an equivalent. It must have been one of the bomb-throwing groups because the FBI came to ask us about her after she'd left Roosevelt Hospital for a trip to Cuba.

The good, committed people I worked with got on with their jobs in a spare, unsentimental way, calling an uncooperative drunk a drunk and a lazy SOB just that. These altruists needed to serve, but they were overconfident because they were working for a big institution and "the right cause." Their supervisors prompted them, and they had understandable feelings of youthful immortality, but I had to warn them, often, that this didn't guarantee safety. We took the courage of the people we sent out very much for granted. Most of what they undertook was physically scary and there just weren't any guidelines worth a damn.

When Gary Walsh received his assignment to 807 West 85th, he made two initial mistakes. He went there alone and he wore a suit. In his neat, double-breasted suit, white shirt and well-shined shoes, he was coming on like a professional.

"I didn't know what you did, how you dressed," Gary said. "There was no information passed from worker to worker until two years later, when I left 807 for good. Then I wrote twenty pages for the next one to read."

Gary's first move was to call a tenants' meeting to explain what Community Psychiatry would do for them. That first meeting, like all others for months afterwards, could be held only in the cellar.

"It was dark, no heat, one light bulb. You'd be interrupted by psychotic outbursts from people there or screaming from people coming in. They came, they started arguing with each other, and they didn't even look at me standing there in my suit. The Hispanics yelled, 'Let's get the blacks!' The blacks yelled 'Kill the Spics!' Some were stripping off their shirts to fight.

"Of course I didn't know what to do. But I picked up the table in front of me and I threw it against the wall as hard as I could. It broke. Everybody turned and looked at me. They *saw* me. They all sat down and we had a meeting!"

When Gary got back to the room he had rented in the neighborhood, he took off his suit—for the duration—and bought street clothes at a secondhand store. Every day he appeared in battered jeans, an old shirt, decrepit sandals. Don't you think that his supervisor, a nice lady who had her office on the sixth floor of the Henry Hudson, gave him a hard time because he didn't look "professional"? Sure she did.

"You could get killed wearing that suit," Gary insisted.

There is always a division between those who work at head-quarters and those on the front line.

After a year in Community Psychiatry we knew the limits of what we could accomplish on the West Side. No one was ever going to do what the public had been led to believe was possible. It was pure delusion to think that Community Psychiatry principles would have any effect in the poor urban jungle. An operation several times bigger than we were couldn't have made a dent in the massive misery there.

To do our job, we progressively narrowed our focus to the people who were the greatest victims and those who were able to respond to our help. We also went after controlling assaultive drunks, child abusers, the ex-cons and other predators who terrorized the helpless in the SROs. Those became our priorities.

I saw so many patients that I made a mental list of the questions that seemed to fit most problems. I could rapidly find out what was needed to improve their general economic and social situation as well as their mental status. Then I'd make calls or write letters—to immigration about visas and stays of deportation, to welfare about checks and case reviews—and I'd use any connection to activate numerous social service organizations in the city and state. I was a kind of West Side ombudsman. As a doctor, my calls carried weight. The letters got results because I signed my name and thereby put my head on the line.

Rabbi Fishman once told me that he was upset enough about a child neglect case he had come across to write to the Department of Social Services about it. His supervisor set him straight:

"Don't sign your name to anything. There's somebody else making more money than you do. Let him be to blame."

That bureaucrat's defensive attitude was common, yet we took the heat in these cases and never got burned. We even made up a game that ridiculed the attitude, calling it "hidden agenda"— the paranoid's reason behind any action. A team captain who was obsessed with the hospital's wealthy board of trustees revealed his lively paranoia by questioning the "hidden agenda" in any hospital policy that affected his team. Everyone got in on the game. You'd hear "Hidden agenda!" when the toilet broke down.

Roosevelt Hospital did not have a hidden agenda for our unit but did have practical objections. The psych beds were filled and their regular outpatient services were doing well. It was only our avant-garde operation that appeared costly. We'd provided good publicity opportunities for the hospital in our few years of operation, but we weren't the sound organization that could show anything like a yearly break-even budget. Validating the welfare patients we saw as Medicaid and Medicare contacts proved a tough discipline for our crew. They saw lots of patients individually and in groups, but the professional hubris might have to be laid aside if each patient contact meant a note in a chart and a form to be filled out. It wasn't hard to see a financial reckoning just down the road.

Gary Walsh had a close one when he was told that his operation at 807 would be phased out because there weren't enough formal psychotherapy contacts with Medicaid patients to pay for all the services he'd brought into the building. And Gary had done a little miracle: daily alcoholism meetings, a recreation program, chest X-rays for all, Pap tests for the women, a first-aid instruction program, bimonthly doctor's visits from Roosevelt. All in all, there was such an improvement in morale that the people who were going to kill each other in the cellar on Gary's first day now set aside a special time to celebrate the birthdays in the building by preparing a communal meal. (It was something like a church supper in the Middle West.) All this was going down the drain because the one hundred and twenty disabled people in that building—a small mental hospital—were not seen as paying their way.

Ten years later, Gary was still angry when he recalled what they'd had to do.

"We collected Medicaid numbers. Every time we said 'Hello, how are you?' to anyone, the 'How are you?' was counted as a professional visit. And whenever there was any kind of meeting, we wouldn't let the people leave until they'd shouted out their numbers and we'd written them down."

By such measures, 807 did show a profit and was reprieved. Other worthwhile attempts, much in the right direction, had to go down the fiscal drain. Bob Clark and Regina Casals, a bright, thoughtful social worker from an émigré Cuban family, decided to build a block assocation on 56th Street between Ninth and Tenth Avenues—a tough block. It was all sweat and legwork. They got the names of a few natural leaders, rounded up the attendance for meetings and started discussions about safety, day care for the block's children and painting the houses. As a result of the meetings, the Eighteenth Police Precinct immediately assigned more patrol cars to the area. It was a good beginning.

But it was only a beginning because Bob and Regina had to move on to reimbursable assignments and the hospital could not replace them on the block project. Without extended direction, the attempt to make a block "family" viable fell apart.

I think the same approach could have been successful with corporate contributions. Equitable Life Assurance was within the Roosevelt Hospital's catchment area, as was the headquarters of Gulf and Western. Why couldn't one of these corporate giants rehabilitate a block, pay for exterior renovating of the houses and be there as the bulwark of the project? I felt that they might be interested in good public relations for comparative peanuts, and that by concentrating, one block at a time, a neighborhood which contained both the corporations and the tenements might be revitalized.

We rarely had time to develop any such innovative ideas.

After three years at Roosevelt, I had an opportunity to go to work in another new field. There had been a great growth in the development of psychiatric services in general hospitals and I was to build a hospital department of psychiatry from scratch. As chief, I'd have the same freedom to make things happen that I'd had in my ombudsman function at Roosevelt, but this time with more measurable results.

When I left the West Side, there were few signs of the comparative improvement due to economics that would come in the next few years. West Side property values escalated with the shortage of apartments in the city. Landlords were offered tax inducements to modernize their rundown buildings for conversion to luxury rentals and co-ops. Since most of the SRO buildings were not covered by rent controls of any kind, the owners could move to dispossess their tenants. The residents had a right to fight eviction in court. But look who they were. How many could hire a lawyer?

Community groups like the SRO Task Force and the Tenants Rights Coalition tried to hold the line against further building conversions. Social workers and tenants charged that sudden, violent evictions took place in some hotels, even midnight "Get the hell out!" raids by hotel employees carrying clubs or bats. In other buildings, they said, dogs and guns were brought in to scare tenants into leaving and the doors to their rooms were nailed shut to make sure that none came back.

The same local citizens who had worked to clean up or clear out the SRO hotels ever since deinstitutionalization had flooded their neighborhoods with mental patients, criminals and derelict tenants were now in a bind. It was true that the worst of them were closing, but the way they were closing put elderly and defenseless people on the streets. Those who couldn't find new housing lived there or in the subways and the bus terminal. When they were admitted to hospitals, they overcrowded the psychiatric units. The papers called them "new derelicts," but they weren't new, just more visible again, out of the SROs.

Things have not gotten better for the mental patients. Everyone now admits how badly they were shortchanged during the dumping period. The state's newest concept of deinstitutionalization focuses on "community residence" homes for small groups of patients in areas outside the inner cities. The patients in these homes would live under a "community support" system, but the communities are resistant. For example, a local department of mental health can rent an apartment, but it's almost impossible to buy a house. Communities have put up all kinds of obstacles to buying property for "residence" homesites.

Of course the credibility gap is still there. People saw the dumping and the danger in the cities; they resent the huge sums misspent to put helpless people in needless jeopardy. And there

78

are other kinds of casualties of the grand plan.

When Gary Walsh told me what had happened when he revisited New York in 1979, I wasn't surprised. He had decided to go back to 807.

"I stood on the sidewalk," Gary said. "When I looked inside the door, there was the same blackness. I caught the same smell of piss. I couldn't believe that I had ever worked there and done any good."

The people outside 807 were beginning to turn and look at him. Gary didn't want to be recognized. He panicked, turned and ran. He said, "I actually ran away."

You can't be a windmill tilter forever.

5 | Expert Witness

When is a criminal not responsible for a crime?

He is not responsible if he lacks criminal intent. Children lack it, and so do the mentally ill. By law, they are not blameworthy.

But how do you measure criminal intent?

The governing statute in New York State is Section 30:05 of the penal code which provides that a person is not criminally responsible for conduct, "if at the time of such conduct, as a result of mental disease or defect, he lacks substantial capacity to know or appreciate either the nature and consequences of such conduct or that such conduct was wrong." Section 30:05 is this state's version of the original McNaghten Rule which had first introduced the concept of insanity as a formal legal defense in Victorian England in 1843.

The issue of criminal responsibility is rarely invoked and should not be confused with competency for trial, another matter altogether. Evaluating defendants as to their competency is what I did at Bellevue. Scores of psychiatrists regularly working for institutions and communities do thousands of such pretrial evaluations each year in New York State.

GOOD GUYS, BAD GUYS

Competency for trial involves the defendant's ability to comprehend and assist his attorney in the preparation of his defense. The lack of *criminal responsibility* is a defense in itself, a rare and specific form of defense at trial called the NGRI. (The abbreviation means "not guilty by reason of insanity," or, according to the latest language in the 1980 New York statute, "not responsible by reason of insanity.")

Evidence to support an NGRI—or deny it—must be given in court by a psychiatric witness who is a qualified expert. When testifying, he is usually working on a free-lance basis. He has evaluated the mental status of the defendant seeking the NGRI and is prepared to demonstrate, under cross-examination, that the facts in the case do or do not fit the legal formula for insanity, depending on which side of the case he represents.

I've worked on both sides of the fence, testifying at times for the district attorney and at other times for the defense. During the seventies, I became an active free-lance witness in the courts. At my peak, I did as many as a hundred legal cases a year, almost enough to make a profession of it. I enjoyed the challenge, perhaps all the more because it remained a sideline to my real professional life.

Sometimes the cases sounded just like the script of a B movie shoot-'em-up. A case that particularly lingers was one of my first and must have taken place just as I was leaving Bellevue. I remember sitting in a Bronx courtroom at the request of Burton Roberts, now a State Supreme Court judge, then the Bronx DA. The action was a competency hearing on a homicide charge. The defendant, a so-called hit man, belonged to a local mob. Frankie B. had been arrested, and for reasons that should have hurt his professional pride: extremely sloppy work in carrying out a mob contract.

Frankie had taken the appointed victim and the victim's girl friend for a friendly ride in the country. Frankie suddenly pulled over and shot the man four times at close range. Another shot—almost an afterthought—killed the woman immediately. The victim was so still that Frankie thought he had finished his work for the day. He threw both bodies out of the car without further examination.

EXPERT WITNESS

The woman was dead, but the victim was playing dead for his life. As soon as the car disappeared, he managed to crawl to a nearby house for help. He reached a hospital in time to survive, and the next morning, District Attorney Roberts interviewed him at bedside. Here, real life deviated from the screen version. The movies would have had the survivor refuse to talk, invoke the Mafia code of silence and take his own vengeance in his own time. But perhaps he wasn't optimistic about how much time he had left. He talked. Frankie was arrested as the shooter.

In detention, awaiting trial, Frankie began to deteriorate. He rejected food. The burly 255-pounder shrank until he seemed a visitor in his own clothes. He complained of hearing voices. He reported seeing visions of his mother floating in the air in a white robe.

Sent to Bellevue for observation and evaluation, he appeared on the ward messy, mumbling and talking off the point. During our interview, I found a clue in his ramblings.

I'd ask, "How much is five and four?"

He'd answer, "Nineteen," hesitating slightly.

That kind of answer, almost to the point but willfully missing the point, was repeated often. It's called "the syndrome of approximate answers" or Ganser syndrome. He wanted to be seen as crazy but wasn't quite sure how to go about it. He was also further down the road toward his goal than he knew. I saw him as a borderline psychotic responding to the pressure of the detention and imminent trial by malingering.

I decided that he was competent for trial. From Bellevue, he returned to the Bronx House of Detention.

The defense lawyer contested my finding and hired two experts to evaluate his client. They came up with a report that he was not competent to stand trial.

On the morning of the competency hearing, the prosecution reviewed its strategy. I sat in Burt Roberts' office going over the two experts' conclusions and reviewing Frankie's symptoms from my own report and recollections: trying to clarify for the DA just how this fellow had demonstrated the pattern of an unstable malingerer. If the DA lost at the hearing and the man was committed, then the defense would have a good shot at an NGRI or opportunity for a plea bargain after Frankie returned for trial from his obligatory stay at Matteawan.

I had met Burt Roberts originally in an angry exchange on the phone, when he shouted at me that I was sending too many prison ward men to Bronx State Hospital. They would promptly escape! It was all too easy to escape from Bronx State and I told him that it was more his job than mine to do something about security there. I think I was having a bad day on N,O-2 and I suggested that the prosecutor come down and complain to me in person. He immediately saw that I was as short-tempered as he. We later became friends and collaborated on other problems in criminal justice, including a way of ensuring that returned "miracle cures" from Matteawan Hospital for the Criminally Insane were not allowed an easy way out of appropriate prison sentences. Now Roberts was suspicious that Frankie might try that.

The DA hoped to find him competent to nail him on that homicide charge. But of course, the defendant could still plead NGRI at the trial and Roberts might have to put up with any wild, crazy thing he might then do to negate the previous judicial finding of competency. I've known of a case in which the malingering defendant stood up and suddenly urinated on the floor— "You want crazy? I'll show you crazy!"

Part of my function that day, as I sat at Roberts' elbow, was to listen closely to the experts' testimony and advise him about inaccuracies. After that, I suggested questions the DA could ask the experts on cross-examination. We both watched Frankie make his entrance; a smiling scarecrow, waving and beaming benignly at a courtroom packed with his people. He waved at the prosecution as well as the defense and the smile was constant. That foolish, inappropriate smile and his general air of being somewhere else were carefully noted by the defense psychiatrists and explained to the court. The judge didn't comment.

Frankie was a pig in clover, playing crazy. He smiled his idiot's smile, held his pose, and the spotlight. The distraction he was causing kept Roberts from making much of a dent in the defense experts. In fact, he was losing points.

But the handsome silver-haired expert then on the stand went too far in his testimony. He had said that he'd found Frankie schizophrenic when he examined him, and now he gratuitously pointed to the courtroom behavior as solid, buttressing evidence.

According to him, Frankie was out of it and had no conception of why he was in court or what was going on. See how trustfully and inappropriately he smiles! The psychiatrist—there's a little would-be lawyer in us all—was invoking the basic legal tenet of *res ipsa loquitur*, "The thing speaks for itself." Didn't that irrational smile speak for itself and point to an inevitable conclusion of "not competent"?

Lawyers can get sore when an adversary's expert shows off with impunity. Both defendant and the expert were doing just this on Roberts' turf! I had worked with him long enough to know that he was generally impressed by psychiatrists. He'd often say (generously excluding the present company) that we were naïve or hired guns. He knew he had to make a move.

The DA stood up. He had a resonant voice. That day it carried across the courtroom.

"What if I told you, Doctor, that Frankie B. fornicates with his mother every Wednesday and Saturday?"

The judge spun around in his chair. Frankie B. surged up—no more silly smile—as he bellowed and lunged for Roberts, shouting and punching the air in his rage. That he could be pushed down in the chair again at all was a surprise and a sign of his weakened condition.

"Doctor?" The DA's voice was properly sarcastic. "Would you call that an inappropriate reaction?"

Frankie B. pled guilty to manslaughter one and took a long sentence in state prison.

The other reason I remember the case was because it was the first and last time I ever sat next to an attorney in the courtroom. That day, I saw myself as Roberts' coach, whispering in his ear, offering strategies. I felt that it was wrong even as I was doing it. Roberts was a very smart man who really didn't need me sitting next to him, and I didn't need the embarrassment of looking unlike an impartial expert. After Frankie's case, I resurrected my usual procedure, which was "Get in, give your testimony, walk directly off the stand, down the aisle, and out."

I had begun to explore the forensic field just after I left Bellevue and while I was employed as a community psychiatrist by Roosevelt Hospital. I was early on the scene at a time when few psychiatrists were forensic witnesses. As I did more and more such consults, I had to set aside at least eight hours a week from a crowded schedule for interviews and testifying. If I could, I'd skip lunch and squeeze the appointments in my office during that time. Or, if I had two free hours back to back, I'd chase downtown to see men in detention: to the gloomy slab of the Tombs Prison on White Street or all the way to West Street and the old Federal Detention Center squatting next to the West Side Highway and the Hudson River. When I had the time, I'd evaluate someone at Rikers Island. Rikers is in the news now, as it was then, because it is dangerously overcrowded. Then it was crowded with men from the Tombs: men in detention, not yet convicted, but housed with convicts. I spent a lot of time racing around for little money in those days, but I had hooked myself on the chance of rescuing "good guys," patients who had inadvertently tangled themselves in the legal process and needed help. It was exciting work. As for the "bad guys," I just wouldn't be interested when their lawyers called.

The phone rang a lot. I heard from lawyers in the Mental Health section of the Legal Aid Society and from the Mental Health Information Service who knew me from the prison ward. I heard from graduates of the NYU Law School where I had taught and from DAs and U.S. Attorneys and lawyers I had otherwise come to know.

Typically, my caller would tell me that there was something very wrong with his client: the guy wouldn't cooperate, the lawyer couldn't understand what he was talking about, or he had a record of psychiatric hospitalizations. As he talked, I'd try to form a mental picture of him, try to decode what he was really saying. I'd wonder—does he know what he wants me to do? Am I hearing the whole story or is he holding back something important to tell me after I've accepted the case because it's bad news? Is this a lawyer who's going though the motions in a hopeless situation because he's managed to get the money from the defendant's family up front? The man who was speaking to me might be straight, but he might just as well be a shopper calling around until he found a flexible psychiatrist who could do something for him.

I wasn't too flexible. A lot of conversations ended abruptly when I would ask, "Does your man have a rap sheet?"

If the answer was yes, I'd carefully explain why a criminal record would usually keep me from taking the case.

A prior psychiatric history was to be expected, but the people whose cases I eventually assisted were not those who had accumulated criminal records of any significance. A single misdemeanor or disorderly conduct charge might be okay: often enough, a mentally ill person, behaving strangely, is not taken to the hospital as a police-aided case but is arrested as disorderly. What I was trying to avoid was a history of willful crime. To me, the NGRI is a defense for a one-time offender only, even if that offense is homicide. Often it is. I would take on many such cases, but "my" homicides would have to be clean. I wouldn't take a repeater, not even those who had committed only lesser crimes. (In my experience, if there are insane murderers who are "good guys," they are not recidivists and have no records.)

If the conversation with the lawyer went in the right direction, I'd ask him to describe the fact pattern of the crime, to tell me everything he knew about his client's social and occupational history and to talk about any eccentricities he himself had noticed. If we were still together at the end of that phase, I would ask him to send me any material he had, a letter recapping the important points of our conversation and a court order for me to see the defendant. When the letter and court order came, I would proceed.

If the client was out on bail, I'd ask to see him in my private office together with one or more members of his family. For one thing, their collective memory was a help. Sometimes hours of digging were saved if I heard a useful comment such as, "George was okay until that slut Sophie refused to see him and started to go out with a rich guy. He didn't eat, he didn't sleep, he just paced around and then he'd mope all day and never talk to anybody. George never got over that."

Monosyllabic George might never have mentioned Sophie. But the victim of his assault, a woman who was a complete stranger to him, just happened to look exactly like her. Once I knew his history, it helped piece together the possible motivation for the crime.

The relationship between the individual and his family was important. I'd ask them, "What's good about him? Do people like him?" People do think in terms of good and bad, and I've noticed that if a person is perceived as good, then the family's solidarity is rarely shaken by a one-time crime, even a shocker. It's the criminal repeaters who finally cool most families.

There are some who never give up. I don't know how often I've told parents to stop making bail and not hire a private attorney when their recidivist son next got arrested. I would tell them that they owed their son the end of that indulgence, and more, that they might want to spare themselves and preserve their money for the future day when he might be arrested on a bigger charge. I would preach the importance of letting go and learning to enjoy their own lives as best they could. If they were believable in doing it, this might give the son an inkling that his parents could change and were capable of leaving him behind. It would help generate his own motivation to change for the better. I think I helped a few so-called drug addicts—no less addicted to drugs than to a lifestyle of goofing and petty crime—to decide to end their sadistic games with their parents. I know I gave the parents a moral rationale by which to end their masochism.

Though I saw men on bail and convicts who had already been to court and awaited sentence, the usual evaluation was with a person who was in pretrial detention. I'd need the court order to see him in what was called "the house of D" and when I got the order, I'd phone the warden's office to arrange the day and hour of my visit.

It didn't help much. I could wait, sometimes for hours, until they found the right man in the right cell block. Several times, a defendant who was finally located actually refused to come down. The wait was always frustrating. I'd be stuck in some dreary cubicle where attorneys interviewed clients or inmates had visitors. My head would throb. What the hell was I doing here? I was always too hot or too cold. In the earliest days, at the old Federal Detention Center, the interview took place with the two of us seated on lethally uncomfortable stools in the medical dispensary, and I could count on a backache, too. I'd wait for the body to appear, conjuring a picture of the man to match his crime.

How often I was wrong! If I was waiting for a confidence man detained on a federal charge, I'd expect a measure of suavity. In would walk somebody toothless, tattooed and shaved bald. While waiting for a man who allegedly turned on a dominating mother and stomped her into the ground, I would picture the typical timid soul quivering with years of suppressed rage. In would come an easy, breezy giant. And on a freezing winter afternoon in the kitchen at Rikers Island, waiting to interview a rapist, I was finally met by a man with a silly smile and fleecy white feathers in his hair, who looked as if he'd been in a pillow fight. I really hadn't known what to expect in the way of appearance for a state hospital patient who made a practice of raping other patients.

The waiting was the worst; the evaluation would sometimes be easier. Occasionally I would just slip right into the routine of the questions without a thought. The man I was trying to reach could be detached and spacey, or bantering and silly. If he had a hostile attitude, it would be important to come on soft. I might even find that I had to first establish that I wasn't some kind of cop. To make him comfortable with me, I'd make a wide detour around the area of his crime and go into the past. He didn't have to answer everything: I'd specifically tell him at the outset that he could say say "I pass on that one" if my question made him uneasy.

Unless there was a special reason, I avoided using a tape recorder. It could make these men nervous. With the clipboard balanced on my knee, I'd fill pages with direct quotes for the report for verbatim testimony in court. As I wrote, I watched his style of communication: his postures, facial grimaces, how he sounded as well as what he said.

I often found out enough in the first five minutes to locate sensitive areas. After half an hour or so, our dialogue would reach and hold a certain rhythm. There'd be fewer notations of IDK and IDR ("I don't know" and "I don't remember") on my pages. Questions were now followed by answers. Once the pattern of response had become set, I could move away from the past and into the details of the crime and arrest. By that time, I wouldn't have to press for the truth. It would just flow. (But if the pace suddenly slowed, the man might be measuring his answers and I'd have to watch out for lies.)

If I took the case for the defense, it was important that I know everything pertinent in the man's history. Confidentiality was not a problem; I would not abuse the trust he placed in me as a physician and there would be no revelations that were later regretted. If I was working for the DA, however, and found enough preliminary information to judge that the man would have small chance at the NGRI, then I set limits, and wouldn't press, even if he wanted to tell me things about other crimes. I didn't want to feel uncomfortable with information that was still unknown to the DA. This had nothing to do with the conflict over privileged communication and the responsibility to report a crime, but with my own feeling of responsibility to the man I interviewed. If I could do nothing for him in court, then at least I could preserve the integrity of the situation by making sure that the interview was not to his detriment. No matter which side sponsored it, every interview was to be therapeutic. Afterward, I'd hurry to dictate my notes (before my memory for details did its twenty-four-hour fadeout). Within a day, I'd be on the phone with the man's attorney.

I'd like to give you a composite hypothetical case, typical of many. A blank-faced, psychotic man, with strangely staring eyes, complains of evolving, nonspecific "nervous" symptoms. In a monotonous voice, he describes such symptoms as sleeplessness, loss of appetite, fear of going outside or aimless wandering. He may also have a more specific and profound symptom: a delusion, for example. This could be grandiose and weird. He'd reveal that he was placed on earth by extraterrestrials on a mission to save the world. Or it could be less grand, but persecutory and equally convoluted. He could, for instance, hold the dark paranoid suspicion that every restaurant he went into had been diabolically visited by the FBI in police uniforms who knew that he'd be coming there and would drug his food. To someone with such disordered thinking, a coincidence of events would be "proof" and produce a crime. Let's say that this man was in a restaurant, suspicious and tormented, when a policeman walked in. He came at just the wrong time, in time to be knifed. Usually, within days, a court-appointed lawyer would have questioned the man's stability and arranged for a competency evaluation at a court's clinic or at Bellevue.

Cases are referred to a place like Bellevue because the pretrial psychiatric evaluation there culls out the most obvious mentally disturbed as not competent for trial, not "fit to proceed." The competency evaluations are the key proceedings by which large numbers of men are diverted from criminal processing in the courts. Instead, they are processed to state hospitals. As mentioned earlier, if the matter is a major felony, the man returns from the hospital for trial as soon as he's judged to be legally competent. He may then take a reduced plea, or decide, after all, to go to trial on the original charge and claim insanity.

Let me refer back to my hypothetical case. This fellow, it would seem, had been given Thorazine at the detention center because of his erratic behavior and, in his brief period at Bellevue, was perceived as already sufficiently rational and contained to be found competent for trial. He was now almost, but not quite, like any other defendant waiting to be tried for his crime, and he might still need an "interpreter."

When his lawyer asked me, "What are your findings?" I could say, "I agree with Bellevue that he's competent for trial. He'll now go along with the idea that he wasn't quite right when he knifed the officer. But he doesn't want to talk about it. And he won't talk about his persecutory feelings or the extraterrestrial beings who influenced him. He's flexible enough to admit the possibility that he's had a nervous breakdown and if I testify to his psychosis, he won't deny it."

"Extraterrestrial beings?" he'd ask.

Remember, a doctor may elicit information from a patient that the latter has withheld from his lawyer (partly because the lawyer would never ask his client such questions). As counsel realized that what I was telling him could point to an NGRI defense, he'd be excited and apprehensive. Probably he'd never done one before.

I could then say, "I think you have someone here who is massively psychotic and has never been so diagnosed. There's a strong relation between his mental state and the crime he committed, so he fits the formula for an NGRI. The crime was witnessed by a restaurant full of people, so I'm thinking you won't be able to use any other defense."

"I guess not," he'd admit. "Is the man competent enough to cooperate with me through a trial?"

I'd say yes.

Next, he'd ask, "What kind of trouble are we likely to run into with the NGRI defense?"

I'd outline the problems that a disturbed defendant who had nevertheless been found legally competent might pose in court.

After our discussion, I would write a detailed report that would be central to my own testimony later. The lawyer could use it for his own reference or also let the DA examine it. If neither prosecution nor defense wanted a plea bargain, the lawyer would formally advise the DA that he was interposing an insanity defense.

A DA doesn't like to hear it. It means problems. Unless he already knows someone he trusts, someone without a defense bias, it's not easy for him to come up with an expert. A psychiatrist may be clinically able, but a poor witness. If he's long on theory, he leaves the jury far behind, or if he can't conform his medical testimony to the rules of evidence, the opposing lawyer will make him look bad. Worst of all is the ambiguous expert because the jury sees that he does not answer the questions put to him.

After hiring one expert, it's unlikely that the DA will shop around for another one if he's unhappy with the conclusion. He is stuck with the expert's report, and if it says that the defendant is insane, he must rely on that advice. A reduced plea or a lost insanity defense—especially in a heavily publicized case—does not gain public popularity.

In this hypothetical situation, the expert hired by the DA makes an independent evaluation and may agree with me. Or his result may challenge mine, saying that in *his* interview the defendant was denying that he ever had hallucinations and now insists that he cut the policeman impulsively in an argument over restaurant service.

Let's assume that the two experts agree. One of the options the DA has is to offer a reduced plea, a process by which trial is avoided if the defendant agrees to plead guilty to a lesser charge. Or he may go forward with a shortened trial prearranged by a conference between the judge and the two adversaries. The adversaries give the facts, the experts present their conclusions, and everyone understands that the outcome of a shortened trial will be an NGRI.

If there's no agreement, the lines are drawn for a battle in court. Usually, neither side welcomes that and it's rare for such cases to come to conventional trial.

In my first year of free-lancing, I got a glimpse of everything I would see in the next decade. I continued to make the kinds of correlations I had made on the prison ward and record the social situations that unleashed violence in dissocial people. I wasn't just seeing frustrated boyfriends and husbands who sopped up enough alcohol on Saturday nights to decide that their women needed killing. Addicts killed their local heroin pusher because he'd cheated them, or because he had cash. Male prostitutes first took their fees and then their clients' lives. And I had a run of rapist homicides the first year. They had a lot in common: brute psychopaths with similar histories of prior sexual crime, aggravated assaults and robberies. At one point, I received a request from an upstate Public Defender to write an opinion on the man he was to defend. I had never seen the rapist. But when I read the materials sent to me, including an account of the crime, and saw a copy of the psychological workup, I felt as if I already knew the guy.

There was the "aggressive sexual behavior as a child, alcoholic blackouts, male prostitution." There were the two competency examinations he passed without question. I had met this type so often that I could almost predict what he would say.

Caught *in flagrante delicto*, without a chance to make the usual "I wasn't there, I didn't do it" defense, this particular guy sounded like a character in a movie coming out of an amnesia bout. He produced this gem: "I remember—the girl was down and there I was on top of her and there was this stabbing thing. . . ."

I didn't have to see him or hear the plaintiveness in his voice. In my report, I said that there was no point in my going further with the case.

The long-distance rapist was an exception for me. Generally, I would not recommend long-distance diagnosis. You must have adequate material and be very meticulous in reviewing it. Even if you are very sure of your findings, you have reason to worry. I remember some occasions when the matter was one hundred percent clear in my mind until I actually saw and spoke with the defendant.

During the sixties and into the seventies, there was a legal technique called the "hypothetical question" which forced you into long-distance diagnosis. At that time, the law allowed a man to interpose an insanity defense but at the same time allowed him to refuse to be evaluated by the state's expert. So if the DA hired you to be that expert, you never saw the accused. You were given pertinent material such as his hospital records and you had access to all the testimony introduced into the case under oath. From these "givens," you had to decide the answer to the "hypothetical question": did he or did he not fit the formula for an insanity defense? Without the evidence of your eyes and ears, you totaled up what was available, made your statement and took the chance of making a mistake.

In 1969, I was hired by the Queens DA and denied opportunity to interview a notorious defendant. The case was widely reported as the "chromosome murder" because the argument put forth by the defense was that the client could not help himself and killed because he had an extra Y sex chromosome. Females have two X chromosomes, males have XY and this fellow's genetic configuration was XYY. The extra Y carriers were soon labeled "supermale."

A "supermale" criminal theory had evolved, based on research studies in European prisons. Investigators noted an undue complement of prisoners possessing the extra Y chromosome. These men had common traits: they were unusually tall, suffered from facial acne, were mentally dull and had been convicted of violent crimes. It was suggested that the presence of the extra chromosome predisposed them to such violence. It was further implied that the defendant in the so-called chromosome murder case, who had these afflictions, had committed the crime because he couldn't do anything else. Because of the supermale Y, he had followed a woman out of a Queens bar and brutally killed her in a nearby backyard.

The killer chromosome premise was a shaky one. Even if the supermale Y made some men impulsive and aggressive, what about the other tall, acne-ridden, mentally dull extra Y carriers living outside the prisons? If these noncriminal Y carriers hadn't committed violent crimes, if even one such chromosome carrier could refrain from violence, then the argument ought to fail. The observable factors of gangling build, acne and dullness are not excuses; other males so disfavored without chromosomal abnormality may suffer yet conform to the law. The XYY theory conflicted with the free-will concept and was an unacceptable liberalization of defenses. Even your genes could free you now! The XYY debate aside, I had to concentrate on what there was to work with. There were some hours of taped material made by the defendant while under the influence of the so-called truth drug, sodium Amytal. The defense considered the contents of this tape as mitigating.

For over an hour, I listened to his uninterrupted, droning delivery. It sounded the way a drugged or hypnotized subject did in the movies. So often at Bellevue, people who wanted to sound crazy borrowed movie mannerisms: the sighing, staring, the wild "Gee Doc, what's happening to my mind?" Here was life imitating art again. It was the same explanation that had solved the mystery of the slurred "drunk" speech affecting young men with drug histories on Ward N,O-2. They were long past the symptoms of drug intoxication or withdrawal. They had no cerebellar brain dysfunction and while they might "bop" when they walked, they never staggered. So why did they always sound stoned?

The answer was, because they wanted to. It was everybody's idea of how a cool drug fiend with a load on should sound. And with a permanent affectation, they would slur away for hours in a kind of "garbage-head" chic.

Now here was the chromosome defendant, also performing for effect in a way that had more to do with the popular imagination than sodium Amytal. We had tried the drug on the prison ward, usually with inauspicious results. You would inject sodium Amytal, a barbiturate, intravenously. It was done cautiously, a little at a time, just enough to get around the censorship his consciousness provided. Questions were asked and slowly answered. When the patient seemed less groggy and bordering on sleep, more of the fluid would be injected. When it went well, it was hard to keep a patient at a level where he'd talk consistently for minutes, let alone for hours.

I listened to those tapes for a long time and concluded that what I heard was not convincing. It sounded like a self-serving defendant in a homicide case, chromosome argument or no. But the case was of national importance because of the precedent it could establish, so I called in other colleagues and told them what I had heard. From my description, they agreed with me.

I explained my disbelief when I testified in court, even while the defense waved the gory glossies of the woman's smashed body in front of me as evidence that the killer who had done that work had to be mad. All I saw was an intoxicated killer and a brutal homicide. The jury agreed and convicted him. That was the end of the chromosome defense.

By the close of the sixties, the NGRI had become a favored legal gimmick. Before 1965, there had been almost no successful

NGRI defenses in the state. Suddenly there were thirty, forty, then fifty a year, more than half of them involving homicides. Under the influence of the Warren Court, lawyers fresh out of law school were zealous to ensure that every due process protection was considered in every case they argued. Some had even seen hallucinating defendants in their law and psychiatry courses. They were quick to raise the issues of competency and responsibility whenever possible.

Ever since the Miranda decision, upholding the suspect's right to remain silent and to consult an attorney before being questioned, lawyers had routinely asked their clients whether they had received Miranda warnings. Now the lawyers complained that Miranda wasn't understood. Their clients were making confessions even after the arresting officers advised them of their right to remain silent! So then the lawyers asked for what became known as Huntley hearings. These were sanity hearings to determine their clients' competence to have understood the Miranda warnings. It could go on and on—numerous hearings playing to empty courtrooms.

Some lawyers were genuine and ethical in their protectiveness of clients; others demanded hearings or challenged conclusions routinely, putting the onus on the judge to grant or refuse their requests. They had covered everything. At appeal, His Honor could not ask, "How is it, Counselor, that you failed to challenge the Bellevue findings?"

I encountered lawyers—real or fancied civil libertarians— who would request psychiatric evaluations at the slightest pretext. For example, who in criminal law was so square as not to identify a skullcap as an "in" thing in prisonwear and nothing else? These psych requests could be part of an obscure legal game plan for a case, or something that might be useful if all else failed.

Here's a paradox I noticed: many of those civil liberties lawyers who proclaimed themselves as protectors of society's victims would represent the most vicious men. They'd claim innocence, failure of due process, brutalization by police, anything. Was it grandstanding? Were they looking for test cases? For every murderous heavy taken up and publicized, there were thousands of less glamorous but more deserving unfortunates. Even militant minority defendants grew uneasy about the motives of these civil liberties champions, finally suspecting a "hidden agenda" that had to do with publicity. I knew that there were lawyers who gave themselves to this work out of principle and at a loss of income, but perhaps they were too anonymous. The news media found the courtroom gadflies and celebrated them. Where they went, the cameras went too.

Sixties thinking lingered on in the courtrooms of the seventies. Talk about determinism and causal psychosocial factors persisted. Criminals were still products of their surroundings, and impoverished minority defendants still deserved extra consideration because they were society's victims.

But behind this logic and seeming benevolence also stood fear. Cocky recidivist prisoners who had whipped the system before, and knew it, strutted in the courtroom. Judges acknowledged that they were easy targets for retribution by the convict or his friends. Some, fearful of the implicit threat these men represented, handed out light sentences—which were of course attributed to their liberalism. Others saved face by letting the administrative judge know that they only wanted to do civil cases. Still others carried guns.

I saw a great many people who believed that they had a license to do wrong because society owed them. Militants tried to push the belief that every crime was equal to a vindicating political action because it was a way toward anarchistic chaos and their desired revolution. This "justification" communicated itself to men who had been arrested. They were made to feel that their rights had been abrogated—even though it might not be true—and as "victims," committed more crimes.

I found this mentality self-defeating. Society did owe every man his day in court. A man has the right to choose not to do a crime. If he seems to have done it, and has been arrested, then he should be given a chance to tell his story and counter the evidence against him. If he can't, and if it is proved that he was responsible for the crime, let him take his medicine. The present state of the art in social justice and criminal rehabilitation suggests that it's the best we can offer.

Fifteen years ago that was not so obvious. The Warren Court had taught everyone to be sensitive about the practice of law enforcement. In those days, if you objected to arbitrary delays or "protective" intrusions which really helped no one and only prevented a speedy trial, you might well be labeled a law-and-order zealot. Psychiatrists in particular were supposed to have a benevolent, permissive social outlook and working for the DA was not popular. I was more comfortable working for the defense, but in time, as DAs kept asking for help in questionable insanity cases, I did more for the prosecution and felt better about it.

There could be difficulties. It wasn't easy for me to tell an upstate DA who had just hired me to fly up and evaluate a homicide defendant that I didn't agree with the prosecution's side. I held a point of view that was opposite to what he wanted to hear. But we both agreed that the defendant was dangerous. I suggested that he use another psychiatrist I knew whose philosophy differed from mine. This doctor had a perfect record of not finding insanity. When he testified, he didn't disappoint the DA at all.

Whenever I did commit myself to a case, I of course wanted to do what I could to help the lawyer who had hired me make the best presentation to the court. In my ready-for-trial collaboration with him, we dealt first with qualifications. Every expert had to have his credentials presented to the court, and if a lawyer was trying to impress the jury, he could drag it out through fifteen to twenty minutes of questions and answers. The expert's schools, societies and honors were all rubbed up to maximum brilliance for maximum dazzle. Far from impressing most juries, I think it bored them.

Before the trial, I would suggest that the lawyer ask me just *one* question, "Doctor, can you give me your qualifications?"

Then, after I was sworn in, I'd go rapidly through the essentials: training at Bellevue, chief of the prison ward, faculty status at NYU in Law and Psychiatry, the Psychiatric Board certification and important memberships. With no interruptions, I'd go right on through the consultancies and affiliations with various agencies, and end with my current job as director of psychiatry at Booth Memorial Medical Center in Queens. The no-frills delivery had a good effect on the jury and prevented the opposing lawyer from cutting me off by "stipulating" my expertise. With the old question-and-answer method, he could more easily have interrupted with "Yes; we know Dr. Lubin. He's an expert and can be qualified."

As a tactic, his stipulation of my credentials could also avoid comparison with his own expert's possibly limited experience. Why should he let the jury hear me respond that I had "done" several hundred homicide cases?

Though an expert's testimony is occasionally taken "out of turn," the usual procedure is prosecution first, as the DA develops his factual case to show why the accused is guilty. Then he rests his case, making way for the defense, who will show why the accused didn't do it, or if he did, why he was insane. (You can defend on the two points, not guilty and NGRI, at the same time.)

At this point, the defense psychiatric witness gives direct testimony. The DA's corresponding expert listens, or if he is not in the courtroom, he is later apprised of the testimony and suggests questions for the DA to use on cross-examination of the defense's man. The DA's expert will give direct testimony on rebuttal, and the DA thus gets his chance to puncture the defense presentation. The witness is then cross-examined by the defense attorney, who will probably try to point out inaccuracies and dispute his conclusion by saying that he did not have all the information known to them. The DA has the chance to smooth out any dents made in his expert when he later questions him on redirect.

Most of the Manhattan or Bronx Supreme Court judges had read my reports or had heard me testify in the Bellevue days. This background might prompt some respect, but lawyers were not intimidated by it and could be very insinuating "on the cross" with questions that distorted the meaning of my testimony. I'd learned a few tricks myself. If I was being baited and the judge or my side's adversary didn't pick up on the sarcasm or insults and object, I'd develop some confusion, and ask the cross-examiner to repeat the question. He'd be wary, or turn dramatic:

ATTORNEY: Are you saying that you did not understand
the meaning of my question, Doctor?
PSYCHIATRIST: Yes. Would you please repeat it?

Rather than emphasize that he had asked an obviously loaded
question, he'd turn to the court reporter and ask that it be read
aloud from the record. Out it came—but in the flat professional
monotone that robbed it of the original insinuation and sting. It
also lost the dramatic punch intended for the jury and broke the
pattern of his questions on the cross. Each time the lawyer tried
to steamroller me with sarcasm, I'd "misunderstand" the meaning
of the question. Finally, he'd cut it out.

Another cross-examination tactic was for him to come on like
the Grand Inquisitor. As it has always been part of my procedure
to give many details about how I came to a conclusion, I could
be very vulnerable on this count. If he attacked me on them,
constantly asking for more clarification and implying that these
items should not have led me to have any answers, I might play
along with him for a while and then suddenly give the inquisitor
much more confirming information than he wanted. I'd go past
the points described in my report to territory he hadn't planned
to explore. The judge could become interested in this new material.
If the lawyer grew panicky over what he'd unleashed and told
me to stop, the judge would usually say, "Go on. You asked for
more clarification, Counselor. Now let the doctor talk!"

Factually, any history leading to the crime, anything germane
to my final conclusion, was admissible under the law and I did
want to be very explicit for the jury. It was extremely important
to have the expert give the dynamics of the case and explain the
reasons for his conclusion within the legal formula for insanity.
This was particularly true where a jury might only vaguely
understand the instructions as to insanity, or when the case was
bizarre, with angels and devils and witchcraft as the stuff of
testimony.

Section 30:05 (McNaghten) essentially provides that a man
is not criminally responsible if he does not know what he is doing
or that it is wrong. Testifying in a witchcraft case, for example,
I might break down the formula for insanity like this:

GOOD GUYS, BAD GUYS

"I think that Mr. X knew that when he pulled the trigger of the gun a bullet would emerge. He knew that the bullet might penetrate the body of another person and that it could cause death. But he did not know that it was wrong. You might say that he thought he was doing something right because the person was a witch who was casting spells and causing death, and so on. He did not know right from wrong."

At the point when I said that Mr. X knew the bullet could kill, it might be all that some of the jurors wished to hear. Juries have a tendency to project their normal reasoning onto a defendant. Is it reasonable to believe that a man who knew what firing a gun meant could have thought he was killing a witch? No, it isn't. But the divorcement of that kind of knowledge—cognition—from its moral value of knowing right from wrong is characteristic of some psychotic people who kill.

Is it reasonable to believe that a mother who poured scalding water on her baby son and then baked him in the oven would expect him to survive this rite of exorcism from Satanic possession? It is not reasonable, but such a case occurred recently. Satanic possession cases do happen and children are flung out windows, burned in furnaces, drowned or otherwise sacrificed by parents or relatives who are preoccupied with the supernatural "mirror image" of moral behavior. The code of good and bad has here gone awry. The people who commit bloody possession crimes may be very naïve and present histories of pious and churchgoing behavior. Religiousness and obsession with sin often keep company with religiosity and psychosis.

Some are attracted to religion as an explanation for their confusion and a balm to their anguish. But close exposure to the mystical aspects of religion can intensify the confusion. Immoral and illegal actions can actually be seen as good by such a mind, one who "kills for God's sake." In others, who are apparently more in control, this murderous distortion is not so clear. They kill for God and to rid themselves of an obvious object of jealousy and hate. These people can be seen as psychotic and willful. This all-important issue of willfulness—this element of self-serving free will in the motivation of the crime—must be carefully considered in each insanity case.

Those who recover their sanity after dreadful deeds often expiate their sins by trying to be found guilty. If possible, they should be protected from jail. Those who don't recover show neither appreciation nor regret. They make no judgments on their behavior because their delusion is still alive. This moral vacuum makes them fit the formula for insanity. But other elements can influence juries to decide against that verdict.

The mother who scalded and baked her child was indicted for his murder. Following hospitalization, the prosecution and defense experts agreed to a verdict, and she was adjudicated as not guilty by reason of insanity without a jury trial. What she did was so repugnant that if she had faced a jury they might well have demanded to see her punished as they would any criminal. The jury may admit to themselves that the bizarre behavior was mental illness, but if it outrages them beyond their point of tolerance, they will still demand punishment, even if they have to make ad hoc changes in the law. It happened to a jury during a "witch" trial that I lost.

I was hired by an out-of-state DA. The area in which the crime occurred was one where rural conservatism still lingered, an unlikely, small-town setting for a bloody "possession" case.

The defendant, Anton, was the kind of boy who was almost too responsible. He had worked after school from the age of twelve until he went into the army. After military service, he was anxious to get home, not only to begin college but to work to support his elderly parents. He fell in love, but postponed his plans for marriage for practical reasons. He took every problem on his own shoulders. He had a disabled sister and he worried about her. It was Anton who prompted his one younger brother to see a doctor about a lump on his body, Anton who read everything about his brother's condition after it was diagnosed as cancer. When he understood that the sick boy had only a few months to live, he took over total care, shielding his parents from that responsibility. He kept vigil at the bedside, rarely eating and sleeping, talking to his brother until he was too hoarse to speak. He refused any distraction and found excuses to break up with his girl friend. He wrote notes to himself about the way she had distracted him, diverted his loyalty. He tore up the presents she had given him as a way of showing his disaffection. He became suspicious and supercritical of her and paranoid fantasies developed. He began to believe that she was influencing his brother's death, and after his brother died, the belief strengthened. He was so confused, disconnected from life and reality and filled with accumulated guilt for having "failed" his brother, that he fused the cataclysmic events of his life into a delusion that his former girl friend was a witch who created the cancer in his brother. Months later, bombarded by psychotic thoughts, he was dreaming of retaliation and had acquired a knife—to protect himself from crowds, he said, because he was now afraid of going out. But he used the knife for something else. By a ruse, he got his unsuspecting former girl friend to meet him at an isolated spot. They had a sudden short quarrel, and he stabbed her many times. Each wound was delivered as vengeance for his brother and meant the extinction of a witch.

When I did an evaluation of Anton for the DA, I found that he had an NGRI defense and reported that. But it wasn't what this DA wanted to hear, and we agreed that I would not be testifying. I was wrong about that. The judge in the case heard of my conclusion and I was told that he would subpoena me unless I testified. One change was, of course, to testify not for the DA, but for the defense. I went back to the town where Anton lived and took the stand as a defense expert.

There was no way that Anton would be permitted to be criminally insane by the jury even if his neighbors agreed with my presentation of him as a hardworking, family-minded, "good" person. (Perhaps my depiction of him made it even harder to imagine.) They wouldn't hear and couldn't realize the destructive effect of the bedside vigil on his personality. They couldn't imagine why he should escape punishment for those many, many stab wounds. No one could commit a vicious murder of a local girl and get away with it. Not in that town. The defense was to lose, no matter what I said. Jury and geography defeated it.

I lost another insanity defense. It was one of the two forensic cases involving the NGRI that I lost over the years. This time it was because the jury displayed more common sense than I may have had when I took the case. I should have paid a little more attention to my own ambivalence.

At first look, Harvey the rapist seemed to fit the pattern of the naïve psychotic who would reveal everything without an iota of insight. He was an inadequate personality with limited intelligence who felt humiliated by his dependent need for the women in his life; first his mother, then his wife. He knew that they thought he was incompetent. Harvey feared that his wife would leave him. He was up to his neck in debt, behind on installment payments, in trouble on his job, and at about the time of the crime, he had signs of psychosis. He wrote letters to John Lindsay, then Mayor of New York, confiding that he was being harassed, and that the women in his shop were throwing spitballs at him. He asked for help. When no cavalry from City Hall came to his rescue, Harvey took his own revenge on women. He haunted the parking lots of shopping centers in the Riverdale area and raped women, at knifepoint, in their own cars. He never cut his victims, but what he did was just as fatal to his own defense. He'd sometimes take money from their pocketbooks: he raped *and* he robbed.

I knew Harvey was psychotic. I realized that the NGRI would be difficult to present because not one but many rapes had occurred, and they were committed over a period of time. But I hadn't quite realized to what degree he had profited in this entirely practical way . . . robbing as a matter of course. He was far more willful than I took him to be, far more the aggrandizing person the jury saw, the man who wanted to ravish *all* their daughters. They considered the evidence matter-of-factly. Harvey was in debt. Harvey stole money. That didn't sound so crazy!

In a sense, I had done what I criticized others for doing. I'd tried too hard to fit someone into the formula for insanity because he was obviously psychotic. The crime of rape was causally related in Harvey's case and I was being a purist in deciding to testify for him. The jury had its own vision: they didn't see the parameters I drew as representing insanity. They weren't motivated by community consciousness like the jurors in the town where

Anton lived: they had a similar, collective reaction to crimes that were willful, repeated and unfair. They were protecting themselves.

I wasn't ambivalent about losing because I believe that it is the jury's right to decide against someone bordering on the psychotic who is also willful. It's their proper function. (Five years later, it was not a jury but a collaboration of judges and district attorneys who saw fit to ignore Son of Sam's incompetence in order to send him to prison. That was *not* their proper function.)

You could easily be nervous about the use of the NGRI in the seventies. Forensic practice had changed dramatically with "due process" impetus toward increased protection of criminal defendants. It made the insanity defense instantly popular, but even the most sophisticated lawyer didn't know who was a good candidate for the NGRI defense. Neither did the courts nor the psychiatrists. Too many men with criminal records were winning these cases and everyone seemed unable to understand that in letting certain kinds of willful psychotics with records win, they were breaking down a system that had been around for over a hundred years. McNaghten was history and with a little care, it could still work.

It was true that the total number of NGRI verdicts was nothing compared to the numbers of antisocial types and malingerers slipping through from the penal system to Mental Health via Section 730 of the state's penal code. (It provided for termination of charges with hospital commitment.) These men could reach the hospitals, make things tough on the other patients or, all too often, walk away from their commitment and the hospital, free and free of charges—until the next time. That was the real danger to the public and no one was addressing it. In fact, the chief of a large processing center was recently heard to say that anyone who bothered to malinger *had* to be sick and ought to be removed from jail and placed in a hospital! I first heard a statement like that twenty years ago. To hear it now, with our current crime rate, was frightening. If this man didn't recognize the public danger, who would?

I had once worked to plug up those abuses in the law when I was at Bellevue. But now I was concerned mainly with the issue of responsibility—NGRI in a confusing, rapidly changing situation. As the field grew, lawyers were actually taking post-graduate courses in how to interpret insanity as if it was a routine defense. A national association of forensic psychiatrists had been formed. After a slow start in the 1960s, which saw federally funded programs in forensic psychiatry fail, the work had become prestigious and psychiatrists were joining the ranks. It was even in style now to be a law-and-order man. Reporters too had gotten on an NGRI kick and were often in the courtroom, anticipating an insanity defense. The whole thing was too casual, and the increased visibility of the proceedings stirred up the old queasiness I'd last felt after Holden disappeared.

I could take responsibility for the accuracy of what I said as an expert witness. I could testify that someone had been insane, but I obviously could not guarantee any safeguards for the public when I did so. By the nature of his illness, the once violent man sent to a hospital might get better and therefore be released. A later exacerbation, also typical of cyclic illness, could make him dangerous again. A grim possibility for an unsuspecting public.

There was some legal concern for men in jail and the beginnings of concern for crime victims' rights, but the inherent rights of the public to protection were still being ignored.

Dangerous men were out on their own recognizance pending trial. At one time, in the late 1960s, New York City had 20,000 bench warrants out for men who failed to appear for trial. Today the number is 100,000! Even if the courts believed that they were not responsible through their malfunctioning for the increase in crime, how could they justify a situation in which a victim or his family were put in further danger from a man who had just harmed them?

I shall never forget one particular case. I was hired by the DA, but I couldn't find for him and once again confirmed the defense view that the man was not responsible. Still employed by the DA, I testified to that. But certain features of the case had so upset me that I stepped out of my compartment as a psychiatric expert and tried to prod that DA's office into action.

The man I evaluated for the Brooklyn DA's office was a small, nearly beardless fellow with a vacuous, haunted look. Call

him Thomas. Though he had a history of psychiatric hospitalization, he had tried to bring some order into his life by taking
college courses and by joining the Army. But he couldn't continue
the college work, he deserted from the Army, he failed in everything
because he was constantly prey to paranoid fantasies. Walking
along the street, he'd be distracted because trucks seemed to be
following him, trying to unnerve him and make him drop his
cigarette, which would mean that they knew he'd had sex with
a relative. Everything around Thomas was charged with threatening symbolism. He located a source of power radiating against
him from a neighbor's house and concentrated his efforts on that
family. He harassed them, damaged their property, threw a
homemade Molotov cocktail against the door of their house (as
David Berkowitz would also do to a neighbor). Finally, Thomas
collected some sulphuric acid in a jar, carried it to the neighbor's
house, rang the bell, and poured the sulphuric acid over the
young child who answered the door.

Badly burned, the child survived. Thomas was arrested, hospitalized, and then—I don't know how this happened either—
released on bail. During the trial, after I had testified to his
insanity, he was found to be living in his mother's house, next
door to the child he had covered with acid!

I made the warning speech I nearly always made by this time
when I testified for an NGRI. I would mention my concern for
danger and the need for an active surveillance system on the
people who won the NGRI. After I left the court, I went directly
to the Office of the Brooklyn DA. I spoke to a friend, the chief
assistant DA, who is now a judge. I asked him to get me a few
minutes with his boss because I wanted to get an immediate
remedy for the threatened family in the Thomas case and I
wanted to explain the need for legislation in future cases. It was
the first time I had done such a thing. My friend went in and
made the inquiry. No, the DA was too busy. I never did get in
to see him. (This vigilant DA was later to demonstrate his determination to protect the public from crazed sadists when he
personally conducted the well-publicized prosecution of the Son
of Sam.)

Thomas didn't revisit his neighbors, but only because he went on a rampage somewhere else first and was rehospitalized.

Caveat publicus.

I think it might have been better if the case had taken place in the Bronx. In the year of the Thomas case, 1975, the office of Bronx District Attorney Mario Merola put out an excellent report about the situation in the criminal courts. It pointed out that the psychiatric examinations were uneven and that imprudent processing of men had made the criminally committed dangerous to themselves, to other patients in the psychiatric centers and to the public, because they escaped so often and so easily. (In the late sixties, I questioned a man about his frequent escapes from Manhattan State, a hospital situated on an island connected to the upper East Side of Manhattan by a footbridge. This was a thin, unimpressive guy who must have hoarded every bit of his strength between escapes, bouts of rape and robbery and recommittals. "How do you get out?" I asked. He looked indignant. "I use the bridge like everybody else!" In early 1980, a man who had split his mother's head with a hatchet some years before used a bridge to get off the island and scared hell out of his family and the city before he was rehospitalized.)

If any of the New York State district attorney offices had investigated the security in a dangerous case like Thomas', I'd have expected it to be Merola's office in the Bronx. He did take a very strong position. I can't help wondering if it wasn't the incredible escape rates from Bronx State Hospital over the years that first made Burton Roberts, when he was Bronx DA, and later Merola so alert to the problem.

After Thomas, my warning statement was a suffix to any testimony I gave. "While I find that this man is insane and therefore not guilty, he killed once and I can't be sure that he won't be dangerous at some future time. I, therefore, recommend that he be kept in a surveillance situation, even after he has improved enough to be returned to society. I ask that the District Attorney's Office and the court take whatever action they deem necessary to make this feasible." I knew damn well we had no surveillance potential under the present law, but with the increase in NGRIs, there must be one. And no one disagreed.

Enough judges and DAs knew what was going on and they had the onus of responsibility to change things. At that time, all I thought I could do as a solo medical practitioner was to make my views regularly known in the court with an occasional appeal to the chief of the state's District Attorneys' Association. As long as I chose to stay in the business, I wanted my opinion to be on record.

I then believed that the NGRI defense should be retained, in spite of its abuse. I thought it could still be made to work by setting up screening panels for proposed NGRI cases and arranging an after-care surveillance system along with other practical modifications. For better or worse, there would soon be a change in the law in reaction to the misuse of the defense. The reform effort was shaping up in Albany with investigative committees and several proposals in the state legislature. The Governor, the legislature and the American Psychiatric Association were looking for formulas of change.

My job in general hospital psychiatry took more and more of my time and interest. I didn't quit forensic work altogether, but refused and referred most of the forensic cases presented to me over the phone. Nearly all the defense cases I continued to do toward the end of the seventies were prescreened for me by a lawyer who shared my nervousness about the unprotected public. He ran the federal division of the Legal Aid Society in New York and would look among his clients for good deeds to be done. We could be "bleeding hearts" together, taking care to help those we thought would pose no harm.

I also looked beyond New York. It was a kick to take one-shot assignments in nearby states. A day trip could take me to Tennessee, or to Washington (where the IRS once wanted me to evaluate a wealthy citizen because he hadn't paid his taxes— they thought that was a crazy thing to do). Generally, I would find that the DAs and defense lawyers out of state were also making frequent use of McNaghten. Everybody was looking for insanity.

I often traveled upstate. The DAs I knew had gotten into the habit of saving the wildest cases for me. I would be called well in advance and an assistant would present the facts of the case in our phone conversation. I could make a quick comment based on what I heard: "It sounds phony and there's no prior psych history," or "Defense case sounds good but I agree that the rap sheet makes him suspect for malingering." Even when I said, "It looks like the defense has a sure NGRI," I might still have to read up on the case and clear time for a trip if they wanted me to come and evaluate the defendant.

I wasn't the only imported talent. They would commonly call in a forensic pathologist and even a forensic dentist to make an identification of an unknown corpse by the fillings and bridge-work.

Small towns were new territory for me. For years, I had had invitations. "Why don't you leave the jungle and visit America?" Now I was doing it and I liked what I saw, even though my usual vantage point was from the county jail.

6 | Murray and the Good Guys

Flying upstate took less than an hour. I'd get off the plane to a subtle change of air, clean, windy, smelling of open country. Someone official was always waiting to drive me into town, and if it was an assistant from the DA's office, we might recap the facts of the case on the way.

In those upstate towns, the DA's staff could know all their cases. I remember that an office I frequently worked for in the seventies had fewer than ten men—while a busy DA's office in one borough of New York City employed 250.

Usually, I'd do the psych evaluation in the county courthouse or the visitors' room of the local jail. Downstate, DAs rarely went to watch an expert work unless the defense attorney put in an unusual request about the way the examination was to be done. Upstate, homicide cases with an insanity angle were few, and as the visiting professor, I attracted a very interested audience. If there were more than several DAs, guards and lawyers in the gallery, I'd reposition the man I was interviewing so that he couldn't see them. Otherwise, he could feel the spotlight and mug for the watchers, or try to keep in contact with his lawyer through winks and signals, hoping for some coaching. When I turned him around to face only me, he was not distracted.

If the defense attorney interrupted my pattern of questions without good reason—it didn't happen often—I'd make it clear that this was not a trial and I was not an adversary. My position was neutral. I was working for the DA, but the information I drew out was what the defense attorney would need to develop his own NGRI case. Defense scribbled notes on what was uncovered, and I would keep digging until I had all the elements for my own conclusion: was the man competent, was he sick before and at the time of the crime and was there a causal connection between the sickness and the crime?

Upstate, the day's work could include a lunch with the DA or a last-minute drink at the airport before my flight was due. I appreciated the pace and the amenities; they belonged to the same period as the old gray stone buildings and Victorian architecture surviving in those towns. The courthouses where I went had tall ceilings, heavy oak banisters, solid brass fixtures. When I admired them, the people who worked in those buildings looked at me curiously. They no more "saw" these objects than the regulars in New York City courtrooms saw the oak-paneled walls and Art Deco fixtures that were there. Upstate, what I admired was solid, serviceable, and symbolic of an older American tradition, more in line with the ideas I'd had as a kid when I believed that law was administered and justice done.

Certain elements that made big-city crime so hard to control were missing here. The city criminal is anonymous and mobile—he takes your wallet, swiftly moves into the crowd on the street or the subway platform, and he's gone. Anonymity was hard to come by upstate. I would almost expect that a sheriff's deputy, driving me to town, would know enough about the defendant in the case to tell me his family's history. Small towns meant continuity. In many cases, adults didn't leave parental homes until they themselves were married. The histories I gathered were of people who went to school, married and started their

114

own families within the radius of a hundred miles of where they were born. Even those who traveled in other states would return periodically to the home base—which still looked like home because neighborhoods changed slowly.

Since who they were and where they lived was known, the risk of detection was higher and the moral pressure on them more pervasive. There was a fear of parents' opinions and what the neighbors would say, or in some cases, how they might be judged by their church.

I evaluated a young woman I'll call Ellen, who lived in a town near the Canadian border. Ellen was certainly psychotic a long time before her crime, yet she managed to conceal it from the family. Circumstances were such that she had to be raised by her aunt and uncle: a good girl, from a respectable background and inclined to religion. She was generally passive and retiring— smiled shyly and said the right things. But at the same time she was covertly and passionately jealous of her more popular and outgoing cousins and classmates. She envied but couldn't imitate them, for she feared the vulnerability that openness would bring. Ellen had no gift for chatter and she made few friends. Her strong religious identification enforced very judgmental attitudes about immoral conduct and "bad" girls. She'd clung to these beliefs because they made her isolation virtuous.

Ellen became involved with an older man who later told her that he was married. He was too religious to leave his wife yet they drifted into sex and, predictably, she decided that she was in love with him. At the same time that she discovered love, she became the "bad girl" she had always condemned.

A few months after the affair began, she lost her job—which she may have seen as punishment—and couldn't find another. Someone claiming to "know everything" was sending anonymous notes warning her to end her involvement. She showed the notes to her lover. He tore them up but she remembered every word. Even after they stopped coming, she was obsessional about them. She couldn't sleep and finally became so phobic that she was afraid to be in the house alone, yet still more afraid of everything outside, where people would look at her strangely as if they too "knew everything." She no longer saw her lover and managed to isolate herself completely. After an initial loss of appetite, she was eating and putting on weight. A single trip to a gynecologist revealed that she was six months pregnant.

Ellen never told anyone. Either she didn't "show" until very late in pregnancy or her family assumed that, holed up in her room, she was eating candy and just letting herself get fat. They were afraid to ask personal questions because of her irritability. She spoke of having long ago impressed her aunt, uncle and cousins with her need for absolute privacy in their home. They respected it.

Ellen would never have considered an abortion and she planned to have the baby out of state. Her phobia against leaving the house may have prevented that until too late. Ellen was alone in her bedroom when the baby came. She delivered it alone, and then stabbed it to death with a nail file.

Its body was found in a laundry bag. The police came and took Ellen to the hospital. They tried to get a statement but she didn't remember killing the baby. She didn't even remember delivering it. Everything had been wiped out by her psychological need to suppress and deny what had happened. She had been strong, rigid. In all this time, she had never confided the story of her mental deterioration to anyone. She'd hidden her conflicts, hidden her pregnancy, deflected any investigation into her fear and confusion. Now these patterns of defense had broken down. Her amnesia was compassionate: what she couldn't remember, she wouldn't have to confront.

When I interviewed Ellen, I had to introduce her to the past year in her life. Her face registered real horror when details had to be mentioned. The tears flowed silently. She reddened and twisted, even though words like "friend" and "relationship" were used instead of "lover" and "affair." She couldn't hear them, let alone say them. Her vulnerability and mortification grew as her emotions were explored. It was almost impossible for her to acknowledge that she had been sexual, become pregnant, then murdered her baby.

Despite the amnesia, Ellen was competent for trial. But she was a broken soul. I responded to her need and felt compelled to come to her support. I explained that she had gone through a total nervous collapse, had been irrational and was not responsible. I said that she was the last person who could have done anything so violent and immoral, and she could not have been in her right mind. Ellen would not be able to understand and digest what had happened to her for a long time. I recommended that she begin treatment at a local psychiatric center. She fulfilled the requirements for an NGRI defense because she was certainly insane at the time of the crime and far from recovered when I spoke to her. The DA followed my recommendation for this tragic young woman.

In western New York, I had the case of a young former soldier arrested for homicide. Roger's problem was his truant, unfaithful wife who wouldn't come home to care for their baby. Their baby but not his baby, for Janine was pregnant and had been abandoned by another man when he married her.

This was Roger's second try at marriage. The first had been happy, but his young wife was killed in an auto accident. His second marriage was something else. It deteriorated swiftly after he lost his job, and there were money problems. Janine couldn't cope with this and soon moved back to her parents. Roger did not condemn her. He tried to court her again until he came to realize that she might never come back. He sent money and clothes for the baby until he began to hear rumors—quickly spread in a small town—that she was spending his money on another man. He went to see her, to confront her with that, bringing food and clothes for the baby but no more money.

Roger found his wife in bed with a man. He punched the stranger and warned him off, but listened to Janine's explanation that she "must have been under a spell." He went home trying to believe it.

During the next few weeks, Roger lived with that scene. What was he to do? A sudden turn to religion brought some solace but not enough. He didn't eat, couldn't sleep and kept telephoning Janine. When he couldn't reach her, he went to church, sat through the sermon, then visited friends. He bought a gun because "the hunting season had opened." When he drove past his in-laws' house, he saw a strange car parked in the yard.

Gun in hand, Roger broke into the bedroom. Again he found his wife in bed with her lover. He shot the man and turned to her. Janine tried to embrace him, crying, "Now I believe you really love me!" Roger didn't listen this time. He dropped the gun, put his hands around her throat and squeezed hard. In another room, the baby awoke and began to cry. He stopped choking his wife; she slumped to the floor, gasping for air. Roger stepped over the dead man's body and went to the sheriff's office.

Here was a man who needed to see himself as a hero. His military combat record was exceptional and he never complained to family or friends about marital problems. He needed her and endured her infidelity, trying his best to avoid the feeling that her actions had made him a patsy. For Janine, he had taken on another man's baby and suffered the humiliation of her infidelity. He had gone "above and beyond." There was no way out for Roger now; he had fallen too far. No matter what the result, he simply had to kill Janine's lover. It was nothing less than the grand gesture a hero makes in defense of his honor.

Though depressed and tearful during our interview, as he had been before the crime, I did not find that Roger was psychotic. I was able to recommend that his mental condition—extreme emotional distress—be considered as mitigating for plea bargaining. This resulted in a reduced sentence.

There's another upstate case I remember solely because of the defendant's curious rationale. He was a burglar who worked only in the daytime. Why? He said, "You can get twenty years for burglary at night!"

Geography influences crimes. Upstate, property held more of its old-time value. Steal a car and you might actually go to jail! Arrest rates were higher there, and at that time, New York City criminals got easier sentences than the natives to the north.

Some of my upstate cases might not have happened in the big city. Where is the New York apartment so spacious that Ellen could have lived there with her family and still secretly deliver a baby? There were no hotel rooms for Janine and her lover to escape to in that small town; in the city, Roger would never have found them so easily. And wouldn't the naïve burglar have learned on any Manhattan street corner that most burglaries are not even *investigated* by the hard-pressed police, let alone result in twenty-year sentences?

On a few occasions in forensic psychiatry, I was asked to be a detective. Once it was to help trap an unknown killer, Son of Sam. Another case involved a multiple murderer whose identity the police suspected. My earliest attempt occurred upstate. Co-incidentally, it was in the same year that I testified against the chromosome murder defendant, and it also involved sodium Amytal.

One day I received a call from John O., a district attorney I knew. John is genially persuasive; otherwise I wouldn't have agreed to come up for an immediate consult and bring some sodium Amytal.

I took a late evening flight. The waiting state trooper, who spotted me so quickly that I knew I looked like New York City, hurried me into his car. We hit a hundred for long stretches on those unlit roads. I tried not to look at the speedometer and I still have no trouble remembering where the car stopped because I was so glad to see the place. It was a motel near a state trooper barracks. John O. was there and so were three anxious-looking people, two men and a woman. They were the principal suspects in the Stennick case. The DA placed them in separate rooms to await my evaluation.

The case involved a young girl who had disappeared while walking home from her cousin's house. Her body was discovered the following day, half-buried in tree branches and weighted with stones. Her blouse was open but her underwear was intact. Dirt, leaves and small twigs filled her mouth.

The death of this eleven-year-old was the only indisputable fact in the case. Almost everyone else involved in it could be regarded as a suspect.

There was the child's own father, a man humiliated by the loss of his wife to someone else who lived in the same town. The father had already been accused of fondling another of his daughters. This same sister of the murdered girl—not a suspect because she was in a home for ungovernable juveniles—had been the

119

early sexual victim of her father's cousin who, nevertheless, remained in the family home. This latter fellow was a man with a history of sexual assaults on his own sister and his stepdaughter as well as on the older Stennick girl. He had a long record of imprisonments and parole violations and was on probation at the time. He had a part-time job and a woman friend whom he entertained in his room in the Stennick house. There was also a full brother of the murdered girl, a discipline problem who had left the father to move in with his mother and her current lover. This lover was known to have an eye for pubescent girls, but he was not a prime suspect. Of somewhat more interest to the police was still another cousin who had a truck and whose memory was unreliable, because he had made a false statement about being unfamiliar with the area in which the girl's body was found.

What could you call this group of people? They were part of a local subculture and the backbone of the county's welfare rolls. The family was known to be violent, promiscuous and guilty of child neglect. They were prone to car accidents (caused by alcoholism) and historically had been involved in crimes of rape. (Even the girl's grandfather had a conviction for it.) This upstate area had a word for them; it was "woodchucks," the local equivalent of "hillbilly." The Stennick case was a "woodchuck" case.

State police had already given polygraph tests to all the suspects, even to the dead girl's neighbors. They had held the first suspect— the cousin on probation who'd already assaulted the victim's sister—for six hours of questioning before releasing him. However, there wasn't enough evidence on any of the suspects to put together a case that would stand in court. A stagnant situation—but now, months later, the DA seemed to feel that something was going to happen. The three principals—father, mother and the thin, eerie cousin—had some intention of clearing up their stories and, who knows, perhaps even confessing. The DA had picked up some hints that one or more just wanted a "license" (excuse) to talk. He thought that a shot of the so-called truth drug would be just what was needed. I had very well-established objections to using sodium Amytal to get at the truth, but the three people had agreed to be injected, and I felt that the idea of the injections, if not the chemical, might bring results and at any rate would cause no harm. So I had agreed, and that was the reason for the wild haste of my trip. I had to get there while they still agreed on it. I was to inject all three of them, right there in the motel.

I interviewed each in turn, only mentioning that I might use the sodium Amytal later. My purpose was to draw them out, to get everything I could without resorting to the injection. The mother was anxious for the chance to clear herself of any complicity in the case; the eerie cousin spoke vaguely, and yet I could see that he was controlling inner anger; the father made many contradictory accusations. I couldn't get clear histories from these people. Who said they wanted to talk? I had a good idea that the injections, placebo or Amytal, would be futile. And what if something went wrong? It was 2 A.M. and I felt shaky after hours of interviewing. I was only half-joking when I told John that I kept seeing these headlines: "PSYCHIATRIST KILLS SUSPECT BY INJECTION, IS INDICTED WITH UPSTATE DA," or "PSYCHIATRIST SUED BY SUSPECT FOR ASSAULT BY INJECTION—DA IS CO-DE-FENDANT."

I said, "This is a mistake." He looked at me and we both smiled, acknowledging the obvious. There would be no injections of anything in the motel that night.

On the way back to the city the next morning, I wrote several pages of notes on the case but there was little of value in what I'd gotten from those three people and I never sent a report. Several years later, I did another upstate case involving a borderline defective who had a history of getting drunk and raping a teenager every four years or so, whenever he was not in prison or a hospital. He was also a "woodchuck" and that reminded me to ask if anything had ever happened in the Stennick case. Nothing new had developed except that the woman I'd interviewed that night had recently died. She was the only one I thought might not be involved in the crime and therefore the only hope of credible testimony. Whatever had been implied was never proved. No charges were made and no trial was possible.

GOOD GUYS, BAD GUYS

I enjoyed going upstate. I would call the cases as I saw them and my recommendations would generally be accepted by the DAs I'd gotten to know. They realized that if I found someone legally insane and this helped the defense, the DA's basic position was not weakened. The mental illness that the defense contended did exist had been authenticated by the expert from New York; therefore the prosecutor's office could not be faulted for leniency. There was a feeling of fair play surrounding all this, and it was responsible for my positive impression of justice in those upstate towns.

Another place in the system where men who cared could make a difference was in the federal courts. Like the upstate offices, the federal courts in New York City have a manageable case load, certainly as compared to the local criminal courts where a busy judge might have to handle a hundred cases on his docket every day!

In the federal courts, contested felony cases could take two or three months from start to finish. Federal practice includes tax frauds, stock and bond frauds, confidence schemes, mail robbery, assorted postal system offenses, counterfeiting, draft evasion, bank robberies, antigovernment terrorism and would-be Presidential assassins. Fascinating stuff. In the close, almost clubby system, federal judges hear the same lawyers and get reports from the same probation officers.

From the sixties through the seventies, I did evaluations in federal cases. I worked for the prosecution—the U.S. attorneys, representing the government—and for the defense. Defense might be private attorneys trying cases in the federal courts, but far more often, my employer was the Federal Defender Services Unit of the Legal Aid Society. Many of my memories of this period are tied up with a man who was the chief of the Federal Defender office of the busy Southern District from 1968 to 1979. He is now a judge.

His name is Murray Mogel. He and I are about the same age, and as boys, we lived in the same section of New York City.

I was working on Ward N,O-2 when he was a Wall Street lawyer. The same year that I left Bellevue and began my part-

122

time career as an expert witness, Murray abandoned corporate law in favor of the Legal Aid Society. For the next ten years, we had a steady working relationship.

Murray always remembered that his clients had families, medical problems and psychological handicaps, and that they would have future difficulties with employment. He took a total view of his cases, trying to break the bad life patterns of people who had gotten themselves into trouble. If he felt that someone was capable of making a fresh start, he'd do whatever he could to make it happen.

There is no question that Murray has an intuitive sense and is so good at his "feeling" about people that virtually all the cases he sent me for evaluation were "good guys" who were in over their heads or completely innocent people arrested by mistake.

One poor soul, whom I'll call Benjamin, had a recent diagnosis of diabetes. The condition worsened, and when he went to work, he occasionally fell into a diabetic coma. Once, found unconscious near his job in a government office, some not-so-good Samaritans threw his body into a subway car and he awakened in another borough. Benjamin was so shaken by this that he became apprehensive about going to work. On the day of his arrest, he felt weak on his feet as he approached his office and sensed the beginning of a diabetic coma. He quickly drank some orange juice from a container he was carrying in a paper bag. Weaving around, drinking, he was mistaken for a drunk by the security guard. When the guard tried to shove him off government property, the confused Benjamin assaulted him. Not only was he arrested for that, but he lost his job.

This was a federal matter and the Defender office got the case. My medical report explained why Benjamin's behavior looked like drunkenness, and the assault case against him was dismissed. He also got his job back. But this case is an example of how other men and women like him, including epileptics, can wind up in jail because their medical symptoms are mistaken for intoxication or criminality.

My association with the Defender unit was good from the first. In the ten years that I worked with the office, it expanded from six lawyers and two secretaries to seventeen lawyers and fifteen supporting people. One thing didn't change: money for psychiatric testimony was hard to come by and Murray would make very persuasive attempts to adjust my fee. When I'd charge the office a preinflationary $100 or $125, he'd react indignantly, goading me, mentioning occasions when he knew I'd waived my fee. It was never just my fee, but always my "exorbitant" fee. Murray never gave an inch. Only on those occasions when I was hired as the sole expert for both prosecution and defense did I break even.

When we met for dinner recently, the conversation between us naturally turned to past cases:

> LUBIN: I had a call from a lawyer down South about the kid with the famous-name credit cards. He's in a jam again. They want to know if I can help.

(This fellow was a nonstop talker who spent three hours explaining why he "borrowed" prominent people's names and went on buying sprees. You couldn't turn him off and he gave us both a headache. He was young, handsome, breezy, homosexual, and psychotic enough so that he made no efforts to cover his tracks. Only months before, we'd gotten him off in New York.)

And Murray had one for me:

> MOGEL: Did you know that the fat gambler with the heart condition finally went to jail?

(Here was a compulsive gambler who was extremely obese. He stole to finance his gambling. I remember telling his lawyer that at age thirty-nine, with his weight and cardiac symptoms, the only thing that might save him was to be placed on a prison diet. Luckily for him, the defense lost his case.)

Because of our special understanding, I was more than usually flexible in accepting some of the cases Murray sent me. It was true that they were "mitzvahs" (good deeds), but maybe I accepted just to hear his reasons for sending them:

LUBIN: Murray, why are you calling with this case? The man has a rap sheet.

MOGEL: Just a few misdemeanors. Drunk and disorderly, you know. He's a nebbish.

LUBIN: But you're calling me on a bank robbery charge!

MOGEL: He bungled it. He was drunk as a skunk the whole time he was doing it.

I saw more bank robbers than any other category of criminal in the cases I did for the Defender office. They were not Willie Suttons. Mine were a mixed lot, frequently pathetic, even clownish, but the sentence they faced was no joke. A bank robber is up for twenty-five years with a gun, twenty without, and that's stiff punishment for an alcoholic who staggers in off the street, demands money and then staggers out again to sit on a curb until the police get him.

Believe it or not, they fit that pattern. They'd walk in bedraggled, with or without a toy pistol. Usually, there was a sorry-looking "Give me the money" note. One who forgot his note completely said afterward, "I saw the loose change in the teller's booth. I asked her for it and she gave it to me." If such a hotshot didn't trip over his feet leaving the bank, he'd amble down the street until the bank guards caught up with him. One of my cases exited the bank and entered the barbershop next door where he was arrested while having a haircut. Failure didn't daunt the drunks: I'm reminded of one we managed to have put on probation instead of in jail and what did he do but go out and try to rob another bank!

As symbols of wish fulfillment, banks also attract depressed, inadequate, compulsive and desperate people who may want something else more than money. They are self-indulgent, crave publicity, or are crying out for help. The way they go about the job suggests the nature of their problems. For example, a black militant group played Robin Hood, taking from the rich (the bank) under full view of the TV monitor cameras to give to the poor. They wanted publicity. So did a psychotic inventor who wanted a backer for his fuelless engine. Others apparently wanted jail. They were ambivalent about the robberies, apologizing to the teller while they took the money or dawdling outside as if reluctant to complete the act. They'd get caught.

In several cases, men who robbed banks were trying to get back at their wives or win them back. So often, a long-suffering wife gives up because the loser she married won't work, or can't keep a job and gets into trouble again and again. He does one dumb thing too many and she leaves. His answer is a "passive-aggressive" act, trying to rob a bank and bungling the job. In effect, he's saying, "See what a jam I'm in now—and it's all your fault!"

Bart, who had a long history of antisocial behavior, wanted to make sure that his wife got that message when she walked out on him. He slashed the clothes she had left behind and smashed the rest of her possessions. Bart decided that he would get himself arrested by pretending to rob a bank. When caught, he came up with the excuse that he wanted to be locked away in jail so that he wouldn't find his wife and kill her! If that was what he wanted, he got his wish. But my own view was that Bart had finally lost his meal ticket and in his anger, did a bad job of robbery. The wife-killing story is strictly post hoc rationalization for still another failure.

The "specific sum" is another odd ploy. I remember, in particular, a young loner who wanted to start a revolutionary group. In each of his bank robberies, he asked "only" for specific sums of money, say, precisely $8,535. By implying that exactly that sum was needed for a political purpose, he was legitimizing his crime. It made him feel less of a robber and more a rebel with a moral cause.

Few bank robbers were as psychologically honest about themselves as the homosexual who told me that he wanted to buy the most beautiful clothes and jewels ever seen on the gay circuit. The robbery was his bid to become "a person to be remembered."

Some of the most outrageous excuses for robberies have been based on jail grapevine advice. In one case, I knew that Malcolm was not enough of a clear thinker to put together two words like "involuntary intoxication," but that was the defense he produced against the charge of bank robbery. His version was that a person named Shadow had dropped a purple pill (purple like the LSD pill most in use) into his grape soda. Malcolm didn't see the pill because of the camouflage, and that made him an unwitting victim of involuntary intoxication who had no idea what he did. I can imagine the men in the detention center coming up with that beauty. But the really weird development was that the jury believed Malcolm's story. When they rendered a verdict of not guilty, the judge was angry enough to comment, "Your verdict is monstrous!"

The defense attorney answered, "Because of the Court's outburst, this jury is now tainted!" He believed that the jurors would be influenced when considering any judge's reaction to any verdict in the future. He told the story around the United States Courthouse and made a real effort to see that none of the "tainted" jurors served in other cases. From a legal point of view he was probably right, but I can understand the judge who'd had it with the "purple pill in the grape soda."

The most engaging bank robber I remember was a serious, round-shouldered, small man who held the courtroom's attention as he explained why his attempt had to fail. He had wanted it to fail and the bomb he had brandished was a homemade wooden dud.

This man, Zachary, was one of the good-deed cases the Defender office sent me. Here was a man who needed one. He was struggling to take care of a wife and five children: two of the children were biologically his; the others, stepchildren from her previous marriage.

When the small hardware business he bought withered and died, he saw no hope in life unless he could make his invention succeed. For a dozen years, on and off, he'd been tinkering with the idea of a fuelless engine that would make a great fortune and benefit mankind. At a very low point in his life, he decided to rob a bank, or better, fail to rob a bank. His object was publicity. He reasoned that the notoriety of being (nearly) a bank robber would give him the opportunity to tell the world about his fuelless engine and attract a backer who would finance its development. This was his story.

I think he would have been a frightened man if he had succeeded in convincing the bank personnel that his bomb was real. He might have had problems with the money, too; how did robbery square with the conscience of a man who asked God for advice every day? But he had no hesitation in grabbing the limelight. There was a good deal of grandiosity in Zachary.

When I interviewed him, he told me that he wasn't afraid of going to trial. He now admitted the bank robbery had been a mistake but would show that his intention was to help mankind with the engine, and this would justify the robbery to the jurors.

I found him to be acting in accordance with a well-established savior-of-mankind delusion, but nevertheless competent for trial. On bail, living with a cousin, and as short of money as ever, he remained in flight from reality by refusing to work. Every moment was needed, he said, to "develop the improved plans for the engine and protect them by visiting a patent attorney."

I never saw those famous plans, but his attorney did when Zachary brought them into court. He clutched them when he went on the stand to testify. There he unrolled them for the judge, confidentially pointing out some problems of design.

"Your Honor, you can see that I really need a mechanical engineer."

"Mr. Prosecutor?" said the judge. "Why are you wasting the government's money by bringing this man into court?"

In its way, it was a very successful defense maneuver. Zachary was found not guilty. The judge said that he didn't have the requisite "intent." He hadn't intended to rob the bank—all he wanted was publicity. I had asked for leniency in my report, saying, "This man is evidently anything but a criminal type, and it would be my hope that the court consider this." The court had so considered and gone all the way. This time the judge had done the good deed.

Bank robberies were frequent in the days of the John Dillinger gang. Then the crime seemed to go out of style. But it's back in vogue today with the handy branch banks everywhere; there's a robbery every banking day in New York City. By the 1970s, there were desperadoes within banks, employees holding responsible positions with ample opportunity for misappropriation of funds. And now they might be female. The Defender office represented several ladies caught with their hands in the till. I knew two of them. One never cracked and the other was a weeper, but both did it for love (and spent the money on their men, whose identities they were determined to protect). I remember the hard case very well.

Roberta had worked for the same bank for twelve years and had been steadily promoted from a teller's job to operations. She was a bank executive when she was charged with the misappropriation of money. "Eight hundred thousand dollars," according to the bank. "It can't be more than one hundred fifty thousand and I didn't take it," said Roberta. She sounded curiously vague for a woman whose function in bank operations was to check out the discrepancies in accounts!

When she was brought into the Federal Defender office, she threatened to kill herself. I was asked to do an evaluation of her on an emergency basis. Another psychiatrist who had seen her thought it possible that she would carry out her threat—what did I think?

Whenever I have trouble extracting simple facts from an intelligent person, there is always the question of evasion. This lady grudged me answers, denied the charges without offering an explanation except some fragmented story about her aunt who was involved with a loan shark, and how she, in kindness, took "some" money to keep her aunt from meeting a gangland fate. The aunt had since conveniently died of natural causes. It wasn't much of a story for a fencer of Roberta's skill, unless she was aiming for a confused, naïve effect. She certainly didn't level with me. But there was an impressive—though controlled—explosive anger in her and I believed in the possibility of a suicide attempt. Since she'd asked to go to jail, I thought it would be the safest course, and the judge remanded her.

Roberta dangled the once real threat of suicide on and off

until her sentencing. One could not be sure. But she remained her surface-cool, enigmatic self, persisting in her denials even in the face of evidence, even at the sentencing. The defense lost, but she came out a winner. She was given a two-year sentence, and since none of the money was recovered at that time, you'd have to call it a win. Someone told her, "Don't think you're going to jail. Just think you're waking up in a confined place, earning two thousand dollars a day, tax free."

I'm sure she thought of it.

Another embezzler I evaluated was quite different. Annette could be described as a sort of clinging vine, a naïve dependent type who had been frightened all the time that she was embezzling $155,000. She didn't keep the money. Most of it went to her lover to keep him with her when he threatened to leave. He was much older and very busy and didn't see her that often. She told him the money was an inheritance. Annette was one of the basically good, bewildered women I came to call "Murray's ladies," and after she served her sentence, my friend was able to help her make a new start. (The sentence was lenient because the money was repaid by her boyfriend—one surprised fellow!) When Annette needed a work reference, Murray found her a job. Eight years later she is still in touch.

Annette was not the first person he boosted back into the world. When a cabbie got in trouble, Murray's first concern was to preserve his hack license. He has tried to get people reinstated in their civil service jobs. And whenever a fallible (meaning vulnerable or not too bright) defendant had a chance to start a new life away from the city, the men in the Defender office would dig down and pay for clothing or find bus fare. There was a special box on a shelf in the office, and in it were three ties, a gift from an alcoholic defendant who'd been given a bus ticket to an out-of-town relative willing to take charge of him. The ties, called "the award," were ritually presented to whichever lawyer had done the latest genuine good deed for a client. The award was given for "meritorious legal service."

The Federal Defender Services Unit of the Legal Aid Society seemed to have a corner on odd defendants. During the years of the Vietnam War I evaluated draft evaders who had other obvious problems: they were disturbed, sexually ambiguous or just pathologically shy people terrified of such Army inevitabilities as stripping nude or sharing latrines. Or, they had grandiose "religious" objections to serving. One Krishna adherent was three hours late for his court appearance because he was at home chanting prayers and staring at himself in the mirror. Government charges against such people were usually dismissed. But even if they had somehow been drafted, I think they would have fallen out from the stress of basic training. I'd seen it happen in the Army, time and again.

Retarded people involved in crimes enlisted my sympathy. Functioning marginally in life, they absolutely screwed up when they tried to show off. They'd follow the big boys into the drug business, and, don't you know, they'd wind up selling to narcotics agents. (Sometimes narcos would use them as cat's-paws to get at the drug suppliers.)

I testified in such a case for the Defender office. The government's psychiatric expert was a well-known doctor and author and his conclusion was that the defendant was shamming loss of memory. But I saw that this man, Phil, had a blind, deviated left eye. A blind eye since birth is a clinical arrow, pointing the clinician to the possibilities of other neurological damage. (I usually check for evidence of epilepsy or mental retardation.) But Phil hadn't even been given a physical exam, let alone a neuro workup. When I investigated, I found that he had organic brain damage, which accounted for the blindness and retardation. Not only was Phil an unrecognized mental defective, but he had been floridly psychotic for years. A courteous, stocky, soft-spoken man, determined to make light of his deficiencies, he asked for no sympathy and wanted to be normal. But Phil was not even able to repeat a sequence of four simple numbers in reverse order. He wasn't shamming loss of memory. The obvious neurological damage won that case.

We had a lot of cases involving postal crime. The postal system seemed to harbor hundreds of disturbed individuals. And it was also a haven for the addicted, for alcoholics and for compulsive gamblers who got into trouble for stealing from the mails to placate the loan sharks on their tails. I remember Arnold, a postal worker who would spend a great deal of his time lecturing coworkers and warning them to stop stealing. On discovering that he himself was under departmental surveillance, he was so angry that he decided to "show them" for their ingratitude. He embarked on a program of theft. But Arnold, though angry and unstable, was basically so honest that he made a botch of it. When his case came to court, his good record over the years weighed in for him and the case was dismissed.

The Defender office represented many "criminals" who lacked any conventional motive. They had nothing to gain from their actions except the satisfaction of their compulsions. How else to explain the behavior of the man who collected mail trucks? He wasn't interested in selling them. He simply couldn't shake the idea that he must jump in and drive one away. Even after he was caught, and released, he did it again.

Another trustworthy, obsessively neat postal worker was caught when he took an electric shaver from the mails. He said he always shaved twice a day and this was the first time in his long em- ployment that he was stuck on the job without being able to shave the second time. He was sorry, he said, and he meant to put the shaver back afterwards. It sounded absurd, but there are some people you have to believe when they say, "I couldn't live without a shave."

If you view the system of trial and punishment as a learning process, it's hard to see what such people could learn from being punished. For them, the most promising alternative approach was the discretionary use of deferred prosecution.

Deferred prosecution is essentially an agreement between the defendant and the government which imposes special conditions on the defendant for six months, a year, or sometimes longer. The conditions involve some mode of treatment: AA for alcoholics, or psychotherapy or psychotropic medications, whatever is "pre- scribed" in each case. During this period, there can be no repetition of the criminal behavior. If the defendant violates the terms of his agreement, he is tried on two charges; the old one and the new one. This helps make for compliance. If he does not violate the agreement, the prosecution will be dismissed.

There is always the temptation to gamble a little, to take a chance on someone who is a good prospect for rehabilitation, if not quite first class. Maybe you'd be right. Or maybe you'd try to do a good deed only to wind up with egg on your face. And you could never be sure about "repeaters."

A repeater goes back and does it again. There are all kinds of recidivists, from those who commit innocuous offenses to arsonists and mass murderers. "My" repeaters were people who'd just keep doing dumb, purposeless things. At one end of the spectrum was Harriet, the mail-order addict who wrote away for everything she saw advertised in magazines. To speed delivery, she wrote for many items at the same time, using a variety of names. Harriet sent for records when she had no record player, clothes when she had no space to keep them, multiples of tape recorders, TV sets, pots and pans, bric-a-brac, unbelievable treasures. As she observed in a moment that was lucid but too late, "They're more expensive than in the stores and I don't need them anyway!" The boxes and packing crates stood unopened in her apartment, the bills were coming in and she couldn't pay. Her game was over and she was charged with using the mails for fraud. This rather silly, fluttery middle-aged lady was terrified of going to jail and threatened us all that if she were sent away, it would make her become "female Public Enemy Number One!" In my report, I called Harriet a harmless soul and stated that the crazy consumer "quirk" would not recur. We figuratively patted her on the back, cautioning her not to buy anything she didn't need. She promised, she swore she wouldn't, and was she grateful for the deferred prosecution!

She did it again. There was another giant buying binge with the same result and I was later told that the merchandise retrieved from Harriet's tiny, cramped apartment filled one of the big bins that the sanitation department uses to clean up after a parade. A calculated risk failed.

If these repeaters were more compulsive than criminal, others did have a kind of purpose. When alcoholics turned in false alarms

133

and repeatedly smashed windows, they had the simple goal of trying to break into jail. Sometimes it was a damaged brain or an instinct to get care. In past years, innocuous alcoholic repeaters were dealt with by drying them out and perhaps offering an explanatory letter to the court. And they did get healthy in jail. There might be some meat on those typically skinny shanks. Their minds cleared, there was less of a glaze on the discolored whites of their eyes, even a deflation of the booze bellies that so many carried. What you had thought to be irreversible damage had improved. This was not the man you had recommended for jail months before! But he'd have to get out eventually, and then get drunk, and do it again.

The windows of the U.S. Courthouse on Foley Square had a peculiar magnetism for men seeking federal hospitality. There's a well-known story about a man who was arrested twenty times for smashing the courthouse windows. The Defender office represented him nine times, nine times over the same route before counsel gave up and said "No more."

This same repeater must have thought he was entitled to a change of venue, because he left the U.S. Courthouse on Foley Square and went uptown. He got drunk enough to smash a window in a government building. But it was his fate to come up in court before a now-famous judge who had earned the nickname of Cut-'em-Loose. Instead of sampling a new jail, the alky was put right back on the street! He gave up on New York and did some traveling: he was hustled out of a few small towns by sheriffs and wound up in Pittsburgh to smash a window in a federal building there. But the judge was wary and said, "See what this man has done in New York." When Pittsburgh looked at his record, the court ordered him to be put on a bus and sent back home to us. Days after he was arrested in Pittsburgh, he was back at the old stand on Foley Square, where he had always been such a smashing success.

Repeaters may be variously more or less dangerous, or willful, and often they're trying to extort something. The suicidals who make a habit of climbing the girders of local bridges are extorting sympathy. It's a passive-aggressive maneuver: "I may hurt me but you'll all be sorry if I jump off this bridge." Those who threaten to damage big targets—to blow up the subway or the reservoir or the tallest building in the city—are extorting fear and admiration for the scope of their ambitions and ignored talents. They often zero in on some area of past grievances in their lives as a reason to extract revenge. Inadequate people are also attracted to targets or personalities prominent in the news and repeatedly threaten them.

There isn't much you can do for them, except to put them out of circulation. In the federal system, incompetent men were then committed for further mental evaluation to the Federal Medical Center in Springfield, Missouri.

Springfield held quite a few would-be Presidential assassins. (I've seen cases where men who were just released would make foolish phone calls, or write letters threatening the President.) Our recent history has made the Secret Service very nervous about such people, however disorganized they may sound. The youngest suspect I ever interviewed was a teenaged girl charged with threatening the life of the President. Angie had a history of juvenile delinquency and she didn't want to tell me that she'd been under psychiatric observation in a hospital. What concerned the President's protectors was her strong interest in guns and the fact that she'd been a crack shot on her school's rifle team. When she called in her threats, it brought down the full might of the Secret Service until it was discovered that her personal weapon was an air rifle! Angie was a damaged person both physically and mentally; once that was realized, she was treated less like a menace and more like a psychiatric patient. But I would want to know whether the people at her school worried about a psychiatric patient being on the rifle team. Those teams are attractive to inadequate people for obvious reasons. A rifle killed President Kennedy, but handguns are the usual villains. The fact that so many unstable people have experience with weapons and access to them guarantees violence and continuing assassinations in the absence of nationwide gun controls.

Psychotic people don't want to be that way. Either they deny the idea of insanity altogether because it is such a stigma and become dissimulators or they deny it because they have rationalized their conduct and stick with their stories in a trial. As mentioned before, there are people with vast, cosmic delusions who won't admit the possibility that they may have had a nervous breakdown and won't cooperate with their counsel. They'd rather go to jail than change that impossible story.

Other defendants, usually mental defectives, won't even attempt a defense. A man like this can be as defiant as he is dull and have a "Let them prove I did it!" attitude. Perhaps he really hasn't a defense and feels his back against the wall. Or he may equate his status as an outlaw with heroism. To him defiance is a sign of strength and asking for help is begging, so it's weak. This is kid stuff, but he may have a mental age to match his behavior. His bad judgment will take him to jail.

Still a third type isn't easily tagged. A man just sticks to a story that runs counter to the facts. It neither gives him a psychological defense nor makes him incompetent. He resists help and that's his choice. When I evaluated a man who denied that he had committed a bank robbery even though the TV camera had taken his picture, the teller had a note in his handwriting and a bank full of witnesses had given positive identification, I didn't waste much time in speculation. That was my mistake, mine and the Federal Defender's and the U.S. Attorney's. None of us believed him.

Let's call him Dennis. He was no repeater. He had a record, an unremarkable one-time arrest for passing bad checks. He was on his third marriage to a younger woman and they had one child. He held down a routine job in a market. And that was all.

Dennis wouldn't move off his denial of the facts. I recommended him as competent for trial. He was convicted on robbery charges and sentenced to eight years. Once he was in jail, his wife left him.

From prison, he kept writing letters protesting his innocence. The jails are always full of self-taught lawyers preparing writs of "error coram nobis" for themselves and other innocent prisoners and the government was not impressed with the correspondence.

Then there was another bank robbery in which witnesses positively identified Dennis. But Dennis was in jail!

There was yet another bank robbery in the same branch as before. The camera took his picture and the witnesses were positive. He left another demand note which was like the first.

The police set up a stakeout near the bank, but the robber slipped through and did it again. Same MO (modus operandi).

There was no answer unless Dennis had a double with his handwriting (but not even identical twins write exactly the same way). Or you could believe that Dennis, who was not in a maximum security prison, would escape on Fridays, rob the bank, hide the money, and go back to prison. Someone on the government side did suggest that, but how seriously?

Then, another robbery exactly like the others.

The FBI called in the New York Police Department's handwriting expert. By now, they had a small collection of identically worded demand notes left by the elusive robber. The expert examined them and agreed that they were all written by one man, but he was not Dennis. The only reason that the notes looked like his work was that both men had had very little education and wrote in a near-illiterate hand with few defining characteristics. The handwriting was similar, not the same.

What did the FBI do with this expert opinion? Very little. For a period of time, until they actually caught his double, Dennis remained in jail. Once they did catch the lookalike, the case against him was very quietly dismissed.

He finally sued the government. He had a dream case: false arrest, time spent wrongfully in jail, the withholding of evidence that he was innocent of the charge, personal anguish and the dissolution of his family as a result of the false arrest. Only he didn't manage to collect—not even a cent!

The men I knew and worked with in the federal courts have moved on to other phases of their careers. Some are professors and judges. The lawyers from that Defender office were convinced of the usefulness of psychiatric testimony, and over the years, I've continued to do cases for a few of them who are in private practice. A psych report I completed for one attorney looked unaccountably familiar. It was a drug entrapment case; where had I seen it before? I went to my files. No wonder I had a sense of déjà vu; the case was identical in fact pattern and in the pathetic personality of the defendant to one I had done for the Federal Defender office ten years before. And the same lawyer who sent it to me now was then the lawyer on the case!

We were still protecting good guys, but there was a commonality to so much of it; we were doing the same things over and over.

Real life crime was nothing like the movie version.

7 | Enter Inspector Dowd

I first met the murderer who called himself Son of Sam in a taunting letter he had written to a New York City police detective. The police approached me with the hope that I could draw a psychological profile of the letter writer and compose an answer that would entice him into contact with them. I had no idea that I'd later be involved in the case as defense psychiatrist. But from the first moment I saw the letter to my last interview with the prison-bound man who might well be killed where he was going, I couldn't shake the feeling that I was part of a movie plot. The case had that effect on everyone drawn into it.

David Berkowitz, known as Son of Sam, became a star of the news media who made his own scenarios of tragedy, teased the police in the best "come get me" tradition until he was caught and contributed a blockbuster finish to his story that was meant to take place in the courthouse. He gave the reporters of the press and TV what they wanted, and in return they hyped him as the hottest case in years. What a run! First, the unknown .44 caliber killer whose

139

victims were chosen at random anywhere on the city streets; next, the announced psychotic, the true "mad dog" killer (by his own admission); and then, in the last act, the repentant convert to what seemed to be born-again Christianity. Something there for everybody. Before this media child was through, he had killed six people, injured seven, and made a casualty of the law as well because of the way that the panicked criminal justice system dealt with his case.

Son of Sam was my impetus for writing this book. I was reacting to the unusual group action by the authorities which effectively controverted the laws protecting the mentally ill by allowing an incompetent man to plead guilty. It was obvious why they wanted Son of Sam in prison. But the decision should have been left to a jury, at a trial, according to the law. The jury might easily have sent a multiple murderer to prison, but even if they had found him legally insane and sent him to a hospital, he might have been of great use to society.

The publicity which raised David Berkowitz to national attention, as it followed him into the hospital, would have forced necessary change. As a "hot potato" in a mental hospital, Berkowitz might have done more for society's need to control dangerous people than anything else to date. His could have been the landmark case. Fear of his escape or release might have forced reappraisal of the use of the NGRI defense and the policies controlling criminally committed patients, as well as the larger problem of all dangerous patients, civil and criminal.

He had said that he was a channel through which greater forces worked. This time it would not have been his demons and angels, but could be the force of much-needed reform.

The letter which was my introduction to the case was addressed to Police Captain Joe Borelli and left at the scene of a double killing on April 17, 1977. Three other killings and four woundings of victims had preceded the April letter which was so obviously a "catch me if you can" gambit for the police. From the contents of that letter, the so-called .44 caliber killer was rechristened by the media. He became Son of Sam.

The police called me a few days after they had acquired the

MR. JOE BORELLI
QUEENS HOMOCIDE

I LOVE TO HUNT. PROWLING
THE STREETS LOOKING FOR
FAIR GAME TASTY MEAT THE
WEMON OF QUEENS ARE Z
PRETTYIST OF ALL. I MUST
BE THE WATER THEY DRINK
I LIVE FOR THE HUNT MY LIFE
BLOOD FOR PAPA

MR BORELLI SIR
I DON'T WANT TO KILL ANYMORE
NO SIR, NO MORE BUT I
MUST "HONOUR THY FATHER."

I WANT TO MAKE LOVE TO THE
WORLD. I LOVE PEOPLE.
I DON'T BELONG ON EARTH.
RETURN ME TO YAHOOS.

TO THE PEOPLE OF QUEENS,
I LOVE YOU. AND I WA
WANT TO WISH ALL OF
YOU A HAPPY EASTER.
MAY GOD BLESS YOU
IN THIS LIFE AND IN
THE NEXT. AND FOR NOW

I AM DEEPLY HURT BY YOUR CALLING
ME A WEMON HATER. I AM NOT.
BUT I AM A MONSTER.
I AM THE "SON OF SAM." I AM A LITTLE
"BRAT"
    WHEN FATHER SAM GETS—DRUNK
HE GETS MEAN. HE BEATS HIS
FAMILY. SOMETIMES HE TIES ME
UP TO THE BACK OF THE HOUSE.
OTHER TIMES HE LOCKS ME
IN THE GARAGE. SAM LOVES TO
DRINK BLOOD.
    "GO OUT AND KILL" COMMAND
FATHER SAM
    BEHIND OUR HOUSE SOME
REST. MOSTLY YOUNG — RAPED
AND SLAUGHTERED — THEIR
BLOOD DRAINED — JUST BONES
NOW
    PAPA SAM KEEPS ME LOCKED
IN THE ATTIC TOO. I CAN'T
GET OUT BUT I LOOK OUT THE
ATTIC WINDOW AND WATCH
THE WORLD GO BY.
    I FEEL LIKE AN OUTSIDER.
I AM ON A DIFFERENT WAVE
LENGTH THEN EVERYBODY

ELSE - PROGRAMMED TOO
KILL
    HOWEVER TO STOP ME YOU
MUST KILL ME. ATTENTION
ALL POLICE: SHOOT ME FERST
SHOOT TO KILL OR ELSE.
KEEP OUT OF MY WAY OR
YOU WILL DIE!

    PAPA SAM IS OLD NOW
HE NEEDS SOME BLOOD TO
PRESERVE HIS YOUTH.
HE HAS HAD TOO MANY
HEART ATTACKS. TOO MANY
HEART ATTACKS. "UGH ME
HOOT IT URTS" SONNY BOY.

    I MISS MY PRETTY
PRINCESS MOST OF ALL.
SHE'S RESTING IN
OUR LADIES HOUSE
BUT I'LL SHE HER SOON.

  "I'M THE "MONSTER"
"BEELZEBUB" - THE
"CHUBBY BEHEMOUTH".

I SAY GOODBYE AND
GOODNIGHT

POLICE LET ME
HAUNT YOU WITH THESE
WORDS,

I'LL BE BACK!

I'LL BE BACK!

TO BE INTERRPRETED
AS- BANG BANG, BANG
BANK, BANG — 'UGH!L'

YOURS IN
MURDER

MR. MONSTER

letter. I was phasing out of the forensic field, and, though I had done an evaluation on a defendant in the well-known Bronfman kidnapping case a year or two before, I thought of myself as almost retired. Yet here were Deputy Inspector Timothy Dowd and his associate, Lieutenant Gorman, wanting my opinion of this letter addressed to Borelli and signed "Mr. Monster." What did I think of "Mr. Monster"?

I studied Dowd. If I did come up with some insight of relative value, how resistant would he be to listening? He didn't have the look of a police officer; my guess, noting those fine-rimmed glasses, would have been clergy. He watched my face as I read; I could feel his expectancy. And I did have an opinion. I remember saying something like, "Are you sure that this was found at the scene of the crime? It's like a put-on."

Dowd was there to tell me that it wasn't. But the thing even *looked* outrageous, and the slanted, blocky capitals drew my attention away from the content. The total impression was of a psychotic killer trying to produce a letter that looked and sounded like a psychotic killer, only more so. A movie publicity man aiming for effect couldn't have done any better. I filed that thought for reference. It was my first intuition of the letter writer. Valid? *The New York Times* of August 12, 1977, quoted him on his first encounter with this same Inspector Dowd. Berkowitz sounded like a meld of Sherlock Holmes and a Western outlaw. "Inspector, you finally got me. I guess this is the end of the trail."

We first talked at length about the time relationships of the crimes. There were three attacks in 1976: July 29, in the Bronx, one person dead and one wounded; October 23, Flushing, Queens, one wounded; November 27, Bellerose, Queens, two wounded. He began his 1977 run on January 30, in Forest Hills, Queens, one person killed; on March 8, another victim killed in Forest Hills (he had taken to prowling those streets on foot); April 17, Baychester, the Bronx, two persons killed and the letter left for the police.

We went over the fact patterns of the crimes and tried to connect whatever we could with the contents of the letter. It is easier to generalize about murderers than other criminals. Murder has the lowest incidence of recidivism of the categories of crime. People kill mainly in passion or while drunk. Their victims are families or friends more often than the total strangers "taken out" during robberies and street crimes. (Recent statistics indicate that the pattern is now changing toward more frequent and casual killing of strangers.)

Contrary to popular opinion, psychotic murderers are only 10 to 20 percent of those who kill. Not uncommonly, they believe they are dictated to by a force beyond their control, and the act of killing relieves the pressure on them. Their delusions include no escape plan and they are caught. The exceptions to this are the multiple murderers: they must be threatening, violent and organized enough to carry off repeated killings over a period of time. Society has much to fear from them. Since they usually choose victims with whom they have no known connection, no particular aggressive focus, they are very difficult to find. Jack the Ripper was one such rare bird, never caught. Today we have the Yorkshire Ripper, Son of Sam, and the Atlanta killer.

These men are different from the usual psychotically driven repeater. I have seen many men who do repeated crimes pursuant to hallucinatory commands, but they lack organization. A rapist I knew had once been only a voyeur—the face at the bedroom window—until one night he heard the voice in his head that made the difference. The voice said, "Do it, do it, do it!" This time, and many times thereafter, he did it. He smashed through the window where he'd been breathlessly watching a woman and leaped on her. Not much organization or precaution there. He was hardly in the "rare birds" league.

I can remember only one case on the prison ward where the violence was packaged with both threats to the public and the organization to carry them out. The papers had a field day with this man too; they called him the Mad Bomber. His first tour on the prison ward preceded my time, but his was a case that was documented there from his first competency evaluation until the last, which came after a long hospitalization and occurred during my tenure. The Mad Bomber was unusual in that he had a fixed delusion. He held a grievance against a local utility company and set bombs because his complaints were not redressed. Son of Sam had no apparent logical grievance. He was a killer who repeated without a clear aggressive focus on any one of his victims.

How in hell did you find such a man? While the policemen listened, I tried every kind of long-shot conjecture in a search for clues.

Did the references to bodies in the letter mean that he lived near a cemetery? Was the name Son of Sam a possible disguise for Samson? Could any real person or family named Samson be identified as living near a cemetery? Samson lost his strength when Delilah took his hair. Was this Sam losing his hair, was he bald, did he blame women for it? Was it worthwhile to canvass barbershops in Queens and the Bronx for particularly eccentric customers who had problems with their hair? Or did Sam wear a wig? Did the one consistent factor of dark-haired victims mean that somewhere in Sam's past, a girl who had such hair rejected him and this made him seek revenge?

(That conjecture was a common one. A lot of women with longish dark hair like the girls Sam killed tucked up their hair under blond or red wigs, which they wore when outside their homes. The wigs were popular until Sam was caught.)

You could play Ping-Pong with this kind of speculation for hours and I knew that such top-of-my-head opinions of what was in the letter were only preliminary to something specific the police would want of me. They were good listeners to the generalities and connections I tried to make as I "freely associated."

I said that the writer was probably schizophrenic. I guessed he was young, white, possibly Catholic, single and a loner. If he lived in an apartment house, he'd rarely be seen by other tenants. If he lived at home with his parents, he'd be isolated in a basement or attic room. I thought the specific placement of himself looking out the attic window, as mentioned in the letter, had some value as a clue.

As I drew up a list of possible eccentricities, I knew that my broad description could fit thousands of former mental patients living alone on New York's Upper West Side. But I had an instant facetious answer to what he might do for a living—he worked on the night shift at the post office. Postal employees were almost a cliché to clinicians. For some psychotics, it was a perfect place to work. They could sort the mail in silence while they hashed and rehashed their bizarre views of life. I could imagine this Son of Sam, seated by himself, planning his actions, thinking his murderous thoughts.

In point of fact, it turned out that he *was* working at the post office in 1977. He was stated to be a good worker on the night shift who never got into trouble. When fellow postal workers made jokes about the Son of Sam, the real article warned them, "Don't make jokes or he'll get you, man!" He would be very earnest when he explained in postarrest interviews that the demons had been listening and those men were tempting fate.

It developed that what Inspector Dowd wanted me to do next was to respond to the letter with an answer that might at least initiate a contact between Sam and the police. I said I'd try.

That night I sat down at my kitchen table, placed the letter before me and concentrated on its details. I looked for familiar patterns. Who was this guy, threatening, teasing, but actually making the violence happen? He had certain psychopathological signs and symptoms that could be addressed, but the willful, teasing obscure references followed no particular pattern. I made notes for each page of the letter.

"Mr. Joe Borelli, Queens Homocide"
That salutation, for instance. It might only be carelessness, but spelling homicide as "homocide" could be significant. Does it refer to homo sapiens or possibly homosexual? I felt sure that this was the kind of schizophrenic who would be into weird puns.

"I am deeply hurt by your calling me a wemon-hater."

I had told the police that this was an obvious neologism for "woman" and "demon," and he used it twice. Berkowitz agreed to that meaning later, at the beginning of his interviews with hospital psychiatrists. But still later, he would find ways to make himself look more rational and insist that "wemon" was only a misspelling. He said, "Women are people too!"

There were fanciful and Biblical references and, above all, movie references. Could Son of Sam be something like Son of Frankenstein? How about such pictures as *Rosemary's Baby*, *The Exorcist* and *Dracula*? Words like "monster," "brat" and "drinking blood" seemed to owe something to all of them.

"Sam loved to drink blood. 'Go out and kill,' commands Father Sam."

If he's hallucinating about vampirism, he's attributing it to a person, Father Sam, and that's not too typical. Most hallucinations are anonymous. Another atypical fact: he's not at all reticent to tell you about Father's orders. Girls are "raped and slaughtered, their blood drained," and that's more movie vampirism. Now there's a little pathos as he says he's a lost soul locked in the attic who looks out the window and watches the world go by. It's a world he can't join because he's "on a different wave length than everybody else."

You said it, buddy!

He says he is "programmed to kill." That's more self-conscious use of television or movie dialogue. "Attention, police, shoot first"—it's right out of the old *Batman* TV show. The many movie references make obvious where Sam spent most of his time.

Now we have a little poetic license creeping in with the sentences about Papa Sam. He's old, he's had a heart attack, his "hoot" (Sam later said it meant "heart") hurts. It doesn't seem too relevant, doesn't quite make sense, but sounds good and may have been thrown in for effect. The monologue at this point is somewhere between semi-Scots and *Mad Magazine*.

GOOD GUYS, BAD GUYS

"I miss my pretty princess most of all."
Why? Has she moved away? Is she a real person, possibly even a victim, or a movie star? This fellow is throwing out possibilities like a smoke screen. It sounds as if he is speaking poetically. I notice that the princess "rests" like the victims he mentions. And why will he "see her soon"? There are so many variables here about what may precipitate his acts. Perhaps he really thinks he's explaining himself. More probably he's looking over his own shoulder as he writes; there is a large element of showing off.

"Monster, Beelzebub, Chubby Behemouth"
Now he's turning sillier on us. It could also be a description of himself. Is he short and wants to be a giant? Is he chubby and wishes he wasn't? "Behemoth" (in its correct spelling) is a colossal beast from the Bible. "Chubby Behemouth" is overkill, but it does sound mysterious and powerful.

On page three, he's back on the hunt to kill. Now the mood changes: the fanciful grandiose references are not at all reticent, despite an attempt to be seen as a would-be good guy.

"Mr. Borelli, Sir, I don't want to kill any more . . . but I must."
More "help me," mixed with willful psychosis. We have a witchcraft thing here; he's saying that he's possessed, can't stop. The beseeching, little-boy tone is noticeable; he drops into it easily and I imagine that he must use it often. I am already wondering whether the Chubby Behemouth may have an NGRI defense. But should a man like this be protected if he's caught?

On each and every page, the main thematic material is ambivalent. He's alternately bloodthirsty and wistful, romantically misses his little princess, explains that he doesn't want to kill but, like a soldier, he's under orders to do it. He says he must honor his father—a commandment from Papa Sam or God or both. He loves the people of Queens and wants to wish them a

Happy Easter with God bless and so forth, but he's still on the job in that borough. The love doesn't get through.

"I don't belong on earth."

He asks to be returned to Yahoos. The police and I struggled with that, thinking that it might come from *Gulliver's Travels*. (Didn't Gulliver have long hair like Samson, and wasn't he tied to the ground in Lilliput by his hair? More hair symbolism?)

Our writer has a good memory and at least a high school education if he read *Gulliver*.

I'm not surprised that he wishes to be returned to the better place he had before, Yahoos. Sounds familiar; Bellevue had more than its share of displaced intergalactic aliens.

"Police, let me haunt you with these words. . . ."

The closing can be seen either as the product of a psychotic, whose censorship system has gone awry and doesn't care if the primitive childish stuff hangs out, or as the psychotic putting us on again.

Despite his playful Hollywood references, I concluded that this man was a dangerous paranoid schizophrenic with a strong delusion. He was totally engulfed and controlled by a drive to destructive behavior, and was making it all operate within an elaborate system of delusional beliefs.

To answer him, as the police requested, I would cut through the trimmings he provided and write to the paranoid's typical symptoms of grandiosity, feelings of victimization and religiosity. He was preoccupied with the issue of good versus evil; I would be too. I'd aim right at the paranoid features and wouldn't bother to be sophisticated. Such bantering, punning psychotics are not as clever as they imply. I decided that the best course was to accept the movie hokum letter he'd written and answer it in the same vernacular. It would be meant for him alone. I thought he'd read it through, and if he recognized the manipulation and perhaps got angry, what difference? He's out there killing anyway.

I couldn't have it typed because the police urged secrecy. I wrote it in longhand, on my hospital letterhead in case someone wanted to call me about editing my choice of words or the logic behind its general content.

I wrote:

> You have shown us that we cannot stop you. You have had the power to kill five people and perhaps more. It may be that you have a mission on earth and the deaths were programmed, as if by commands from a powerful person, in order that their young blood somehow helps people close to you to have less suffering. We cannot know this. We do believe that even if you are acting as a demon or a monster programmed to kill, you are, at times, strong enough to stop yourself from killing some of the people you could have killed.
>
> You may be able to control the sometimes cruelty of those commands by rising above them, perhaps reflecting a greater force. You can show the courage to contact either myself [Borelli] or an intermediary of your own choosing. The world must learn that you are simply not another woman-hating coward with a gun. If you delay, too many false stories may have been told and you may not be believed. Now, before it is too late, grasp this opportunity to talk with us and other government officials, who will be able to verify and thus ensure that you be able to tell the true story of things that have happened to you and what you may have suffered.

I had to draw on what I thought he was saying; my answer rambled but the tone was right. I fed his grandiosity by admitting that he had the power to kill five people, but then I also gave him an excuse. I mentioned that he had a mission on earth and said that maybe it was okay because he followed a command (command hallucination) or that he had to do what he did to mitigate someone's suffering. I again played to his grandiosity with "We cannot know this"; it meant "You're smart, because you do." Then I appealed to his ambivalence, to the good boy in him—the flip side of evil—and suggested that he had shown

148

great strength and generosity by not killing all those he could have killed.

In the second paragraph, I told him that he was strong, perhaps a stronger force than evil. I made it a heroic act to contact Borelli, or someone else. I emphasized (as if I were on his side) that the world *must* learn that he was not ordinary, not your everyday woman-hating coward with a gun. (No paranoid thinks he's ordinary, and this was one who said he'd been specifically singled out for a mission by Papa Sam.)

In conclusion, I appealed to the paranoidal victimization beliefs that I figured to be part of the package. That was the reason for "Don't let false stories about you continue to be told." I told him that government officials (and the world) would greet him and confirm that he had suffered. He could tell his story to the widest possible audience.

Yes, I had fired a scatter-gun in his direction. Even ordinary citizens would recognize the ideas in this primitive series of compliments and requests as having a purpose, but the man I was trying to reach might understand it uniquely. He might impulsively act on it and make a mistake.

I wondered what the police would make of my movie-style rhetoric. I wasn't too surprised when Dowd came back the next day and asked for a shorter version.

SECOND RESPONSE

We have seen that you have had the power to kill. Perhaps your mission on earth was to help the suffering of some by the deaths of others. If you were programmed to kill as a demon or monster, you were also strong enough not to kill some of the people you could have. You may contain a greater force which controls and rises above sometimes cruel demands. You have the courage to contact myself or another person of your own choosing. Do not delay—false stories will spread—the world must find out that you are not just a woman hater with a gun. The story of what happened to you must be told.

GOOD GUYS, BAD GUYS

The shortened version was a little bare, but the police wanted the condensation and maybe they were right.

In both letters, I was careful not to challenge the delusion, which would only make him hostile. I did not say that he was sick and I did not say that he needed help. Just the opposite. I suggested that *we* needed help and he was the only one who could supply it. Son of Sam, teasing and triumphant, might hook himself on this bait.

Inspector Dowd said that he and the chief of detectives thought that the letter was a good idea and might coax Sam into making contact with the police. I was fascinated by the idea of using the news media, which I knew had dangerously influenced some vulnerable people, to undo some of that danger. My letter appealed to him, as an obvious movie buff, in terms of the universal scenario: good guys versus bad. The shift that the news media had gradually made in our original understanding of those terms, suggesting that if bad was not good it was at least deserving of attention and analysis, might be of help now. He could believe that we might understand why he had to do those bad things.

We have come a long way from the black and white hats of the early cowboy pictures to the current sophisticated heroes who are not quite heroes: the less-than-pure protagonists played by Clint Eastwood, Lee Marvin or James Coburn. It has been shown as acceptable to do wrong for a good purpose, righting a grievance or saving fellow citizens. A hero can therefore be an outlaw. The natural correlative of this change is that the appearance of "good" may actually conceal hypocrisy and evil. A few steps more in this confusing direction and the heroes are just like the villains. But they are still admired and inspire imitation.

When media teaches, acceptance of its "truth" can be tragically uncritical. There were vulnerable children who tried to fly out the window after watching Superman. These were juvenile emulators of a hero—but what about the women we saw at the Bellevue Psychiatric Admitting Office who deliberately took overdoses of barbiturates after Marilyn Monroe died that way, or the Beatles fans who shot themselves after John Lennon was killed?

During the time that the Vietnamese War was on TV, suggestible mentally disordered persons went even further in aping what they saw. There were several cases of people dousing themselves with gasoline and setting themselves afire because they had seen Vietnamese Buddhists do it as a form of political protest. Other kinds of people tried to imitate what had excited them on TV. In 1979, a civil suit was filed against a television network because a nine-year-old child had been raped with a mop handle by a group of children, just the way they had apparently seen it done on a TV movie only four days before the assault.

In Florida, the defense in the Ronnie Zamora case directly blamed TV's "bad lessons" by saying that Zamora had been intoxicated into committing murder by his steady diet of TV violence. The contention failed to convince the jury; young Zamora was no stranger to his victim and an attempt was made to rob her.

It is true that the news media give life to certain criminals. Widespread publicity is essential for hijackers, hostage takers, or political extortionists equipped with bombs. They nearly all claim to be doing it for a good cause, implying heroism or martyrdom. Without media coverage, these terrorists wouldn't exist. Whoever heard of the Symbionese Liberation Army before its members kidnapped Patty Hearst? The media made this "army" of five a coast-to-coast movement and a danger to the nation—for a time.

The connection with Son of Sam is that the cumulative effect of news as theater—incident after incident, protest after protest—adds to the osmotic blurring of "good" and "bad." The audience for violent theater can simultaneously love and hate the latest criminal celebrity (acceptable antihero). Sam would know that the public's curiosity wouldn't be satisfied until he and his history had been examined in camera close-ups. In this show-biz atmosphere, Sam—a creature influenced by the media-made confusion of values—might not be unwilling to turn himself in for the same contorted, heroic, show-off reasons. He would give us the message that he was saving us all from demons and would expect to enjoy the results of celebrity.

GOOD GUYS, BAD GUYS

The police did something anomalous with my letter: they didn't use it and they didn't ignore it either. They took phrases from the second version, for over the next few weeks I heard fragments of it (attributed to the police) on TV and read them in the news. Dowd called once, apologetically. I think what prompted the call was the appearance of the four-sentence "letter" to the Son of Sam in the tabloids on April 29, 1977. It appeared as a memo on the Police Department's letterhead:

NEW YORK POLICE DEPARTMENT

Thursday, April 28

NOTE TO MEDIA: You are requested to use the following in its entirety:

Son of Sam,
 We now know that you are not a woman hater and know that you have suffered. We wish to help you and it's not too late. Please let us help you. Call Police Captain Borelli or Inspector Dowd at 844-0909 or write them at the 109th Precinct, Flushing, New York.

So much for the letter.

When Commissioner Michael Codd went on television to appeal to the killer, he spoke in generalities. He asked Sam to give himself up because he was a sick man and needed help. Of course that wouldn't work. (It didn't work in the movies, and it was the wrong way to manipulate a grandiose schizophrenic.)

Now, because there were virtually no clues, the police had to wait until the maniac who was so clearly playing games with them contacted the press again in a June note to Jimmy Breslin, *Daily News* columnist. By that time, he was into a media "head trip" and I felt that any possible vulnerability to surrender had passed.

That was correct. The Son of Sam, in an interview with a Kings County doctor after his arrest, said he thought that Breslin was "obsessed with the shootings" and he had sent the note because he wanted more publicity for his first victims as well as an acknowledgment of the demons. In other interviews, he re-

152

affirmed that he had had no intention of turning himself in; in fact, he was ultimately disappointed in the results of his letter to the columnist and even blamed the shootings that came afterward on this failure.

He attacked again on June 27, 1977, wounding two persons outside a Bayside, Queens, disco, and then again on July 31, in Brooklyn, blinding Robert Violante and killing Stacy Moskowitz. I couldn't help wondering if my original letter could have been at all helpful in preventing these last crimes or whether it might have been a deterrent to the massacre he was planning for the steets of Southampton when he was finally captured on August 10.

I did get the chance to ask him. How I came to take the job of defense psychiatrist in the Son of Sam case and to work with his lawyers will be detailed a little further on. For the moment, I want to concentrate on one aspect of that cold morning, January 2, 1978 when I first interviewed him in the psychiatric prison ward of Kings County Hospital in Brooklyn.

My purpose, as usual, was to determine competency and to explore for possible material which could be made the basis of an NGRI defense. And I was curious. Kings County was a nostalgia trip, like coming home to Bellevue. It was the same kind of big processing hospital, serving the borough of Brooklyn instead of Bellevue's Bronx and Manhattan.

I had been there before, but never to the psychiatric prison ward. Coming up on the building, I felt the same excitement and apprehension that used to accompany my morning walk into Bellevue. I found my way to the sixth floor, no thanks to an officious hospital guard monitoring the main floor elevator. He didn't care that I had a court order to go to the prison ward. Just like old times!

As the elevator stopped at the foyer waiting room, almost on the entrance gate, a Bellevue gloom and dinginess met me. There was a short delay as a Corrections officer checked my court order signed by Judge Corso. He groaned a bit at seeing my tape recorder, but he let it go in with me. There had been "errors": an unauthorized, taped interview for which someone had persuaded

Berkowitz to sign a release, a picture of him in his cell that had somehow reached the newspapers. They didn't want any more problems.

Passing through the gates on the Kings County ward, I saw a vignette from my own past on N,O-2. A middle-aged doctor was edging out of his office, careful not to turn his back on a hulking, angry-looking patient who followed him. As he moved toward the safety of the Corrections officers' area, the doctor avoided eye contact and spoke quickly, something about needing more information at another time. His outstretched arm as he pointed toward the ward made a barrier between him and the patient: "Go back there." I could see his expression and I knew that fear was this doctor's daily partner, a working condition of his job. I wondered how many years he'd been putting himself through the wringer and I felt sorry for him.

In the little interview office, I located an outlet and plugged in my tape recorder. Bringing it with me was a purely defensive reaction. Everyone else who had interviewed Berkowitz had made tapes, and though I rarely did it on a forensic consult, this time I felt I might need the evidence of Berkowitz's answers.

Outside in the corridor someone shouted "Gate." Berkowitz came in, wearing hospital pajamas. He was exactly as pictured; heavily lidded blue eyes, the smile photographers had called "silly" or "evil" or "the glazed inappropriate smile of a psychotic," depending on who was describing it. The former Chubby Behemoth had lost weight on hospital food, but he was still a soft, polite, apologetic fellow with the boyish, beseeching quality so often noted. I had to remind myself that this was a multiple killer. As we began to talk it was obvious that he wished psychiatrists would let him alone. But then I could see that he had decided to use the talk as a diversion. He had nothing to do all day, nothing in his cell but his bed and his Bible. As if cued in by my thought, he was soon talking Jesus. I recognized that the preaching had become a tactic. He was practicing his all-embracing rationale, using it to fend off harsh reality and any interviewer's questions. Whenever we approached a sensitive area, Berkowitz would retreat into Jesus or answer with ambiguous grunts. Pauses

154

stretched into lapses as his mind went elsewhere. He was dreamy at times and said he felt sleepy from his medication. I knew that the doses in fact were minimal. They certainly didn't keep him from hallucinating when he talked to me.

He'd evidently had destructive hallucinations for a long time, and I was immediately alerted by his reference to the fact that he could sometimes control himself.

A voice in Korea had urged him to "kill some of the lifers" (lifers are Army career men).

"But I wouldn't do it. I refused to do it."

"You could rise above the voices sometimes?" I asked.

He answered affirmatively.

At this point, we had talked for more than an hour and I was satisfied with what I had elicited from him in this first session, but his last response struck me and I turned to the subject of the Borelli letter. Berkowitz had already been questioned about it in other interviews and, after hesitations, he had usually mumbled that he had forgotten what was in it. What he did remember, and complained about, were the names he had been called in the press. Woman hater! He liked women, loved women, didn't want to harm them. Nobody understood anything.

I already knew that he hadn't heard Commissioner Codd's televised appeal to Son of Sam. He had been told that the Commissioner had said that he was a sick man who needed help and should give himself up. Would he have done so if he'd heard that message?

Berkowitz's answer was entirely predictable. In every interview, he had insisted that he wasn't sick.

I made an abrupt decision to show him the letter I had written to him and pulled it from the Son of Sam file in my briefcase. What if he'd read it eight months before and realized that someone seemed to believe that he was possessed by demons but could rise above their commands sometimes and not kill?

He read it slowly now and seemed confused. Would it have impelled him to make contact with the police?

First he answered "Yeah," then amended it to "I don't know." Then he wondered aloud, "But there was no letter like that."

No, there wasn't.

It probably would have made no difference in this case. But he'd written to Borelli originally because he saw that name in the papers. I remained convinced that if the news media could help to create such monsters, it could somehow help to control them.

8 | Demischmutz

"That's a name the demons gave me."

D. BERKOWITZ

On August 10, 1977, David Berkowitz was arrested by the police as he emerged from his Yonkers apartment for an evening of "hunting." He was in his car as the police approached and had his favorite .44 caliber Bulldog in a paper bag on the seat beside him. But he offered no resistance. In fact, he smiled.

The following day, he was confined in the prison ward of Kings County Hospital. Six months later, I was called to the case as first psychiatrist for the defense. By then, several doctors had interviewed him many times on the subject of his competency for trial.

On August 12, pursuant to the usual judge's order, he was examined by the staff psychiatrists at Kings County, Drs. Daniel Schwartz and Richard Weidenbacher. They saw him six times in formal psychiatric examinations, and the transcripts of those sessions ran to 400 pages of questions and answers. On August 31, Dr. David Abrahamsen, an independent expert hired by the Brooklyn DA on behalf of that borough's case, began several psychiatric examinations of his own.

157

GOOD GUYS, BAD GUYS

The fact that Berkowitz had ranged through three city boroughs for his crimes created special legal problems. Though the crime that finally caused his arrest and the beginning of his prosecution was committed in Brooklyn, he was wanted just as fervently in Queens and the Bronx, which had their own lists of victims and jurisdictional rights to him. The law might have sanctioned three separate trials in three boroughs, but in practice it was an impossible idea. The courts and district attorneys of Queens, Brooklyn and the Bronx would have to devise some tripartite formula for trial. Son of Sam would require a special arrangement. From the beginning, he made a mess of the usual procedures.

Months after his capture, the case was still in the headlines, the crowds still gathering in front of G Building at Kings County, magnetized by the thought of him somewhere inside. The case had always been a media circus; reporters and photographers falling all over each other to get close to a just-arrested grinning killer, reporters arrested for breaking into his apartment and lifting items that belonged to him. He complained that paintings given to him by his father had vanished, and missing too was a scrapbook in which he had listed natural disasters around the world for which he felt personally responsible. (That could have been important to the defense case.) Enough souvenir objects had vanished to prove sticky fingers on many hands. A Corrections officer at Kings County got in trouble for trying to sell a bogus interview he'd persuaded the prisoner to sign. Illegal pictures of the monster sleeping in his cell reached the papers. His relatives needed real protection from the press and television; even friends and former coworkers were hounded for anything they could contribute.

"Berkowitz fever" was running high. But the jurisdictional problems of his case had not been solved.

I knew that the Brooklyn DA had announced a date for the competency hearing that would initiate his borough's prosecution for the killing of Stacy Moskowitz and the blinding of Robert Violante. I happened to be in the Bronx DA's office on other matters when I heard that the three DAs were meeting to decide to agree that the conclusion of the first Brooklyn competency hearing would be binding in Queens and the Bronx. A hasty bias to find him competent could lead to a mistake. I told my friend, the Bronx chief assistant DA, that the wrong decision in this direction would later embarrass the Bronx office if, as I suspected, the defendant was currently not competent for trial. Although I knew that one competency hearing for all boroughs was almost a practical necessity, I still decided to call District Attorney Mario Merola and tell him my concern.

When Schwartz and Weidenbacher of Kings County submitted their report on Berkowitz and found him incompetent for trial, that concern seemed academic. At this point there was still no defense psychiatrist on the case, and with such a finding, one wasn't urgently needed. But then the Brooklyn DA's expert disagreed. Dr. Abrahamsen said that Berkowitz was competent and fit to proceed for trial in spite of "some paranoid traits." Confronting the judge at the October competency hearing was a sharp division of expert opinion.

As Dr. Abrahamsen was leaving the stand after his testimony, Brooklyn Supreme Court Judge John Starkey, presiding, asked him two questions. One concerned the premise that the defendant might have been rejected by a woman. Was that possible? The doctor answered that it was. And was it then possible that the young man's sexual frustrations could have led him to retaliate by killing other women in revenge for his humiliation by one? Answer: also possible. Judge Starkey then made his finding, overturning Schwartz and Weidenbacher's opinion, supporting Abrahamsen and the Brooklyn DA's point of view. David Berkowitz was now officially competent for trial.

Shortly thereafter, Judge Starkey stepped down from the case. He did so after it was alleged that he had allowed a journalist to look at the then-sealed transcripts of the Schwartz-Weidenbacher psychiatric interviews. The competency matter was then assigned to State Supreme Court Judge Joseph J. Corso. Everything would have to be done over!

This time, the new judge could still choose to accept the Kings County doctors' recommendations, find him legally incompetent, and commit him to a hospital. On his return, a year or two later, an NGRI could be available to him. Competent now or competent later, the interposed insanity defense would still have to be resolved by a jury at trial.

As months went by, there seemed little movement on the case. The competency hearing would be repeated in Brooklyn, so it was unlikely that the Queens or Bronx DA's offices would need an expert. I hadn't thought of working for the defense.

On a cold December afternoon, I was tinkering with my old car in the garage where it was immobilized when the mechanic told me that one of his other customers knew who I was and wanted to reach me. The man was Ira Jultak, Berkowitz's lawyer.

Several defense lawyers had come and gone. First there were Philip Peltz and an associate, Ira Leitel. I knew Peltz fairly well and just two months before I'd done an evaluation for Leitel of a would-be Kojak, an incompetent bank robber who shaved his head, sucked lollypops and owed his persona to television. But Peltz and Leitel were out of the picture, and Mark Heller, an attorney hired later by a Berkowitz relative, was also not permanent. Now the latest defense team, the ones who would go the distance, were Leon Stern and Ira Jultak.

Since Dowd's visit, I'd wanted a closer look at "Sam," but the prospect of working on the defense side was not so comfortable. I could do it for professionalism, or because it was exciting to be part of a hot story—but my real reason for accepting was curiosity.

When I got together with Jultak, I gave him my precondition for doing the evaluation. If I found Berkowitz to be competent and further thought him responsible under the law, then I'd obviously be of no value to the defense. The attorney was to understand that I might use any information I had acquired if a district attorney decided to call for my services at a later date.

He didn't hesitate in agreeing. Then, to introduce me to the materials he had given me to review, he told me what had happened in the previous months, summarizing his contacts with DAs, judges, psychiatrists, Berkowitz's family and Son of Sam himself.

The killer who emerged was much as the newspapers had described him; the eccentric loner who got out of the Army and

160

went on a murderous binge. He heard voices that told him to kill speaking through demon dogs. He also had typical ideas of reference, so that nothing in his world occurred by chance. A particular victim would be waiting as he passed by, and at the same time he'd hear the voice ordering him to kill. He was operating in a preordered context; even the convenient parking place for his car while he stalked the victim was demonically arranged.

Very crazy—but at the same time, the complicated vicious acts and evasive behavior had taken place over such a long period of time. How much willfulness was mixed up with his madness? My questions would have to reach beyond the howling demons and command hallucinations in order to determine how he came to his bizarre plan. But first, a mountain of material; hundreds of pages of transcripts and reports that would later be admitted as evidence and released to the press. From these sources alone, there was extensive history as well as many clues to the behavior of Son of Sam. I read for hours.

He was adopted at birth and David was originally his middle name. He always referred to Nat and Pearl Berkowitz as his "real" parents, remembering nothing but affection in the house. He was sure he was like any other kid—even though he often thought of killing himself. Most kids, threatening that, would have a grievance to point to, but this fellow insisted on a resolutely normal, happy childhood. Then again, he would say that he had no pleasant memories and saw monsters constantly. His father confirmed the nightmares, finally prohibiting the watching of horror shows on late night television. Maybe it was too late. The boy's monsters were very real to him. He was later to say that they were visitations from his demons, trying to get in touch. "I think the demons wanted me since I was a child."

By his own descriptions, Berkowitz loved thinking about death. He said he enjoyed poems about dying. After his mother died—he was fourteen at the time—the adolescent boy would visit the cemetery frequently, lingering at her grave for a few moments of "conversation" and convinced that she heard him. But then he roamed the cemetery for hours, looking at the headstones of the young dead, particularly drawn to the graves of children and teenagers, and above all, young girls. He would sit musing beside their graves, wondering if they'd had a chance to enjoy themselves in those short spans of existence. Pretty girls had the chance, he decided, because of all the admiration and attention that came to them. Ugly girls missed out. Life was unfair to his mother; she too had died young.

The doctors questioning him remarked that he'd caused quite a few early deaths himself. David agreed. "I thought it was unfair that she died so young and yet I killed young people. Strange. I can't explain it."

Even while his mother was alive to keep watch on him, he was a problem in school. "A truant," he said. "A clown." Obviously, school didn't interest him and although he claimed a straight A average for one year, school records show that B minus was his most consistent level. On at least one occasion, behavioral problems and disturbances in class sent him to the principal's office.

It's not certain how much his parents knew about these troubles. His father, who worked long hours in the family hardware-variety store, would have little chance to compare his only child to others and find him different. People who knew the teenager remembered a quiet, polite boy who would help out in the store. He studied Hebrew and went to temple with his father until the confirmation age of thirteen, but it was pro forma, and religion, at that point in his life, never "took."

The good boy set fires. Much has been made of the fact that he set fires at the time of his killing spree and recorded 2,000 arsons in logbooks, but arson, like the death obsession, was a sign of illness with him since childhood. He set fires in street trash and there were later attempts to burn buildings in which people still lived. In Yonkers, in 1976, he threw homemade firebombs at two houses and told the police that he hoped the people who lived there would be destroyed. He'd tried to burn them alive but of course they only *seemed* to be people. Actually, they were demons, protected by demon guards, and he could enjoy the idea of demons roasting to a crisp. He failed, because "the guards beat out the flames" and laughed at his foolishness.

When he lost his mother, at the age of fourteen, he only knew that she was "away" for months and did not visit her in the hospital until shortly before she died. Understandably, he was confused. As a result, his confusion about her death fitted into his delusion and fortified it. The demons had murdered her, he said, and done it in order to break him down. The taboo against talking about death and illness was probably why David did not know that his mother had had a mastectomy for breast cancer several years before he was born.

Their Soundview section of the Bronx began to deteriorate. It had been heavily European, the kind of place where Italian and Jewish families brought folding chairs down on the street to share gossip and good weather. Now apartment doors were locked. Family by family the old neighbors moved away as blacks and Hispanics moved in. The boy was isolated on his own block. He said he couldn't reach the kids who lived beyond it; the blocks served as natural boundaries to insiders and outsiders alike. He'd come home after school to an empty apartment; mother dead, father, as always, working. Even when he was truant from school, he'd hang around the apartment. There was nothing else to do, until he managed to get in with a gang of his new Puerto Rican neighbors. For a fat Jewish kid, it was an accomplishment.

Now he was part of another world, fighting invading gangs from other blocks—just like *West Side Story*—drinking cheap whisky on the rooftops, moving to the bongos but never shooting up with heroin when some of the others did. Not for him, he said. When they did drugs, he drank beer. He was saving himself.

The neighborhood got even rougher. It may have been the burglary of their apartment that brought David's father to a decision to leave. They'd had an application in at the new development called Co-op City, and in 1969 they moved to a comfortable apartment there.

Co-op City was the refuge of Bronx families who had fled disintegrating neighborhoods and should have been an environment in which a David Berkowitz could feel accepted and valued. He reentered a middle-class world, met other teenagers and dated a few girls.

"We were all clumsy together," he said. "We didn't know how to do much except kiss."

He also joined a mountain climbing club and took up weight lifting. He joined the auxiliary police and rescue fire squads around the giant apartment complex. People there told the press that young Berkowitz took his fire fighting very seriously, worried about saving old ladies, and was impressed with uniforms. But none of the new clubs and enthusiasms seemed to last, and his history does not reveal close friendships with girls or boys.

In 1971, there was a major change in David's life. His father married a widow with grown children. Discussing his new step-mother, he made the right polite noises: "Dad was happy and that was all that mattered." Once complimented on that generous point of view, he did a quick turnabout. Yes, he did resent her new stricter rules that cramped the freedom he'd enjoyed. Nothing was the same after she came.

At his father's insistence, David finished high school. As soon as he graduated, he enlisted in the Army. He gave patriotic reasons, but he was also uninterested in going to college and felt he might "learn something" as the recruiting poster promised. Also, he wanted to get away from home.

He tried for combat duty, but the Vietnam War was winding down and the next toughest assignment he could get was the infantry in Korea. He enlisted for three years. After sixteen weeks of basic training, he went overseas.

Korea, in his own words, was a mad, absolutely unreal place where everybody went crazy. But he never described any of his own actions as crazy. Instead, he'd say that his behavior was "strange," or he'd say, "I don't know why I did that."

(As a convict, he would use the same words when he later recanted his story of demons in jail. The reporters asked him why, if there were no demons, no talking dogs, no satanic hench-men, he committed the murders? What was the reason? He answered that he didn't know why; he didn't know what made him start to kill or what made him stop.)

Berkowitz's overseas hitch from December 1971 to January of 1973 was two years of waiting for something to happen. He looked at North Koreans from a distance, along the boundary fence, by the bridge over the Inchon River. While waiting, he picked up the habits of soldiers everywhere.

He drank, visited prostitutes, perhaps was accepted in Korea as never before, a man in a man's world. He bitched about the wholesale corruption of the Army lifers, who he said sold stolen service equipment and food to Koreans at inflated prices. And he joined the drug scene, using uppers, downers, "maybe a dozen trips" on acid, but still no heroin. He said he was careful because he never liked to be out of control.

As an ironic footnote to his Army career, David Berkowitz— from the maximum security prison at Attica—applied for a veteran's disability pension. His claim provoked an avalanche of indignation in Congress and the press. It's hard to assess what he meant by "damage" sustained in Korea, but the significant point was that an obvious personality change appeared there. It may have been triggered by drug abuse, the work of LSD or mescaline on his central nervous system, but it surfaced in letters he wrote to his father and to a girl friend. The much-quoted letter of August 1972 still remains ominous:

> They taught me how to fight, [he wrote], They taught me about weapons, demolition, control, self defense—all of these courses will come in handy some day. I plan to use them and it's not going to be the way the lifers want me to use them. I will use these tactics to destroy them the way they destroyed millions of people through the war they started. One day there will be a better world.

Yet his Army service record suggests he was regarded as a good soldier, one with potential for a permanent Army career.

After his service in Korea, Berkowitz was sent to Fort Knox to complete his tour as an administrative clerk. He told others that he missed Korean amenities, the cheap liquor and clean prostitutes. (There is some question of credibility about his tale of sexual experience there.) In Kentucky, liquor was easy but sex—he later said—was out of reach at the prices charged in Louisville. He also rationalized abstinence by making the Louisville girls "dirty" or "not pretty," but there were no more sexual contacts after 1973.

He was lonely, depressed, out of sync with other people. He "knew" they hated him. Some force was making it happen. He said he stopped taking drugs in the States and fell back on alcohol. But he found a better antidote for emptiness when a barracks buddy took him to a fundamentalist Baptist church. Everyone was accepted, and the young soldier walked down the aisle to receive Jesus with grateful tears in his eyes.

From then on, he buttonholed anyone who would listen to his lectures about the new compact he'd made with Jesus. And the convert felt a beautiful kindness surrounding him while he was a member of that proselytizing group: men and women singing, swaying, holding hands—a family.

But, as he often said, he couldn't stay with anything very long. His religious interest waned. After some weeks, complaining that he'd lost the faith (and the transportation to get to church), he went back to drinking. Faith kindled again when he got out of the service in June 1974, and there was a brief attempt to carry the gospel message to unenthusiastic family and friends in Co-op City. Was he naïve enough to expect that Nat Berkowitz would understand why his son had become a born-again Baptist?

Without encouragement, he again discarded his interest in religion. It was like his on-again, off-again commitment to Jesus in the last, pretrial months of his stay at Kings County. (The Christian answer was finally dropped when he began to hear the demon voices breaking through his prayers.)

Shortly after he came home from the service, his father and stepmother moved to Florida. A holdup in the family store was convincing proof that the move was necessary, but David's father had kept his son's frightening letters from Korea and was worried about his ability to cope with New York life on his own.

Alone, Berkowitz floundered. He had no social or occupational connections. In 1974, he took a test for postal service employment, but heard nothing further about it at that time. In a vague attempt to better himself, he enrolled for courses at Bronx Community College, but seemed to resent pressure put on him to make some definite choice of career. He was a shadow student, never participating in class, absent more often than not. Bored? Perhaps. But he gave another explanation. Noises "just started" in his head and the racket kept him from studying. He dropped out.

No friends, no direction. Instead of dating, he had porno pictures. He drifted in and out of minimal jobs that paid the rent. He was a cab driver, an apprentice in construction, a security guard and finally a night clerk in the post office. While still attempting his college classes, he worked nights at the job that most effectively isolated him from human contact. As a guard for IBI Security, he was permanently assigned to a big truck yard as a roving handler for two trained guard dogs.

One was a huge German shepherd, the other, a mean crossbreed he thought looked like a wolf. From eight at night until six the next morning, the dogs were all he saw. He called this a terrible, lonely job but it was undemanding and required only that he stay awake.

At this time, the noises in his head, growing steadily louder, were disturbing his sleep. He thought other people *must* hear them. He didn't know what was happening to him, especially when he "heard" dogs howling when he was nowhere near the guard dogs. Then, with the noise, came sounds like words and he thought he heard a message he could understand. Dogs who howled and gave him orders became demon dogs who would give him orders to kill.

They tortured him by keeping him awake and would only relent and allow sleep after he fulfilled the commands. He understood that it was part of a grand satanic plan in which demon armies had specific tasks. The dogs were demon soldiers who wanted him to kill young girls to supply them with blood. That was his assignment.

Desperate in his fear and loneliness, Berkowitz made another try to attach himself to something. He began to think of his biological mother. He had discovered that his name at birth was Richard David Falco, and he confronted his father with this, asking for more information about her. Sleepless, bombarded by voices, and with his father far away, he made a search to find another parent.

With the assistance of an organization called ALMA (Adoptees Liberty Movement Association), whose mission was to help adoptees find their roots, he located his mother. She led him to his older sister—half sister, actually—who was very sympathetic. For a while David saw a great deal of her and her family. He was a brand-new uncle. But his homicidal delusion had already gathered too much momentum, and he would break contact when the demons told him that he must.

In addition to his new biological family, Berkowitz acquired "courtesy" relatives through his stepmother. A warmhearted, pleasant couple—call them Harris—accepted the young man as a kind of cousin. By 1975, he was seeing them several times a month. For someone so withdrawn, it was a real achievement. He could relax, even sleep a little at their suburban home. They saw him as sensitive, crying at other people's troubles, and didn't know quite what to make of his eccentric sense of humor. It seemed to come and go. But his smile stayed fixed.

Then his father sent out a signal for help, complaining from Florida that David had written him a terrible letter full of ravings. "People spit and kick at me as I walk down the street!" (This was 1975.) The old man asked the Harris couple to see that his son went to a doctor.

How could they? David revealed nothing to them. It would have been just about impossible to confront the shy young man who was their frequent guest with the suggestion that he was "mental." So nothing was done and the family continued to see him at intervals. But they did witness one shocking incident. It was during a family dinner party when his parents were up from Florida. Suddenly he began to jeer at his father. Next he was talking about a General Cosmo or some 6,000-year-old man called Sam who inhabited his body. As they watched, he changed—bristled, shouted, glared impatiently at their failure to understand, and ran out of the room. Upstairs, his father found him moaning and hitting his head with his hands. The demon voices had attacked him in someone else's home!

He wouldn't explain what had happened and I can understand the Harrises' reluctance to pursue it. A little more insight was given them when they arranged to meet his half sister. She described her own feelings when he began a sudden, elliptical conversation with her, talking about his mysterious mission. She hadn't understood, but it sounded so strange and frightening that she cried.

They feared that he was suicidal. No one seemed to be afraid *of* David Berkowitz as much as they were afraid *for* him. They didn't feel like targets.

But they could have been. Berkowitz admitted to his questioners that he was worried about demonic revenge on his relatives. "There were always boundaries," he said, because of his "assignment," and he could not tell them what he was doing. So, before he got too close, and without explaining, he phased out the visits to his mother and sister and kept only minimal contact with the Harris family. On July 29, 1976, he'd been fishing and returned to their house. That night, after he left them, he would kill Donna Lauria. He could have gone home for his gun, but it is just as likely that he had it with him, ready for his mission, probably in the car next to the fishing rod. After the first shooting, he would always keep his gun within reach.

Donna Lauria was the first person he is known to have killed, but this was not his first attempt at murder. He was preparing for that in the winter of 1975.

The apartment he had rented at that time was on Barnes Avenue, not far from Co-op City. He had already trailed people on the street and now he was going to do what the voices demanded and kill someone with a knife.

Could he have studied how it was done? He said he had a sudden taste for books about murder, but as usual, he didn't know why. He only knew that he had to kill someone and was carrying a knife around with him.

Berkowitz thinks he just happened to be driving on Co-op City Boulevard on a cold December night when he saw a young woman crossing the street. He heard a sudden voice: "Her! She must die!" A parking place was handy. He hurried out of the car and walked up behind her. Before she could sense his presence in the winter dark, he began to stab her, or stab at her, through her heavy coat.

It didn't go the way he had seen it in the movies—one thrust with the knife and the victim drops. The woman jumped and struggled, rolled away from him on the ground, screaming. Astonished, he thought she was getting stronger, as if he were pumping life into her with the knife! Her screams numbed his ears and he ran off in fright. By the time he made it back to the car, a few people were alerted, looking for the source of the screams. But he was safe.

As he would after every hunt, Berkowitz watched the papers to see how he had done. But the woman, for whatever reason, did not report the stabbing. He was discouraged because his knife had hardly a drop of blood on it.

There's a mystery about that night. Berkowitz, at one point, indicated that he had stabbed *two* women. But whether he'd tried his luck with one or with two, he failed on the job. No sacrifices for the demons. No one known to be dead.

He avoided Co-op City after that. In fact, he moved all the way to New Rochelle in February 1976, resenting the extra expense, because rent had been far more reasonable in the Bronx. Yet he'd had to leave. In his evolving delusion, he'd come to think of himself as the victim of persecution by a variety of evildoers, later identified as members of the demon army.

Berkowitz had cannibalized his entire background for useful material to construct his delusion. In particular, he stole concretely from his Army service. His murders were done at the orders of a paramilitary organization, led by a General Cosmo, with all the staff officers jockeying to move up in grade. The local GHQ of the demonic host was guarded by demon dogs "circling the perimeter." When hunting for victims, Son of Sam liked to say that he would "make a sweep" through the territory. He was still a soldier.

His hallucinations and delusions pursued him and a pattern of flight from them was set. Each new apartment he rented fell under the control of a new master demon who was responsible for turning the screws tighter, causing more howling, roaring, orders to kill, less sleep. He was said to have used his stereo to blot out the demons' noise with another kind of sound. Imagine him, trailing extension cords as he moved around the rooms, his headset clamped tight to his ears!

A nice quiet landlord in New Rochelle was transformed by his delusion into Cosmo, the demon general of the region. Demons of rank were everywhere he looked, howling "Blood!" He fled Cosmo by moving to Yonkers (in May 1976). It was an equally bad move, for the demonic plan placed him next door to a man named Sam Carr. He made this neighbor the Papa Sam of his letter. There was no escape because he had no money to move again. He thought the yards behind the nearest houses were full of hungry demon dogs. To relieve the pressure of their constant howling, he bought a rifle and shot two of them. One was Carr's own black Labrador. The voices weren't satisfied; they said he must kill people for them, or hundreds of other humans would die in earthquakes, plane crashes and catastrophes around the world. He had failed with a knife. Now he'd have to get a special gun to do the job.

In mid-1976, Berkowitz decided to visit an Army buddy in Texas, where it was legal to buy a gun. He first visited his father in Florida, but told him nothing. In Texas, he bought a .44 caliber pistol and two hundred rounds of ammunition. There was no particular reason for buying the heavy .44. He said it was all they had in the store and that his friend bought it for him.

It's of interest that he felt better when he was visiting in Texas. Once he got out of New York, he wasn't bothered so much by the voices. He told one psychiatrist who examined him that they had "disappeared." But he seemed surprised by their suggestions that he should have stayed where he felt better. No, he had to return to New York. The mission was there.

On July 29, 1976, the day he went fishing, Berkowitz used the evening to cruise one of the nice neighborhoods he favored, where he thought people were better looking and cleaner. A phrase he used has echoes of cultism: "People clean, washed and ready to be killed." Nothing but the best for his demons.

As he drove past two young women seated in a car, he heard the staccato hallucinations that triggered all his homicides: "There. That was it. Do it!"

He pulled over and went after the one girl he knew that the demons had chosen, walking to the car, firing through the windshield while the splintered glass poured down on her, his senses frozen in the moment when he pumped out all the bullets in his gun. In later attacks, when he'd gained more confidence, he became more sparing with his ammunition. By then he was using the combat stance, the crouch and the two-handed grip. (Witnesses said that John Lennon and President Reagan were shot this way.)

The papers told him how well he'd done, as they would each time he succeeded on a mission for the demons. But he was able to judge his success before the early editions came out by how peaceful he felt, how much the demons let him sleep. If he'd managed to kill a healthy young female for the demons (and later kill males for the demon wives), they'd all be so satiated with blood and sex that they'd let him sleep for a long time.

How did the demons have sex with his victims? Berkowitz evaded such questions. In the interview record, he sounded prudish, with much talk about good girls having respect for themselves, and utter denials that the killings had been done for his own sexual motives. Maybe they made him do it, but he loved his work, or the hunting aspect of it, and could speak about a sharpening of his senses at the moment of the kill. "My eyes would sharpen—very clear like pinpoints—I could almost see the bullet." Afterward, there was the reliving of the moment, the strange but good recall of his sensations during the act. That recall would ease his tension and the demonic howling, until next time.

But what happened to the victims afterward? Berkowitz thought their families might not want to know. Grudgingly, he revealed that the demons snatched the souls, took them to the attic of one of the demon houses in Yonkers, chained them up and had sex forever, endlessly raping and molesting them. The souls, which "look something like the body," he said, could have no peace, no sleep.

From the beginning of his case, David Berkowitz was conscious of his press. Later he actually prompted reporters about his attacks. It took a few killings before the media began to identify him with proper respect as the so-called .44 caliber killer. Then, through the Borelli letter in April of 1977, he gave them another tag for himself. He was Son of Sam. His June letter to Jimmy Breslin was meant as a rebuke to the news media because his chroniclers hadn't included his first success in the "Sam" group of victims he had been building. Donna was his bride-to-be, promised but not yet delivered by Father Sam. So he wanted to set Breslin and all the readers straight on the importance of the night when Donna "got hers."

He was just coming into murderous stride when he wrote the Borelli letter. He had killed five times before he started to play "Catch me" and drop the garbled hints which he insisted were perfectly clear instructions on how to do it. He couldn't resist playing games with the police. Later excuses that he couldn't give himself up because the publicity would embarrass his father were pure pseudologic. Obviously, he wanted to look like a good guy who was trying, at least, to break the demon hold on him. He couldn't help but represent himself as the battleground between good and evil forces. If he failed to kill selected victims—as in June 1977, when he shot at a couple and only wounded them— then he could conveniently rationalize his failures into victories for the battling powers of good. "An angel must have deflected the bullet," he said, sounding exasperated as well as awed. Good triumphed whenever he failed. He had it both ways. As he contrived it, he couldn't lose.

By the late spring of 1977, he was working nights at the post office and the tormenting hallucinations kept him from sleep.

173

GOOD GUYS, BAD GUYS

The demons were closing in and his delusion was taking unpredictable turns.

A young man moved into the apartment below him. This neighbor could not be a human being, he thought, because thunderous noises and messages came through the walls to harass him. He plotted revenge. How often people seek revenge on their neighbors for "voices" coming through the walls, the TV, or even in on their bridgework!

Berkowitz felt under surveillance, so the man must be another demon put on him by the higher-ups. He gave him a special name. (The assignment of colorful and fantastic names was a remarkable feature of his delusional constructs.) Thus, Craig Glassman became Gregunta Glassinto, a demonic spy. At one point, Berkowitz was so annoyed by the sounds "Gregunta" was sending through the walls and floor to deafen him that he made a Molotov cocktail out of a wine bottle and threw it against his neighbor's door.

The roaring and shaking, the tricks and noises his persecutors favored seemed to be straight out of *The Exorcist*, and of course he admitted seeing the movie.

Not content with firebombing Glassman, Berkowitz tried to bomb the nearby houses of the innocent Carr and Neto families. He identified them respectively as Father Sam's headquarters and of all things, a demons' rest hotel. But he was not successful in any of his firebombings and he said that the demons had laughed at his powerlessness.

In July of 1977, Son of Sam decided to threaten the city with a special anniversary killing to mark the first year of his work. The media blew that up into scare headlines but he let Anniversary Day, July 29, go by and moved again on the thirty-first.

He went to Brooklyn, scouting along the perimeter highway that circles much of that borough, and encountered a couple sitting in a car. Since his killing of April 1977, he'd understood that he had a mandate to kill couples. The demons were especially vindictive about couples.

But this time, they hadn't arranged a parking space for him. Son of Sam parked next to a hydrant, got out when he saw a

174

police car approaching, and went to a nearby playground. From there he could see the traffic police putting a ticket on his windshield. He made a mental note to pay it. He had already paid five parking tickets.

No contradiction there, according to Berkowitz. He'd been raised by parents who paid their bills and so did he. He mentioned that he hadn't paid one bill, but explained that he had withheld the money because he didn't like the way that company did business.

He insisted that he was law-abiding.

His convenient psychotic system let him make such statements. The law to him was the higher law of the demonic army, the law that superseded New York state law and "even the Supreme Court." In this particular instance, demonic law hadn't said anything about parking tickets and he was therefore supposed to pay them.

The parking ticket led to his capture and the prosecution for his attack on Stacy Moskowitz and Robert Violante. He had fired four bullets into the car, thought he killed them both, and didn't stay to discover that Robert was blinded, not dead. As usual after a killing, he went home and slept.

By now he felt that his assignments were a lot of work; he was really tired of murdering one or two people at a time. Suddenly there was a lot of "upheaval" going on in the demon army and his masters conveniently produced a new directive. There would be one last big job, an assignment to kill as many people as he could at one time, and he virtuously noted that he expected to be killed in such a wholesale operation and "end his miserable life." On the other hand, it was also a chance for a flashy finish, using the last of his .44 ammunition and all that he had for another automatic weapon. He'd hold out till the last bullet and go down when that was gone.

The first Saturday in August, he drove out to the Hamptons planning to "make a sweep" along the crowded main street of the resort area, killing as many people as he could. The day had been clear but in the evening it rained so hard that the main street was deserted. The forces of good had interfered, for the moment, with his Saturday night shootout. He gave them direct credit for that.

Certainly, the rain saved many lives.

On August 10, when he was caught, the killer was temporarily back to business as usual and meant to go hunting in neighboring Riverdale. He spoke of it as a dull night. But he had bigger plans for another giant shootout. The loaded machine gun in his car was ready for a mass killing in a discotheque far out on Long Island. The police closed in on him first and the terror of Son of Sam ended.

As noted, I first evaluated David Berkowitz on January 2, 1978. He was pleasant and courteous to me but it had been six months since he was arrested and he'd understandably developed a resistance to psychiatrists' interviews. Even his affiliation with the church since his imprisonment had affected his ability to answer questions. He wanted to avoid talking about the past. Now he was determined to look neither to the right nor to the left, but to follow the Scriptures and preach the gospel.

To make things more difficult, he was busily engaged in "covering over" certain facts in his history. This is a defense used by an individual who, on recovering, finds that the psychotic beliefs he once held are untenable. Berkowitz would say different things to me about the same subject at different times, and his equivocations were so frequent that answers to questions about the killings were always ambiguous. There was no way to judge his sexual motivations or capabilities. I couldn't determine if he could commit rape or whether his preoccupation with puritanical religion had prevented aggressive sex but somehow allowed him to become a multiple murderer instead! He would have forgotten his motives, or there might be a retrospective falsification of items all the way from childhood to his most recent recollections of the killings.

His inconsistency was a factor, but the information already on record spoke for this as another acting-on-a-mission series of murders by a probable paranoid schizophrenic. His delusions of persecution were typical to start with: people shunning him,

176

singling him out for their hate. He could easily have had the usual fantasies of revenge. But his sleeplessness and hallucinations worsened until a very complex delusion evolved on those fantasies, ending in the bizarre Son of Sam configuration. That wasn't typical at all.

I was struck by the peculiar evolution of sleeplessness and dogs howling. In the beginning, he'd made a deal with the dogs on his night job as a security guard. They were to keep watch while he slept. But then he began to distrust his "team" because they'd howl capriciously when there was no threat. The howling followed him home, where he "heard" it off duty, while trying to sleep. He might awake, sweating and disoriented, ready to resist a burglary. Inevitably, in an evolution typical of the onset of psychosis, the howling noises were joined by hallucinations of voices. They became command hallucinations, ordering him to kill.

In the grand delusion that followed, he first made dogs into demons and then evolved an elaborate delusional system. Its scope set this case apart, as did the nature of his crimes.

He had probably been a borderline psychotic for years, preoccupied with monsters and arson, but what had triggered the year and a half of homicidal violence? I was to discover that he'd done outrageous, aggressive things in earlier years, and that his later psychosis paralleled these earlier times in motives and patterns of behavior.

Berkowitz's total pattern was a search or a series of searches that became a life mission to find his identity. He swung to wild extremes of acquiescent or aggressive behavior: a student, then a truant, someone who set fires, and for a while, a fire fighter. He was a patriot when he joined the Army but went from patriot to radical, from gung ho *for* the service to a man out to get it. When he left Korea for Kentucky, he would swing back in the other direction, radical into Christian convert, no longer against a system but wanting very much to be a part of the democratic religious ideal, equality before God. The man was incredibly ambivalent about good and evil, and it was obvious in a name the demons had chosen for him. "They called me Demischmutz," he said. Berkowitz denied that he knew that "demi" meant "half" but admitted that "schmutz" meant "dirt" in both German and Yiddish. So, "half dirty"? If it wasn't a coincidence, it was just right, a perfect extrusion from the unconscious where everything in this man's life had been condensed into a revealing, delusional behavior pattern. His demons had him figured out.

His religious interest didn't last, and neither did a straight role, the good son looking for a job and thinking about college. His delusion took over and he was back to fire setting, on to killing—both during the same period of time. Yet, even as he killed, he made moral pronouncements: he would give himself up if only it didn't bring shame on his parents; he would help the police to catch him, if only they'd follow his clues. Though he was "just a dog" to the demons and had to obey, he was still a constant fighter who battled them. He didn't want help in this lonely battle. Only he could beat them, but he almost always lost.

Even after he was caught he switched back into a former role, the reawakened Christian in God's welcoming arms. This enabled him to tell the parents of the young people he had killed that if they would only listen to him now, he'd bring them peace and make them feel whole.

My basic purpose in interviewing Berkowitz was to determine his competency and criminal responsibility. I had to decide how much of his homicidal behavior was locked into his delusions. In his engulfing system, he seemed to pick and choose details to arm his pseudologic. And if he could do that, could he at any level have controlled himself?

These questions had to be answered, but something else kept intruding. When I wrote the letter for Inspector Dowd, I had imagined the killer to be a media creature. I found the reality to be that, and more. In childhood, television and the movies fed his obsessional fantasies, told him how cops and robbers, demons and angels were supposed to act. It wasn't hard for him to write his own scenario: demonic demands, search-and-destroy combat missions, bullets through the windshield in the old Chicago style. There were so many movie images to draw on. The movies even provided him with the structure for dealing with the press. He prompted them by the predictable notes to the police and columnist Jimmy Breslin. They'd fed him; now he in turn fed them with more killings. All he had read and watched on the screen was recombined, not only for his crimes, but for the police pursuit. He piled cliché on cliché, and then, just like in a "possession" movie, abrogated responsibility for anything he had done by blaming it on the demons. He even blamed them for his creation.

As I drove home from the first interview, the snowy streets on that holiday morning were deserted. There was time to speculate on how movie demonology could produce the cues that would help to model someone with the right paranoidal potential into a multiple murderer. If I were the demon in charge of script and casting, could I provide the right kind of film formula to turn on a "possession" murderer? The many men I'd known who had committed this kind of crime could be my sources.

The star of my epic would of course be a schizophrenic on a mission, unremarkable looking, as so many of today's heroes seem to be. To make the audience know that he was different, I'd have to rely on the good old visible stigmata of mental illness. His eyes would look "wrong." They'd be vacuous and seem unfocused or have a telltale shining quality. (Contact lenses could do it.) Then I'd want my murderer to have a constant sheepish smile, the kind of smile I'd seen in many young psychotics, teasing or smug, saying "I know something you don't know." The smiler's secret is that he is listening to his hallucinated voices while we can't. And I'd lay it on thick by adding a tentative, yet chilling giggle that appeared at inappropriate times. Richard Widmark used it in a movie when he pushed an old lady in a wheelchair down a flight of stairs. On cue, my star's appearance would make you uncomfortable.

As for childhood background, let him by all means be an orphan or an uncommunicative adopted child with problems. (What psychiatrist hasn't noticed how many of these go awry?) The only child would be a mystery to himself, out of touch with what made him happy or sad, shifting rapidly from one emotional extreme to another. Other children would not be attracted to him and he'd lead a solitary life, bothered by monsters and ghosts, spending an enormous amount of time on fantasy. He'd dream of visiting aliens from space who'd recognize him as one of their own and take him away with them. I'd probably write in a quick scene or two showing his surreptitious hobbies: maybe a little vandalism, or setting fires.

Parents can miss such signs, but bad behavior at school forces them to take notice. This character wouldn't have obvious mental signs like being withdrawn, hallucinating or showing paranoidal anger. Instead, he'd be reported by the school as a disruptive clown in class. How many patients (who have no sense of humor) tell me they were called clowns in school? I won't forget a six-year-old from my training days at Bellevue. He would rub slices of white bread onto the filthy floor, offer me a slice and, after I'd said "No," let me see his threat to eat it; then he would do it. He would "playfully" take a woman visitor's glove, fill it with water from the fountain and present the bulging thing back to her. This outrageous stuff, getting "bad attention" at the risk of any punishment, was hard to control because people laughed and gratified him. (This cute little boy, who couldn't stop being bad, was diagnosed as a pseudopsychopathic schizophrenic.)

Back to my story. A teacher would detect danger signals in his classroom behavior and suggest a visit to the child psychologist. The mother would dutifully put him into treatment and the friendly, grandmotherly psychologist (that's how I've cast her) would have a scene in which she'd explain her findings to the worried parents. She'd tell them that she has made a diagnosis. Their son thinks in a special autistic way which explains why he lives within himself and can't seem to see himself as part of the great world around him. It also explains why he skips thought associations and goes off the point in answering their questions.

Mother wants to know if this has anything to do with the way he can't make up his mind.

"We call that ambivalence," the psychologist says. "He can like, dislike, trust, distrust a person all in a short space of time. But nothing has changed about that person except *his* perception in his own mind."

180

Father doesn't follow this. "Just what's wrong with him, Doctor?"

The kindly psychologist now provides the nugget of information that Hollywood likes to tuck into such stories for credibility. She's comforting, but talks of Dr. Bleuler's required indicators of schizophrenia.

"Everything we've mentioned is typical, and there's something else we call an affectual disturbance. It's why your boy smiles so much, even when he's hurt."

"Who knows where he got that?" the father mutters. It's a reminder to Mother that it was her idea to adopt a child. The smile can probably be blamed on the biological parents.

The psychologist would not be able to do much with her patient. Maybe his mother and father are disappointed by the slow progress (parents have been routinely conditioned to expect too much). Dad decides he'll grow out of it and discontinues the costly treatment.

Our boy goes into a turbulent adolescence, still getting as much emotional charge from "bad attention," doing the wrong thing, as he does from doing what's expected of him.

Telescope the plot line. His mother dies of mysterious illness and he adds this loss to the other anxieties beneath his bland exterior. His father is rarely home and he's left alone in the crumbling, crime-ridden neighborhood, menaced by tough kids. He knows he must get in with a gang to survive. But how to prove himself with them? Some kids impress by walking on the edges of roofs or jumping between buildings. Our character's too chicken—and too shrewd— for that. But he's taken into the gang without half trying when they catch him at one of his hobbies and realize that he's the biggest torch in the neighborhood! They call him Pyro, short for pyromaniac. They follow him around to see what he'll burn next.

A change of scene: Pyro moves to a better neighborhood. The audience, who knows that the story has a bloody ending, is confused by the suggestion of a hopeful future for him as he is seen doing normal teenage things and is the good boy his father imagines him to be. But the scene where's he's acting as a volunteer fireman is followed by a flashback of him setting the fire! Shock and outrage as they see him in a crowd as the firemen arrive. The message is that arsonists are often voyeurs of their own work; it's true and something to think about. Look for the man with the smile at the scene of the fire.

My creation is constantly trying to decide who he is. Does he feel better when he's bad, or when he does good things? The reward for being good is often to be taken for granted. Bad behavior puts you in the spotlight, but it's dangerous—and jail definitely scares our murderer-to-be. He dreams of aggression, even heroism, but he's passive, and in everyday life he can't even manage to stand up to people. They think he's polite. But he avoids arguments because he can't win them, and each time he acquiesces to someone else, he takes an emotional pummeling because he must pretend he isn't angry. The audience sees that he is *very* angry and knows the dammed-up emotion will break out later.

He'd like to imitate the patriotic heroes in the war-and-glory pictures he's addicted to, so he makes a sudden decision to join the Army.

Fade in: soldier days overseas. Too late, he sees that it's all a mistake because Army life is nothing like the movies. It's awful. Maybe we could have him crack a little, send letters home implying that he's God on earth, or become such a hell-raising, pill-popping radical that he does time in the stockade.

Back in the States, finishing his enlistment, he finds drugs less available and shifts to liquor. But he feels empty. Enter religion to fill the void.

A lot of people suddenly come on religion when they are at odds with society. (And too many, after arrest and imprisonment, write books about how they found God in the cell block.) Religion is an acceptable reentry for anyone who needs a fresh start. When our ambivalent character reverts from drinking and fornicating, he takes it too far. In one wild swing, he becomes not only a convert but a preacher. I'd have him be guided by a good voice he hears in the wind to smash up his collection of liquor bottles.

His friends stand around in awe and anguish as the bourbon dribbles away. Now he'll preach to anyone who'll listen.

Does this revelation last? Not at all. It dies for lack of attention once he's a civilian again. But he has nothing to replace it, no idea of what to do with his life. He can't seem to make decisions. He's alone, and feels abandoned. Some of that inner anger begins to surface.

Because he knows he needs someone's help, he begins a search to find his long-lost natural mother. This is a movie must, a standard procedure for lonely, adopted children. And he manages to find her. In a tearful scene, he starts on the role of long-lost son. But he can't enjoy the new family life. He has too many secrets, and the biggest one is that he's now enmeshed in a mission of grand design that will remove him from the company of humans. So he leaves his relatives.

Working nights in a dead-end job, there's too much time to brood on his life. He's an insomniac, but manages to relax in the dark of movie theaters; he is one of the millions whose sense of reality is so vague that they're apt to take their behavioral cues from the screen. Movie fare is large helpings of dread and horror, *Omens* and *Exorcists*. Plots are repetitive: innocent individuals come under demonic control and are made to do brutal things. Even if they kill, they can't be blamed for it because demons have isolated them and totally directed them, preordering every detail of their lives. Our man, sitting through *The Exorcist* again and again, is getting a steady message. He realizes subconsciously that if he were under such control, it would explain why he can't get his life together, and even why he hears noises in his head. If he were the demons' creature, he could be far more outrageous than the little girl in the film. Let Satan give him the word, and he'd be glad to sell his soul!

Close-up: he's reading for the role, studying the stories of other famous murderers. He reads about Jack the Ripper. I'd have him note a character in that story called Diemschutz (Demischmutz?), who found the body of one of Jack's victims. Jack the Ripper, never caught—something to aim for! There's wonderment as he reads, then resolve, and it's clear that he's formulating his own script. Being under demonic control has freed his creative powers. In partnership with the voices in his head, he becomes author, producer, director and star of a wild, delusional scenario of death.

The camera tracks him as he kills and kills. In close-up after close-up, the gun explodes in our faces.

On this rampage, the good/evil character finds a way to be moral and outrageous at the same time, deploring killing as he kills and announcing that he's doing good. (Movie schizophrenics on a mission must always do good, whether it's bombings or assassination or multiple murders.) The logic of this needs decoding; in his case, he's saving the majority of us from the demons' greater revenge by offering up a few human sacrifices. We're supposed to be grateful that he's trying his best.

Someone must now be made to acknowledge the power our man holds over life and death. He contacts the media, baits the police, all the usual stuff. I could never leave a killer's note out of such a story. He protests a little, like the movie killer who scrawled "Stop me before I kill again" with his victim's lipstick. There has to be a scene—it's obligatory—in which police and psychiatrists huddle over possible clues, plotting strategies to bring him in. But he has all sorts of reasons why he can't give himself up.

So he goes on. But he will slip, a small slip, and it leads to capture. It comes when he's feeling cocky because nothing can happen to him. The world has finally adapted to his Hollywood requirements of how it should act. He's satisfied that it revolves around him.

What a relief when he is taken off the streets! The audience is treated to close-ups of his capture, long panning shots of the threatening crowds around the courthouse, and then the argument about what to do with him begins. He decides to take charge of his own case. In his cell, he makes the one move possible to neutralize the feelings of anger and vengeance against him by announcing that he's back with God, redeemed, and seemingly able to blot out the past with his Bible. All he needs to forget past errors and face the future is faith. We're lectured on faith: I'd even throw in a scene in which he opens his Bible and asks us to pray with him!

A typically ambivalent swing has brought him to the side of the angels, but it's not quite enough and he promotes himself. Now he's a Christ-like figure capable of dispensing love and peace. Why not to the families of his victims? He knows that they need it. He wants them to listen to him and they probably will for the simple reason that they can't believe what they are hearing.

How bizarre can a plot get?

This is as far as I would take my story, ending on the note of ironic frustration which is favored nowadays because it implies realism. With all the clichés I've tried to toss into my story line, it's clear that my prototype creation couldn't top the real-life saga of Son of Sam. The team of Hollywood, Berkowitz and demons had created a screenplay that needed nothing more to "explain" another mass murderer. As it stands, it's an ultimate.

The fun was over. I'd just have to get back to reality and my job, judging Berkowitz's competence for trial.

His primary goal now was to get into jail and preach the gospel. He was consistent in that, in all his interviews, and resisted my attempts to uncover his pathology. He did his best not to look mentally ill. Where a line of questioning pressured him and intimated that he might be abnormal, he answered with pat generalities.

But it was important that he cooperate. We should know if specific command hallucinations preceded the crime that was currently being prosecuted in Brooklyn, the death of Stacy Moskowitz. He had committed six murders and there might be subsequent trials. If there was to be a successful insanity defense based on his delusions and hallucinations at this juncture, it could set a precedent for the later trials.

Berkowitz was preoccupied with the idea that going to jail would be a reward (comparatively) while a mental hospital would be punishment. If he went to prison, people would see that he wasn't trying to get out of the charges against him with the Sam story. It would legitimize Sam. But if he went to the hospital, it would mean that he was crazy, and who would believe a crazy man talking about demons? He was so set on going to jail that he threatened to stand up in the courtroom and call his lawyers liars if they pursued an insanity defense!

I think his aim had been to go to prison from the time of his arrest, but it was actively reinforced by Mrs. Ollie Smith, the gospel preacher who visited other wards at Kings County and who was eventually allowed to see him. As his spiritual adviser, she allegedly told him that he had a mission to preach in jail. She had a vision of it. He also said she told him that it was immoral for a Christian to avoid punishment. He could willingly be moral for Christ, reject the NGRI (which was his way out) and be believed about the demons because he had done so. But Berkowitz's judgment was so poor that he could not appreciate that it was illogical to imagine being able to preach the gospel in prison, that in fact it was dangerous. He ignored the likelihood that he would get hurt.

There were other reasons for preferring jail besides carrying out her prophecy and being believed about the demons. Berkowitz saw himself in many roles. One of them, not the preacher or the demon fighter, but the fan of other murderers, required that a big-time criminal go to prison, not the hospital. He admired the Boston Strangler (the book about him kept strange company with Billy Graham's story on a shelf in his apartment), and Berkowitz liked to point out that the Strangler was sent to jail. He was wrong on several details of his hero worship: the Strangler first spent time in a mental hospital before he went to Walpole Prison, and second, he was murdered in prison, possibly for less reason than confronting convicts with sermons.

On those occasions when Berkowitz was not concealing, it was clear how delusional he still was. Many months after his arrest, he was adding finishing touches, incorporating just-received revelations into the body of his delusion. At each interview, he might have an "I never realized till now" kind of insight and put more pieces into place in his construction. He was so suggestible, so transparent that you could watch him seize on a possible explanation for his crimes and make it operate retroactively.

There were good days and bad days. At Kings County, he'd slammed his hands against the bars and screamed when the demons were getting at him. He had torn up his room—and then helped to straighten the furniture. Mad but dissimulating, he disguised his incompetence behind the shield of religion and the loud determination to let justice take its course. David Berkowitz succeeded in confusing everybody.

The conflict and ambivalence over good and evil in his mind, which had created the Sam delusion, also explained his current incorporation of Christ into his delusional system. I believed that he was acting "as if" he were a convinced Christian but would retain no permanent commitment to what he was saying. The Reverend Thomas Wallace, pastor of the Kentucky church where Berkowitz was baptized, told me that the few weeks of participation the young convert had had there could not have yielded the behavior he was showing now. His piety was part of his delusion, not a true change, and would last as long as Christ held Sam at bay.

The defense faced a problem in getting a difficult patient to cooperate and the worry that the court system might not be able to ignore public pressure. How could it beat the combination of first Mrs. Smith and then God telling their defendant that he had to go to jail? It was absurd.

Yet he did change his mind briefly when I saw him in January; he was thinking aloud about the possibility of an NGRI. Then he changed it back again. When I went to see him for the second time, in March, he was adamant for jail. Despite this, I didn't really think that the court would find him competent over my explanations at a sanity hearing. I could point out how his psychosis prevented him from cooperating with his attorney's view that the NGRI was the only defense he had.

After all, I was the third psychiatrist to find him incompetent.

His case would be handled as in other cases when psychotic men refused to defend themselves. He would have to go upstate to a hospital, and then, when his improvement destined him to return for a trial, he'd have the same opportunity to cooperate with the NGRI. But the punishment he was now blindly demanding by pleading guilty and receiving sentence would not be his until after he'd been treated, or until there had been a trial.

There had been a recent and very pertinent federal decision which endorsed a judge's order that a presumably unbalanced defendant at trial *had* to interpose an insanity defense, even over the same defendant's objections. I speculated on events to come:

1. If the Brooklyn court somehow conveniently managed to find Berkowitz competent in his present uncooperative state, they wouldn't also accept his guilty plea. They would see the need to interpose an NGRI. The judge should follow the federal precedent pointed out to him and order it.

2. Whether he liked it or not, Berkowitz would have to have his sanity judged at an open trial.

3. If he lost the NGRI and went to jail—so be it.

4. If he won and had to go to a hospital, then the legislature would be forced to act by public pressure and address the policies that made dangerous committed men, civil and criminal, such a continuing problem to the country.

5. I thought that Berkowitz, whom everyone agreed must never get out, could help make those easy escapes and easy releases a thing of the past.

And I thought I had considered every angle.

9 | Face of Madness

Two court-appointed psychiatrists have reversed themselves and declared "Son of Sam" suspect David Berkowitz mentally competent to stand trial, it was learned last night.

Dr. Schwartz and an associate, Dr. Richard Weidenbacher, reportedly changed their position after Berkowitz informed them that he now believes, as a born again Baptist, that he is "serving Jesus" and hopes to preach the gospel, should he be sent to prison.

. . . This now puts all the psychiatrists who testified at the competency hearing, including one hired by District Attorney Eugene Gold who said that Berkowitz was competent, in agreement. However, the defense is now expected to ask for a new competency hearing and bring its own psychiatrist into court.

That psychiatrist, Dr. Martin Lubin, Chief of Psychiatry at Booth Memorial Hospital in Flushing and former Chief of Forensic Psychiatry at Bellevue Medical Center, . . . already has interviewed Berkowitz in the prison ward of Kings County Hospital.

—*Newsday*, February 25, 1978

I could see my first premise die. How quickly my scenario had collapsed!

189

Jultak, who had been keeping me informed, said that nine days after my interview with Berkowitz, he was examined again: by Dr. Schwartz on January 11, by Dr. Weidenbacher on the twelfth. The reports of those mid-January examinations gave "the security of his belief in Christ" as a reason for Berkowitz's improvement and apparent readiness to take moral responsibility for his acts.

"I found Christ on December 3, 1977," Berkowitz told Schwartz. It was the fourth or fifth such finding he had made since Kentucky. In this case, his meeting with the evangelist preacher, Sister Smith, had prompted the rediscovery. Now Berkowitz reported hearing Jesus "with an inner voice" and reported that "the demon holds are broken on me: God has rebuked them from bothering me, talking to me, having contact with me."

He'd been talking that way on January 2.

According to the transcripts of the doctors' interviews, Berkowitz had said, "I want to make Mr. and Mrs. Moskowitz happy. Tell them how much Jesus loves them. I could change their whole lives if they'd only let me."

He also felt he could bring peace and joy to Bob Violante, the man he had blinded, even more peace and joy than he'd had with sight.

When Dr. Schwartz remarked, "That may be so. Perhaps you're not the best one to tell them this: they may have some ill feelings toward you," Berkowitz answered, "Sure, sure—that's, that's—but God has forgiven me and that's the main thing."

He was totally responsible, he said, because he should not have listened to the demons and followed the devil. He sounded a familiar note: "The trial will accomplish nothing because, first of all, I am not insane and second of all, people wouldn't listen to me about Jesus if I told them I was sick, but I'm not, they wouldn't understand."

The first time he made that statement, he didn't want an insanity defense because "people wouldn't believe" him about the demons. Now it was because they wouldn't believe his ministry. I had the feeling that any rationalization would do, and sure

190

FACE OF MADNESS

enough, he later presented the prosecution with nineteen reasons why he wouldn't take an NGRI!

I studied the reports but couldn't see the basis for a changed opinion. The demons' hold was not broken, they did come back later, and though he was again able to revert to Christ, it was with less confidence. He was still complaining of demonic harassment in the period between those mid-January examinations and March. I had similar reservations about his accepting moral responsibility. His desire to preach to the families didn't mean any concern for them. It could even have been a sadistic interest in their shock and disgust.

However, I had to see if there was a logic in the doctors' reversal that I had missed and on March 3, I reappeared at Kings County. Berkowitz began to lecture as soon as he saw me, and it was still psychotic gibberish; he was not expounding fundamentalist belief, he just sounded nuts. A court order had finally prohibited the preacher, Sister Smith, from visiting him, but clinically speaking, that order had come much too late. She'd had access for months. (I wonder what she thought when he later turned on her!)

March 3 was a replay of my January 2 interview. Yet two doctors had just declared him competent and that was a stopper. I felt that they had erred and his apparent improvement was superficial. Yes, there were Christians who believed in demons, but not as Berkowitz did, and not with his kind of history.

If the status of competency would allow the prosecution and the defense to cooperate for a speedy disposition of the case, then there was one way I could conditionally accept the doctors' findings. If he would take an NGRI, I would find him conditionally competent and, potentially, he could still have a fair trial. Otherwise, it was too wrong.

I interrupted his preachments—not easy!—and presented the reasons for making an insanity defense. His family was begging him to do it, his lawyers never stopped urging it as his only course, and the Reverend Mr. Wallace had volunteered to come from Kentucky to talk to him about the importance of cooperating

191

with his attorneys. Ignoring the obvious absurdity of his desire to preach to the convicts, why was he so sure that he wanted to plead guilty and go to prison without a trial?

I had an idea of what lay behind that desire. It was the pure terror of being in the courtroom, going through the trial, listening to the recital of his crimes, hearing over and over that he was insane. But he could avoid that ordeal, and look penitent, by insisting that God wanted him in prison and pleading guilty. He did seem moderately impressed with the idea that his pastor would come to New York if there was hope that he'd cooperate with the NGRI, and he even seemed to be listening to my other arguments. At least there was no more preaching! I left Kings County with the feeling that I'd dented him a little and that his family might reinforce it with a follow-up visit. Jultak's weary verdict later was yes, he did appear more cooperative. But I could see that he wasn't too impressed.

Several days after this visit, Dr. Schwartz called me to ask my opinion. I told him that Berkowitz, though psychotic, could be thought "relatively competent," but I could maintain my position only if he did not relent from his cooperative status vis-à-vis the NGRI. I was contorted in this position and I'd have to explain the conditioning factor to the judge at the hearing. If he spoke to Judge Corso before that date, he might tell him so.

Just then a phone call came in from the judge and Schwartz cut short our conversation to speak with him. I believe Dr. Schwartz did explain my position.

Minutes later, Jultak called me. He had just visited Berkowitz. Cooperation was out! Berkowitz, compliant for a brief time, had changed his mind again and would again plead guilty in order to preach in prison.

Back to Square One.

I told Jultak that after the fact of the call from Schwartz, he might want to tell Judge Corso that because of these unrelenting vacillations, I would have to testify that the defendant was incompetent.

On April 5, a harried Jultak called to tell me that I had to submit a report to Judge Corso. I could address it to him and he would see that the judge got it. So I dictated three pages reviewing the atypicality of Berkowitz's history from childhood through the bizarre psychosis as a soldier and Son of Sam. My report ended:

In recapping then, I believe that he is incompetent because his judgment is impaired at a psychotic level, in a manner consistent with the other evidences of psychosis in times past, and that what we are observing is not mere religion but religiosity, a well-known condition observed in paranoid schizophrenics. (See American Diagnostic and Statistical Manual DSM-II.) If he were to remain somewhat delusional and hallucinatory at a controllable level, such that he could be induced to cooperate by allowing you to interpose an insanity defense, then I would say that he might be of sufficient relative competence to proceed. Since this is not presently the case, I must reiterate my conclusion that he is incompetent.

Sincerely,

Martin I. Lubin, M.D.
Diplomate
American Board of Psychiatry and Neurology

I mailed that report on April 5. On April 7 the papers announced: " 'Son of Sam' Suspect Is Facing Trial Soon." The story in *The New York Times* announced that State Supreme Court Justice Corso planned to start the murder case "if the hearing next Wednesday finds Berkowitz fit."

It further reported that, according to Judge Corso, the fitness hearing would be closed to the public and the press, a full transcript of the hearing would be released, and he had studied all the psychiatric reports involved.

On the next day (April 8), *Newsday* ran the following story:

BERKOWITZ TO PLEAD GUILTY IN MURDERS

New York—David Berkowitz has decided to plead guilty to the Son of Sam murders without trial, and discussions are already under way about his possible incarceration in an upstate prison for the criminally insane.

. . . *Newsday* has learned that the judge has already become involved in elaborate planning for the anticipated guilty plea, even to the point of alerting State Correctional Services Commissioner Benjamin Ward that the state prison system would have to decide where Berkowitz should be placed.

Disposition of the case? There hadn't even been a hearing—call it fitness, competency, sanity, whatever you like! On the eleventh, an article in the *Daily News* underlined what I, personally, could expect:

"SAM" DOCS TO TESTIFY

Only one of the four psychiatrists who will take the stand at tomorrow's closed-door competency hearing for David Berkowitz will testify that the alleged .44 Caliber killer should not go to trial next Monday for the murder of Stacy Moskowitz.

That testimony by defense psychiatrist, Martin Lubin, is expected to have little bearing on the ultimate outcome of the hearing.

The April hearing was in the same converted day room at Kings County that had served as a "court" for the first competency hearing in October. Dr. Schwartz was the opening witness. Because of a problem in my own schedule, I would testify the next day, out of turn, and Schwartz would return for cross-examination by the defense.

On the stand, he defended his position and testified on direct examination that the defendant could weigh evidence relative to using the insanity defense or pleading guilty. In support of this, he gave the nineteen reasons that Berkowitz had provided for wanting to plead guilty. The doctor felt that these did not reflect that his reasoning had been blocked by a demonic structure.

These were the reasons:

1. To save the taxpayers' money.
2. To save the attorneys' time.
3. Because Sister Smith wanted him to. She had a vision of it.
4. To go on trial in an insanity defense would stir the demons against him.

194

5. No one would believe him about demons at a trial.
6. It would be cowardly not to plead guilty and it would take courage to do it.
7. A good Christian can't plead insanity.
8. Because he wants to be a minister but can't do that in a mental hospital.
9. Society demands he plead guilty.
10. It doesn't look right to plead insanity.
11. He must confess to sins before people as well as God.
12. An insanity plea would accomplish nothing.
13. He would never leave a mental hospital if he went into one.
14. People hate him and therefore he can't get a fair trial.
15. In a mental hospital they'll open his head.
16. God wants him in prison.
17. It really doesn't matter, any place he's sent would be for the rest of his life.
18. To see him in jail would make victims and families happy because he would be suffering.
19. The guilty plea has to happen because that's justice.

The prosecution used these items as a basis for questioning the experts. They sidestepped 1, 2, 3 and 4—no wonder—but on my cross-examination by First Assistant District Attorney Greenberg, I was asked why items 10, 14, 18 and 19 were not the normal reactions of a competent man.

Something most unexpected happened on that first day. While Schwartz was on the stand, Ira Jultak saw Berkowitz writing something. Jultak picked up the paper and circled the message: "Sister Smith gave me a lot of those ideas. I must dispose of these demons once and for all."

Jultak passed the note to Schwartz. The court adjourned early. Schwartz had an immediate interview with Berkowitz and made the tape of that interview available to all the principals in the case.

When I came in to testify the next morning, I heard that barely audible tape. It did more than confirm again how sick he really was; it also affected my testimony that day.

On the tape, a delusional Berkowitz was once again with the demons and complaining that his spiritual adviser, Sister Smith, was in league with the devil. No way could this be interpreted as fundamentalist belief!

He had turned on her. I wondered if it would be an embarrassment to the others, and then I knew it was going to be handled. The newspapers, in their insistence on the outcome of the hearing, were obviously right, and the weariness of the defense lawyers told its own story. What happened here today didn't matter. The results were a foregone conclusion. But that was all right for the goal I had in mind.

When Berkowitz was found competent, he'd plead guilty and the whole question of his insanity relative to the killings would be buried. All the causal factors could be lost unless they were on an official record as testimony. For that reason, I wanted to get in as much as I could about his lack of criminal responsibility—yes, background for the NGRI defense—and his psychosis. I would underline the fact that his zeal to preach in prison was only a continuation of previous psychotic missions and that his apparent religious concern with demons and angels was a symptom called religiosity. My testimony might be superfluous, but it was going on the record even if I had to testify aggressively to get all my points in. Eventually the transcripts would be released to the public and the material would be read.

I took the stand on the thirteenth. Facing me, to my right, sat Attorneys Jultak and Stern and defendant Berkowitz: to my left, Brooklyn District Attorney Gold and First Assistant District Attorney Greenberg. There were a court reporter and Corrections officers. The room was like a bleak stage stripped down to essentials for a hasty drama. The missing ingredient was suspense.

Jultak had me recite my qualifications. I explained how I reviewed materials and had interviewed the defendant, his family and even his former religious mentor before I came to a conclusion. Naturally, defense wanted me to testify to the ways in which Berkowitz's psychosis inhibited him from defending himself. I told the court he had not been able to help me with the description of his crimes, or the causal connections between the hallucinations and the acts because he would begin to hallucinate when I pressed him. He generally heard voices when he became anxious.

The tape of yesterday's interview with Dr. Schwartz revealed that he was actively hallucinating again. Now he heard the devil's voice—he was sure of that—saying, "Don't plead to being insane, you've got to allow yourself to be punished."

Careful to point out that this voice was not a function of logic or religion, I launched into a brief history of other periods when he had heard voices: command hallucinations in Korea and the isolation in New York when the hallucinations evolved into commands and the construction of an elaborate theory of demonic possession with a quasireligious quality.

The Son of Sam letter and both versions of my answer to it were offered into evidence by the defense. Both versions of my letter were unpublished and the prosecution seemed startled by their appearance as evidence. District Attorney Greenberg objected: "Your Honor, the doctor has admitted that at the time he wrote the letter he had never met David Berkowitz and he had no idea of what the man who is sitting here, the subject of this hearing, is like."

That, however, was just my point. I had not seen him then, but I was able to recognize that he was a psychotic on a mission and my later interview with him proved it. It wasn't even such a diagnostic coup because I had seen so many recognizable, classifiable paranoid defendants who were acting on missions. "Mission" was the key word of my letter and I would verbally underline its meaning throughout my testimony.

There was a brief recess while the prosecution compared my answers with the original Son of Sam letter to Borelli. I had shaken them by pulling these unpublished answers out of nowhere and placing them as Defendant's Exhibits B and C. I surmised that because Greenberg handled the subject gingerly in comparison to the way he went after me later.

After recess, I continued on direct testimony with Jultak and made more points about the relevance of missions. Berkowitz had told his half sister about a mission and she cried because he sounded so irrational. His present zeal in wanting to preach in prison was like his psychotic missionary zeal in putting church tracts through the Army mails in Kentucky. I spoke about his being on a demonic mission, under control of the command hallucinations, and identified it as a fairly common symptom in psychotic defendants.

In sum, I said, "We are dealing with a psychotic, hallucinating man who has refused to cooperate with his family and his lawyers. I don't believe that with his history and his refusal to use the one possible defense he has, joined to the history of repeated psychotic missions, he can be conceived as anything but incompetent for the upcoming trial."

Jultak's questions gave me the opportunity to talk about the general nature of paranoid schizophrenics such as Berkowitz. From there we moved into religiosity as part of the package of symptoms. The handbook DSM-II was introduced and placed in evidence as Defendant's Exhibit D. DSM-II was then the standard handbook for psychiatric diagnosis, and one could usually be found in every psychiatric ward. (They produced a Kings County prison ward copy.) From it, I quoted the definition of "Schizophrenia paranoid type" which included the sentence "Excessive religiosity is sometimes seen." Still referring to that definition, I described Berkowitz as a grandiose schizophrenic who would act pursuant to his hallucinations. I recounted his inability—and unwillingness—to talk about events proximal to his last crime in Brooklyn. When Jultak asked, "Do you think he would rather plead guilty than help his counsel?" I could answer "Yes."

While I was testifying, Jultak introduced into evidence the report I had written for Judge Corso. As a way of underscoring my conclusion, he asked me if I was sure that Berkowitz wasn't feigning. (Berkowitz? A malingerer? I'd seen my share. This was not a simulator but a dissimulator, a man pretending to be *sane*. I didn't care how many times he recanted his demons!)

After that, Greenberg put me on cross-examination.

Then and throughout the hearing, the prosecution had certain lines of attack. The obvious tactic was to counter any impact of my testimony by chipping away at my credibility as a witness and to maintain that the insanity defense was not at all available to Berkowitz. If Greenberg could produce evidence to show that the defendant was able to make reasoned choices, then my logic in making him incompetent because he wouldn't take the NGRI was faulty. I think I was to be disposed of by cross questioning on some of the nineteen points Berkowitz had given as reasons.

I had the feeling that the DA was mentally circling me and looking for an opening. He did attack my credibility but not my professional credentials. He attacked along the fringes; when and how many speeches I'd made to the DAs' Association, how much, if any, concrete work I'd done for the Criminal Justice Coordinating Council. When I didn't remember specific names, dates and places, he asked me—deadpan—if I remembered how often I'd interviewed David Berkowitz.

He picked up on my answer to the Son of Sam letter, saying that since I lacked information, I had drawn a very general picture that didn't necessarily apply to David Berkowitz, sitting there. The DA was specifically trying to knock out any importance attached to the idea of a mission. I had to reread my answers and explain them phrase by phrase.

Next he challenged my testimony that Berkowitz's behavior in wanting to avoid trial and preach in jail was part of a continuing psychotic mission. He was trying to normalize Berkowitz's responses by showing that they were not illogical under the circumstances and were even shared by other people. We went round and round about what might be wrong with wanting to preach:

Q. Aren't there people who plead guilty every day?
A. I guess so, sure.
Q. Aren't they exhibiting the same thing you see in David Berkowitz?
A. No.
Q. Why not?
A. Because they might not be psychotic.
Q. Well, how does that impinge on his ability to make this reasoned choice?

A. Because it is not reasoned.

Q. Well, he gives reasons for it.

A. No, the reasons are illogical.

Q. Well, is it illogical to . . .

A. Preach the gospel in prison?

Q. Right. Let that be the question.

A. Yes, all right. He is untrained to preach the gospel in prison.

Q. Now what is illogical about wanting to do something like preaching the gospel, though you, Dr. Lubin, feel that he is unqualified for it? Are there not people you meet every day who are fired to do things, who have hopes and you privately believe that they will fail or not qualify?

Here the defense counsel objected to the form of the question. But the Court allowed it. Several times the Court would explain why a particular direction of testimony could be explored: "There is no jury here."

I had a rather wordy answer for the DA that I hoped would dispose of the subject.

A. I think that you have a certain kind of mental condition which involves wanting to preach the gospel, that it speaks for itself, that it is entirely consistent with the mental disorder. There are people trained to preach the gospel and they go forward on preaching . . . there are people untrained that may wish to go forward and preach the gospel. It was my opinion that he was untrained, wanted to go forward and preach . . . and that it was pursuant to hallucinations and delusional beliefs.

Q. Are you familiar in any way with the fundamentalist religions that pervade parts of the United States?

A. Moderately, yes.

Q. Are you familiar with the backward preachers, the sidewalk preachers?

A. Yes. That was the reason I called up Reverend Wallace to establish whether in fact he could have been imbued with an atypical kind of Christianity and the Reverend assured me that it wasn't the case. I think I mentioned it in the report, too.

Q. What did the Reverend assure you?

A. That it was not the case.

Q. That what was not the case?

A. That he was not imbued, to his knowledge, with an atypical kind of Christianity that would involve his preaching on street corners as Berkowitz told me he did.

"We are talking about now!" said the DA. He was suddenly anxious to move the action out of 1973 and Wallace's opinion of his convert. He had started to press on the fundamentalist connection without being aware that I had called Wallace and had the rebuttal information ready.

This information was so important because the debate about whether Berkowitz was displaying religiousness or psychotic religiosity was apparently going to be the key issue of this hearing. By authenticating his "religiousness," the Kings County doctors had made the point of controversy inevitable. Their report indicated that he had improved and stabilized because he was moving away from his unique beliefs and closer to a certain theology held by other people. The prosecution took that and ran with it, building an argument for competency on Berkowitz's desire to preach. They would try again and again to identify Berkowitz's beliefs with those held by fundamentalist Christians.

And they also used his nineteen points as examples of reasonable beliefs. I was questioned thoroughly on number fourteen: "People hate him and he can't get a fair trial."

The DA asked me why it was illogical for Berkowitz to decide that people hated him after killing six and wounding seven. Wasn't that a reasonable conclusion?

During my cross-examination I answered that question:

A. No, that's false. I think he could think that people could hate him. I think that to the degree that he thinks people could hate him and how it would affect his thought processes about going forward on an insanity defense may be [reflective of]* a pathological mental state. It's a degree of hating and a kind of hate.

Q. How do you know that people hate him?

A. Well you—I responded to your question. You said is it possible that people would hate him for having killed. I said that if you kill a lot, people hate you and it's entirely possible.

Q. Yet he expresses that thought you say is a sick and illogical thought?

A. I didn't say that.

Q. What did you say?

A. I said that if the belief about being hated is so pervasive and reaches an illogical proportion vis-à-vis his defending himself, then it reflects a mental illness. Then I cannot say that it has a logical quality. It's gone beyond what I consider to be logical. Why should he think that he could not get a fair trial in Brooklyn? It's possible he might get a fair trial in Brooklyn. It's possible.

(I knew that didn't sound like a neutral expert, but I'd had it. I would fence with this DA to the degree that the judge and defense attorneys didn't keep his inquiries relevant.)

When the item of Brooklyn was exhausted, the questions relating to the nineteen points continued in the same disputatious way. The question about Berkowitz feeling hated was an absurd question. Others I spotted from the list were: What was wrong with Berkowitz wanting to be punished for what he'd done? And another: He'd said that the guilty plea was justice, and didn't that show he had a sense of justice?

This type of question, which isolates specific judgments, is always tricky to answer. A basic belief in each case may seem

*In several places, the record of verbatim testimony is garbled (yet still comprehensible) because I or others spoke too rapidly for transmission by the court reporter. On this page, "reflective of" was mistakenly recorded as "effected by."

normal and shared by others, as the DA constantly emphasized, but if the belief is in the company of other symptoms of mental disorder, other factors having to do with Berkowitz's psychosis, then it may not be normal at all.

For example, Berkowitz certainly had sufficient intelligence to listen to his lawyers, but that did not make him competent because his hallucinations compelled him to ignore their advice. The NGRI was available to him, but his illness stopped him from cooperating with his one possible defense.

When I stated this in testimony, the DA jumped me for saying that Berkowitz had the defense. "Are you making that judgment as a lawyer?" he asked me. "Are you trying to make the idea as a lawyer or are you sticking to medical ideas, psychological and psychiatric ideas?"

I asked him if there was some other defense I didn't know about.

"Doctor, I will ask the questions," he responded.

We could wander astray in his attempt to play down the NGRI. At one point I heard a question that belonged only in a trial after the defense had been interposed.

"Based on your examination of this defendant, what is there about your finding that makes you believe he did not know the nature of the act of shooting Stacy Moskowitz?"

I inquired, "Are you asking me about the responsibility defense at this competency hearing?"

The judge remarked that we were going beyond the scope of the hearing. Indeed we were.

On the whole, the DA made a tactic of finding alternative terminology for the psychiatric words I used, as if to deny that they applied to Berkowitz. At one point he remarked that he found no meaning in the word "psychosis." Later, when Dr. Schwartz was on the stand for redirect testimony, the DA used such terms as "reasoning process" to describe the frequent vacillations and Berkowitz's tendency to tell whichever doctor was questioning him what the doctor wanted to hear. This was a desire to please, a normal "reasoning process." Further, in disputing the fact that Berkowitz was as suggestible as all the doctors said,

Greenberg cited the length of time that Berkowitz had been able to ignore the continuing advice of all the people who felt that he should take the insanity defense. For months, he had had the "strength of mind"—as the prosecution put it—to resist. Dr. Schwartz's testimony explained that there was no such element of choice involved. At that time, Berkowitz's delusions said that he had to reject it.

The definition of delusion came under prosecution scrutiny as well, but the big obstacle to be disposed of was "religiosity." Here I couldn't give an inch. Berkowitz's distorted view of something akin to religion obsessed and controlled him so that he could not cooperate with his attorneys, make judgments relative to taking one defense over another or even converse in a logical way.

On the afternoon session of that day, while I was still on cross-examination, Greenberg zeroed in on religiosity. He had done a little homework during the lunch break and confronted me with the handbook DSM-II, saying that he couldn't find a definition for the word. Where had I gotten my definition? The sentence I'd quoted under the diagnosis of "Schizophrenic, paranoid type," "excessive religiosity is sometimes seen," was not sufficient. He wanted a definition of the word per se, and seemed to suggest that it had no special psychiatric usage. Religiosity was excess religious zeal and that was all.

We fought that back and forth. On redirect with defense counsel Leon Stern, I was able to differentiate religiosity from religion, especially from fundamentalist Christian theology. Greenberg was still not satisfied, and on recross he would lead me through questions about tribes and religious cults who had unusual practices, asking if their unusual forms of worship indicated to me that there was something "not right" about their mental status.

When he asked me, "How can you say that David Berkowitz, by exhibiting religion, is suffering from religiosity?" I answered that his mission to preach the gospel was not religion—it was psychosis, like all his other missions. His preaching was religiosity, not just religious fervor but the accompanying indications of mental disorder which added up to a clear diagnostic conclusion.

Again the DA came back at this point, comparing his religious missions to something legitimate like a call to the priesthood.

I said something about a qualitative difference.

The DA asked, "And *you* make it quality?"

I tried to counter sarcasm with humor. "Yes, that's why you have me sitting here as an expert."

I wasn't his expert. His expression spoke for itself when he said, "No, he called you" (meaning Jultak).

I pointed to his boss, the Brooklyn DA, and said, "He's called me in the past. Schwartzwald last called me. He belongs to you."

Schwartzwald was indeed another assistant DA in the Brooklyn office. I saw Greenberg look at his boss. (Apparently they didn't remember me as their expert witness on the Thomas case in 1975, when I'd gone to this same DA's office to ask for help in changing the law to protect the public against another dangerous psychotic. This was ironic.) They realized that they had once used my expertise, which made it difficult to cut me down now.

From my point of view, the religiosity issue was not lost in this exchange. And the prosecution's other tactic of trying to normalize Berkowitz's ideas through frequent reference to the nineteen reasons came to grief during defense counsel Stern's cross-examination of Dr. Schwartz.

The doctor testified that Berkowitz had told him Mrs. Smith wanted him to plead guilty, to preach in prison and bring Christ to other prisons throughout the state. She had also told Berkowitz that the insanity defense was wrong, that it would be cowardice for him to plead it, and that the only right thing for a Christian to do was plead guilty.

In other words, reasons 6, 7, and 10 on that list.

Stern further elicited that Berkowitz had told Dr. Schwartz that all the items in sum and substance were directed or told to him by Mrs. Smith. She had influenced him completely. But now he'd rejected her and substituted her for his demons as an agent of the devil. We had all heard the tape. So where did that leave the list of reasons the prosecution was presenting as indicators of his competence for trial? The doctor's dilemma was clear in this exchange with Leon Stern:

Q. . . . So they are not significant, are they, Doctor?
A. Not as reasons, not as motives, but to, as evidence of his—
Q. His present desire?
A. Of his vacillation.
Q. Of his vacillation?
A. Of his looking outward for some kind of guidance and justification and reasoning and so on.
Q. Exactly, and it is true, is it not, and you have subsequently learned that all of these items or most of these items were actually the feeling and influence of Sister Smith?
A. Yes, sir.
Q. All right, and it is true, Doctor, that you are still not sure whether this defendant, David Berkowitz, is fit to stand trial presently.
A. I think I have to say that I'm not sure, and the main reason is, if I may, because he seems—
Q. Well, you are not sure, Doctor?
A. Yes, okay.
> MR. GOLD [Brooklyn DA]: I think the witness should be allowed to finish his answer.
> MR. STERN [defense]: You can redirect him.
> THE COURT: I will let the doctor finish his answer.
A. Because he seems to change from one moment to the next.
Q. Whatever the reason, Doctor, at this point you're not sure, is that right?
A. I am not sure because I am not sure if this is what 730* means in terms of mental disease or defect.
Q. You leave the definition of 730 to His Honor, Judge Corso.

*730: New York State Code of Criminal Procedure describing competency.

A. Beautiful.

Q. What I am referring to is psychiatrically, Doctor, your opinion now is that you are not sure whether it's because of vacillations or whether it's because of other conditions that you subsequently learned about prior to—or subsequent to the time that you made the report, that's what I want to know.

A. And because I'm not exactly sure how the definition applies in this case.

Q. All right.

Dr. Schwartz went on redirect by Greenberg, but nothing could be salvaged of the nineteen reasons. In fact, it was elicited that Berkowitz finally admitted that these were not real reasons. He "didn't know why"—he didn't know why he would plead guilty. With his rejection of Sister Smith's teachings, he was still working on the shoring up of his beliefs, but was now saying that it might not be un-Christian to take the insanity defense. But he didn't know why he would do that either. We were back to "Would he or wouldn't he?" again.

Unsurprisingly, the Court moved the hearing along to other considerations. Judge Corso asked questions about Berkowitz's intelligence, his minimal contact with reality and whether the stress of a trial situation could make him more permanently psychotic.

The testimony of the Kings County doctors was that he couldn't become more psychotic. But there was a divergence between Dr. Schwartz and Dr. Weidenbacher about Berkowitz in any trial situation.

Schwartz said, essentially, that he wasn't sure of what Berkowitz might do because of the latest vacillations. He did suggest that there could be outbursts in the courtroom that would necessitate a recess from the trial until the defendant had recovered. That had been his pattern at Kings County: violence and peace, sudden outbursts, sudden recoveries.

Weidenbacher, who testified after Schwartz, did not diverge from his March report of competency. Agreeing that Berkowitz

was sick, he nevertheless found him fit for trial in spite of vacillations. His viewpoint identified Berkowitz far more closely
with fundamentalist belief than did his colleague's.

There was no question about our agreement that Berkowitz
was a paranoid psychotic, but I disagreed with them both on his
being competent. I directly disagreed with Weidenbacher because
I felt that the main area of Berkowitz's incompetence was his
inability to aid his counsel. I could still maintain my admittedly
contorted position that if he cooperated, if he could accept an
NGRI without vacillation, then he might be conditionally competent in order to have his day in court. But by now I didn't
expect that to happen.

All of us wanted the case to be over. The columnist Murray
Kempton wrote, "Put him away. He's driving us crazy!"

There was still one more psychiatrist involved in the case,
Dr. David Abrahamsen, the people's psychiatrist engaged by the
Brooklyn DA's office. His findings had been used from August
1977 until now. He made a pretestimony examination of Berkowitz,
and testified on the morning of April seventeenth. The following
exchange is from the conclusion of his cross-examination by Jultak:

> Q. Dr. Abrahamsen, is it your testimony that David Ber-
> kowitz told you as to the date of your report, March
> ninth, that the demons had gone from him?
> A. Yes.
> Q. And he no longer believed in the demons as such?
> A. Yes.
> Q. Doctor, I show you Defendant's Exhibit E and ask
> you to read the two statements on there (handing Exhibit
> to witness). Will you read the second sentence on that
> page, Doctor?
> A. "I must dispose of these demons once and for all."
> Q. Doctor, if I told you David Berkowitz wrote that as
> late as last Thursday, do you feel it would be of any
> significance to you?
> A. Yes, it would be if this is his opinion about it, if this
> is a constant opinion. But with regard to the demons,

he has been oscillating, he has been flexible in the sense that he is saying, going back and forth about this—and this was what he wrote on Thursday, you said?

Q. Yes, sir.

A. Now I want to say the first line is that "Sister Smith gave me a lot of those ideas." I do not know to what he is referring there.

Q. Does the second sentence show you that he still, in effect, believes in demons?

A. Mr. Jultak, with all respect to you, sir, you cannot really out from one sentence state what it says here, because he has said something about that, and I don't believe that from a moment—we cannot, at least I cannot, decide whether or not this is so.

Q. Would this tend to indicate to you that he could be vacillating back and forth about his demons?

A. He can vacillate, yes, he can.

Q. And would he show you that up until last Thursday, at least, he was still vacillating as to whether or not he heard the demons?

A. That I cannot say anything about.

Q. Do you feel, Doctor, that it is a function of Mr. Berkowitz's personality that he can be made to feel different about any topic by virtue of a good strong conversation?

A. That he can be made to feel different?

Q. Can he be manipulated?

A. Pardon me?

Q. Can he be manipulated?

A. He possibly might be. I do not know for sure but I do believe also this: he has also a strong ego.

Q. Doctor, in summation, then, would it be fair to categorize your testimony that David Berkowitz is absolutely fit to proceed at this time?

A. Yes.

Q. Would it be fair to categorize your testimony that he is not now under any psychosis?

A. Yes.

Q. Would it then be fair to characterize your testimony as excluding any diagnosis of paranoid schizophrenia?

A. Oh, absolutely.

Q. There is absolutely nothing that would suggest to you that this man might be a paranoid schizophrenic?

A. Absolutely not.

MR. JULTAK: Nothing further.

THE COURT: Any redirect?

There was none, and no further witness on either side.

The hearing adjourned on April 17 at 10:30 A.M. Judge Corso's decision was reserved until he could fully review the testimony given.

On April 25, one week later, the waiting was over. I was fascinated to read the account of the hearing as published in *The New York Times* on the day Judge Corso's decision came down (April 25, 1978):

BERKOWITZ IS JUDGED COMPETENT
A MURDER TRIAL IS SET FOR MAY 8

. . . "The testimony indicates," Justice Corso said, "that defendant has given full consideration, pro and con, to the legal alternatives available to him and understands them. It further indicates that he is appropriately addressing himself to the immediate problem confronting him."

Justice Corso noted too that during the hearings the defendant's conduct had been orderly with "no emotional outbursts, disruptive behavior or bizarre conduct." Also, he said, "Mr. Berkowitz has a complete understanding of the process of trial and the roles of the judge, jury, prosecutor and defense attorneys" and "he has had a working relationship with his attorneys up to the present time." . . .

I was now willing to bet that even when the transcripts of this closed hearing were released, there would be no surprise, no shock, no public stir at all! And I wasn't disappointed. The weight of popular opinion rolled over any discrepancies in the testimony and was solidly with the Court.

The trial itself was scheduled for May 8. Under an unusual procedure worked out with the city's administrative judge, the courtroom in the State Supreme Court in Brooklyn, where Berkowitz was scheduled to be tried, was transformed by judicial order into part of the Supreme Courts of Queens and the Bronx. The three judges, Judge Corso (Brooklyn), Judge Kapelman (Bronx) and Judge Tsoucalas (Queens) represented all the boroughs involved and each would preside in turn.

The trial was short. Afterward, a columnist reviewed the statistics: "Berkowitz entered what was to be a Brooklyn courtroom for half an hour, would become a Bronx courtroom for 25 minutes and would finish as a Queens courtroom for 35."

The New York Times of May 9 noted how smoothly the opportunity for Berkowitz to make a wholesale plea of guilty had worked in practice: how the defense attorneys rose before each section of the three-part session to express their belief that their client was not competent to stand trial and was defying their advice. With equal smoothness, each judge accepted the guilty plea. It technically may have been a trial, but in effect it was a ritual performance centering around the penitent defendant.

But on that same day, May 9, 1978, the *Times* published a speculative article about the possibility of Berkowitz changing his mind and deciding that he should have pleaded not guilty by reason of insanity. Many lawyers said that he could argue that even though he had spoken the word "guilty," the three judges who accepted his plea had before them enough information to suggest the possibility of an NGRI.

For example, there were the tapes introduced in that first (October) hearing to determine his competency to stand trial. In them, Berkowitz had talked about the demons who had commanded his body and carried out the six murders with which he'd been charged. Naturally, the issue was skirted. The judges individually went through the ritual of asking the defendant if he knew what he was pleading to—generally managing to ask only those questions about the killings which would avoid eliciting the subject of motives. He could have ruined everything by starting to talk about his demons again.

Berkowitz might have been following the intention he had announced in his mid-January interview with Dr. Weidenbacher. He'd said then that he wasn't going to talk about the demons in his prison preaching because "the demons have received enough publicity already and it's time to give God publicity." He behaved prudently and did not smile. He didn't want to sound incompetent any more than the judges wanted him to sound that way. All the motives meshed.

By pleading guilty, he did lose his chance to make the big courtroom speech that he used to mention. This was to have been the fireworks, the oratory that would either warn New Yorkers about demons or bring them to Christ, depending on which way he was vacillating at the time. But his fear of being in a real trial was greater than his grandiosity. He was a sober, hangdog defendant.

The trial was tough and frustrating for Ira Jultak and Leon Stern. The many months of detention had been wearing enough and now their worst fears were realized as they stood watch while their psychotic client pleaded guilty. He wanted to go to prison to preach and the public wanted him there for punishment—although paradoxically, the insanity defense which he and the public rejected for different reasons would have been a greater punishment for Berkowitz than anything the judges provided.

Monday, May 22, was the day of the sentencing. The preceding Thursday, Berkowitz had shown some unusual curiosity by asking Jultak if they would once again be in a certain room in the Supreme Court Building for the regular pre-court-appearance pep talk. And from Kings County, Dr. Schwartz reported a "gleam in his eye" as Berkowitz discussed his coming court appearance. The "cat ate the canary" smile was back: Berkowitz was enjoying a secret.

Jultak, uneasy, phoned me four days before the final proceedings. I trusted his intuition of danger and when I asked if there was an unbarred window in that particular room, Jultak confirmed it. "That might be Berkowitz's secret," I said. "He could be a 'jumper.' "

Jultak duly called Corrections and there were extra officers assigned to Berkowitz's transfer from Kings County to the Supreme Court Building. Still Jultak didn't sleep the night before the sentencing. The months of frustration were ending with the fiasco of sentencing, but both he and his partner were relieved. They'd been trying to protect a confounding, insane man in a hostile environment, a double jeopardy situation. The frustration of being forced to let Berkowitz dictate all the moves was crippling, as was their disappointment with the legal establishment. Jultak had been an assistant DA until shortly before he was retained by Berkowitz's father, and he was incredulous that the attitudes of the DAs, judges and psychiatrists arrayed against his client could be so "extraordinary." But what bothered him in his fragmented sleep was the image, flicking in and out of his consciousness, of Berkowitz in his light blue suit, flying out the window into space, again and again.

In the morning, when Berkowitz entered that room, he suddenly lunged toward the window, but his timing was off. When the officers tackled him, he kicked one and bit another, wildly struggling to get free. Jultak's dream was happening before his eyes. Even more manpower was needed to keep this one madman down; after a sporadic struggle, he was tightly bound and held to prevent any unexpected movements when he was thrust into the sentencing courtroom one and a half hours later.

They should have thought of gagging him too. As he was pushed into the courtroom red-faced, torn, wild-eyed, he began to chant, "Stacy was a whore, Stacy was a whore." Stacy's mother, crying, "You're an animal!" rushed from the courtroom, but she couldn't escape his voice as he shouted after her, "That's right, that's right. I'd kill her again, I'd kill them all again!" When people in the courtroom shouted threats at him, he screamed back. The outbursts ended abruptly when half a dozen officers pushed and dragged their manacled prisoner out of the courtroom and into a small waiting room.

Judge Corso postponed the sentencing to order yet another psychiatric examination on June 12, despite courtroom shouts

213

demanding immediate revenge. The other judges concurred. Later, Berkowitz would blandly say that his courtroom behavior was "invented" at the last moment after the suicide attempt failed.

Again calm, again sounding like a polite teenager, he admitted that his plan had been to go out that window. He'd imagined himself lying in a pool of blood on the sidewalk after the fall. In the casual, matter-of-fact way so typical of persons with his illness, he explained that the jump was to have been a public sacrifice to the demons. Ambivalent to the last, he admitted that he hoped, perhaps half-expected, that angels would rescue him in midair and take him away. If the angels came, that miracle would have restored his waning faith in Christ. If not, then dying would have been satisfactory.

When the suicide failed in action, Berkowitz said he had tried outrage in the courtroom; he had done it hoping that someone would come forward and kill him. At one point, a maddened victim did leap to his feet, but Berkowitz was closely surrounded by court officers. Everyone present in that courtroom would have been searched or watched: Berkowitz might have remembered that obstacle from the movies he'd seen and the mysteries he'd read.

I wondered about the private feelings of the justices who had agreed that he was competent. They felt it was a necessity, an expedient priority to get him into a jail instead of a mental hospital. The public—and probably the judges too—distrusted the hospitals and felt that Berkowitz would be back on the streets in two or three years if the release procedures of a successful NGRI were later applied. But whose fault was that? The judges and the DAs had had the power to stop the drift of the law-in-practice to this ruinous point. They were years late in facing that responsibility.

The judges also didn't want to face the press. Still agonizing over their sentencing dilemma, they clamped a gag order on talking to the media. I hadn't been in the courtroom and hadn't heard of the gag, so when the *New York Post* called me at my office I answered the reporter's questions. The *Post* quoted me: "I would not doubt that he [Berkowitz] had written his own scenario. He was going to participate in a certain way, commit suicide in a certain way. He was the captive of a corny conception of going out in a blaze of glory."

The TV news shows wanted me for interviews. Suddenly I was a hot item, a seer, the one psychiatrist who had said from the beginning to the end that Berkowitz was incompetent. What did I think about the case and did I feel vindicated?

Privately, I felt angry with myself about the case. I hadn't believed that the deck was quite so stacked from the beginning, hadn't believed the defense lawyers when they insisted that he'd be found competent. Even after testifying in hundreds of cases, I'd never imagined the possibility that such an extraordinary arrangement could evolve between district attorneys and judges. I had known from the beginning that I wouldn't ask for a fee and I now felt that much of my energy had also been wasted. It was too late to get out, and at the same time I was fascinated by the unbelievable chain of events.

This was a case like no other. I had been asked to act as an expert; I knew a few things about the man and yet I was not being heard. The police had not used my response to the Son of Sam letter (I don't count those four lines in the tabloids) and then the court had virtually ignored my conclusions at the competency hearing even as Berkowitz read his Bible and hallucinated before us during my testimony.

He'd gone on to plead guilty without a hitch and the prosecution's luck still held. Even the public reaction to the transcript of the hearing, which had been released at the time of the trial, was as apathetic as I'd guessed. There were a few articles after the trial with such headlines as "Defense Plans an Appeal" and "Berkowitz Files Show He Did Many Arsons," but the voice of moderation from the *Times* urged us to "put it behind us." There was only faint damnation in the press of what had happened and the general idea seemed to be that we should hurry the business to its conclusion, get the defendant off center stage. It was *sic transit* Berkowitz until he began to smile in Kings County and prepare a few surprises for his appearance at the sentencing.

He had been quietly strange at the closed competency hearing, taciturn at the trial, but finally, at the sentencing, he was the

215

true Son of Sam. Reporters only heard about his attempt to jump, but then they saw what he could do in the courtroom. Murray Kempton wrote, "Suddenly it was there, the naked face of madness!" Not suddenly, but through plan or accident the public finally saw it in a close-up.

Through the months of involvement, I had typically avoided publicity. Now I didn't hesitate to talk about the case. I gave a few TV interviews and in them, tried to include some observations with a psychological content. On a news show, I said that although he was psychotic, it was possible that David Berkowitz had made a final attempt through his courtroom violence to reestablish authorship and control of the mad scenario he'd commenced a year before. When I looked at that show later, I realized that it mattered only to me that the tape editing had made what I said incomprehensible. The editor knew what people were interested in—they wanted Berkowitz making it to the window and flying through the air. They were not involved enough to listen to the background of the case or think about what it could mean, even though I wanted to tell them. I was the curiosity of the week, Son of Sam's shrink—that's all.

Hours after the violence in court, I'd called Ira Jultak and we'd talked about his premonition of the suicide attempt. He was down, disillusioned about the impact of politics on the legal profession. I felt that the DAs and judges must have been involved in an uneasy collaboration since the time of the joint plea acceptance. They had negotiated the sitting in one courthouse for expediency, hoping Berkowitz would behave, and it had really gone sour. No wonder that the Supreme Court judges could actually be heard arguing, shouting, cursing after Berkowitz's chants had unnerved them and he had had to be dragged out of the courtroom. The *Post* carried a story about it and Bronx District Attorney Mario Merola's reaction to the gag rule on May 23:

> A furious Mario Merola today prepared to challenge a gag order in the David Berkowitz case by ordering the minutes of a top level meeting of judges as the press ban was imposed. . . . Following the court session, the principals were summoned to the vacant anteroom to decide their attitude toward the press, according to one source.

The meeting soon disintegrated into a wild exchange of shouts and screams at times so loud that it carried clearly to the corridors where court officers shifted in embarrassment. The consensus of the judges was, "Don't talk to anybody." They promptly put it into an order so strict that the judges involved would not even tell reporters why it had been imposed.

. . . The gag rule was clamped on lawyers, judges and prosecutors in the case.

. . . Merola, nearly livid with rage, stormed from the courtroom, furious at the gag order and frustrated by the failure to wind up the Berkowitz case with his expected sentencing.

I couldn't help but sympathize with him. Of course the Queens and Bronx DAs should never have allowed the obviously questionable Brooklyn competency finding to be binding in their own boroughs. It all went back to that. But even if they had initially agreed, there should have been some skepticism about accepting as competent the guilty plea of an insane man, even if the whole city wanted the case over and done with!

Merola had told the court to "bite the bullet and sentence him today" after the outburst that postponed the sentencing, and it was true that Berkowitz could have been sentenced without being present in the courtroom. Whether Merola believed in Berkowitz's insanity or not, he was a strong ally in any effort to control abuses by and against criminally committed mental patients, and what he recommended was the only logical action, considering the course that had been chosen. All the public agonizing over legality, all the delays and calls for still more reports would come to the same thing.

Sure enough, we were offered another round at charades. The papers said that Judge Corso would be forced under state law to order another competency hearing if either the defense or the prosecution contested the June 12 finding by a court-appointed psychiatrist, Dr. Weidenbacher. I was quoted correctly as saying that if there was now to be a ruling that Berkowitz was incompetent because of his behavior in the courtroom, then the first finding that he was competent to stand trial would be put in doubt. A lawyer added, "If he was incompetent on May 22, he was probably incompetent on May 8." And a Brooklyn judge who asked not be identified said, "Once a defendant is declared unfit at any time during the trial process, the entire process becomes tainted, especially when he has been confined in a mental institution for more than a year."

I'd said, reluctantly, that I would testify at a hearing that Berkowitz was incompetent to be sentenced, but I was relieved when the defense team didn't actively engage in contesting any competency finding to be judged in the Brooklyn court.

I too had had enough of it.

But I did go back to Kings County one last time on June 6, ostensibly for the legal purpose of considering his competency for this last sentencing formality. (Judge Corso had lately said he'd sentence Berkowitz on the twelfth no matter how he behaved in court or what his next psychiatric examination showed.)

This time Berkowitz was heavily sedated and thick-tongued. But as we talked and the medication's effects lessened, the material flowed. We had a long interview. He said again that he had been doing his best to be killed by someone in the courtroom—but he added more to his post hoc explanation of why he had tried to jump from a courthouse window. Now he said, "All the time I was sacrificing other people, it was time I sacrificed myself, don't you think—isn't it only proper?"

One last good-guy think, one suicide as a quid pro quo for killing six people and injuring seven. It was all he had to offer.

On June 13, 1978, Berkowitz went back to the same court and received a sentence of twenty-five years to life on each of the six killings.

Within several weeks upstate at Attica, he had been evaluated by four psychiatrists, found to be mentally ill and was committed for treatment to the Central New York Psychiatric Center at Marcy.

He was back in Attica State Prison perhaps four months later.

On February 23, 1979, he arranged for a news conference in an apparent effort to scuttle a book project on the police pursuit of Son of Sam. He was very moralistic, expressing great aversion to the idea that his former lawyers might make some money from a book sale through the history and experiences they had acquired defending him. He didn't want a cut, he just didn't want them to get anything. In an effort to undermine the project, he recanted his demons (again!) but came up with a different explanation.

He smiled when he told the media people that he'd made up the whole Son of Sam thing. The demons, the talking dogs, the satanic henchmen who ordered him to kill were faked, he said, "just invented by me in my own mind to condone what I was doing."

Then what was the motive of the murders? "That I really can't say," he answered. "I don't know what started it and I don't know what it was that caused me to lose interest. I just don't know."

He went out of his way to demonstrate how well the new Berkowitz had adjusted to life in Attica. The food was decent, he said, and "not like the kind in the old Jimmy Cagney movies." His cell was comfortable. "It's really home," said Berkowitz. "It's like a small apartment. I spend most of my time in there."

In later interviews, he speaks of more comforts—bright curtains, an orange toilet seat. The public would be upset if they knew how comfortable he was. Outrageous. And in his pictures, he's smiling.

The news reported something else I expected to happen when Berkowitz was slashed in the neck by another inmate, causing a wound requiring 63 stitches. He was in the news again when it became known that he had asked for a veteran's disability pension because his psychiatric troubles had started in the Army. The public outrage when that was reported caused Berkowitz to say that "someone else" had made the request in his name. He used the media to complain that "someone else" had been pocketing money that belonged to him.

Prison seems to have made him more articulate. He spends a lot of time in correspondence, offers moral advice to youngsters and replies to the kind of women who write mash notes to murderers. He'll be heard from in the future. I was interested in the fact that he felt conned after pleading guilty when he found that he couldn't preach in prison after all.

We cannot easily measure other criminals, sane or insane, by David Berkowitz. More than anyone else before him, he frightened the people of New York City. More than anyone else, he demonstrated how insanity and willfulness, mad and bad, can coexist in one person. And more than any case I can remember, he embarrassed us. How absurd the contradictory arguments of experts could be, how "convenient" it was for the courts, under heavy public pressure, unabashedly to reinterpret the law to fit the need! And the news media—they helped create the monster, then encouraged his career with the exploitation which repelled and fascinated us.

Yet the sensational coverage of the Son of Sam was the very stuff from which another monster like him could arise. We are only beginning to explore that connection and the problem it presents. It could hardly be more important to our increasingly media-oriented and violent society.

Epilogue

This epilogue will be a wrap-up of the main themes of the book, including the influence of the Berkowitz case and the changes in New York State's NGRI and competency laws which followed it. I will also add to a topic touched on in Chapter 7: my interest in how the broadcast and print media may affect crime.

I had hoped that the Berkowitz case would act as a catalyst for change in the laws relating to the mentally ill, and it did, but only with the reinforcement of two other outrageous cases.

One was the case of policeman Robert Torsney who shot and killed an unarmed black youth in Brooklyn in 1976. He was tried and found not guilty by reason of insanity. His mental condition was ascribed to a form of epilepsy. The public reaction was indignant: everyone felt the NGRI was inappropriate. But the case is far from over in its implications. I quote *The New York Times* editorial page of February 17, 1979, for a review of the later developments in the Torsney tangle:

221

GOOD GUYS, BAD GUYS

The case of the policeman Robert Torsney has taken another bizarre turn. The white officer was acquitted on a controversial plea of insanity by an all-white jury. . . . Now he finds himself locked in by the very laws he used to his advantage. They permitted an insanity defense, but also required that he be committed to a mental hospital until he can prove that he is sane and no longer dangerous. An appellate court has now ruled that he must remain in the custody of hospital psychiatrists who don't think he's sick.

At least one of Mr. Torsney's keepers thought there was never anything wrong with him. None found any trace of the "psychomotor epilepsy" his defense lawyer said seized him on Thanksgiving 1976, when he killed Randy Evans without provocation and calmly walked away. The Mental Hygiene Department, his custodian after the insanity acquittal, soon said that he was not sick and petitioned for his release. A judge agreed, but now the Appellate Division disagrees.

The lower court found uncontroverted evidence that Mr. Torsney could be released safely under restrictions. But five judges of the Appellate Division unanimously found the same evidence unpersuasive. Some of the doctors who favored his release turned out to know little about him, or did not take adequate account of the stresses that might trigger another outburst. The court said that even if Mr. Torsney had no psychomotor epilepsy, there remained an "impulsive and explosive personality disorder reactive to stress."

Unquestionably, this was fallout from the Berkowitz case. When a judge agreed to Torsney's release in 1979, the Brooklyn district attorney appealed, causing the release order to be vacated. Torsney was thus kept in the hospital until midsummer while defined as normal by doctors who, of course, would not be treating him because of their conclusion!

The Brooklyn DA's office was using extraordinary methods. They wanted the psychotic Berkowitz in a prison and the sane Torsney in a hospital, perhaps out of fear that the laws were inadequate or because of political pressure. What they did had an *Alice in Wonderland* quality, but the egregious manipulations were no fantasy and the desperation behind this exposed the chaos in the operation of legal procedure in the state.

Real efforts to correct the situation had been under way for some time, but it took one more tragedy to achieve the momentum required for change to take place. A known dangerous mental patient, Adam Berwid, was given a twenty-four-hour pass from a state hospital on Long Island without officials having provided prior warning to his former wife or to the police. (Berwid's file was supposed to have red notations on it, or flags, indicating that he was dangerous.) He had threatened to kill his ex-wife when he went into the hospital: that was validated by the Nassau County DA's office, a judge and his wife's lawyer. Nevertheless, he was released for the day. He went to his wife's home. Within hours of his release, she was screaming to the police emergency operator, "He's killing me!" He did kill her before help could come.

There was an immediate public outcry and a departmental inquiry into the practices of the Office of Mental Health. The Nassau County Grand Jury, impaneled a month after the murder, criticized the state for having "no written guidelines or procedures to follow" when potentially dangerous mental patients were released.

Newsday referred to the six-page grand jury report which said, "The decision to release is now solely within the prerogative of the treating physician . . . without fear of the release being unauthorized or the physician being held insubordinate." The two state hospital doctors who had arranged for Berwid's pass were reassigned from clinical to purely administrative duties to await departmental or legal developments. The circumstances of his case prompted other action. The state legislature, specifically referring to Berwid and the grand jury report, passed a bill requiring the Office of Mental Health to notify law enforcement agencies and any potential victims before releasing mental patients who might be dangerous.

Fear created by Berkowitz impelled change in New York. But many states had their own gruesome multiple murderers as impetus for reform. Illinois had the Gacy case—one man killed thirty-three victims. California had two notorious cases of multiple homicides. In one, a frustrated politician killed the popular mayor of San Francisco and a city councilman. In the other, a known

223

psychotic killed strangers and ate their viscera. A sympathetic jury found the first defendant, White, to be emotionally disturbed and deserving of a reduced plea under the laws of that state. Chase, the psychotic killer, was found sane and sentenced to prison where he managed to commit suicide. As a result of this confusion, bills are pouring into the California legislature recommending change in the state's liberal laws.

By early 1978, the New York State Department of Mental Hygiene submitted a report to Governor Carey entitled *The Insanity Defense in New York State*. The department advised of a major need for change in the law. The old NGRI was to be eliminated. A scholarly history indicated that it was no longer appropriate, that it had criminalized the hospitals and that the mental health needs of insane criminals could be dealt with otherwise.

In lieu of the NGRI, the mentally disturbed criminal would be handled under a diminished reponsibility concept designated "diminished capacity." It would enable psychiatric testimony to be presented to explain that a man was unable to form the required criminal intent to commit a particular (more serious) crime. The offenders could be given reduced pleas and shortened sentences based on successful testimony. By this replacement for the NGRI, no criminal would be going to hospitals anymore. Convicted disturbed individuals would be sent to prison but would have access to clinical psychiatric services there. A budget had already been provided and expanded mental health services were in place in New York State's prisons. Protests over the recommendations were heard from various sources for various reasons, however, and legislation did not go forward. Instead, the governor set up a special law revision commission whose task it was to submit a recommendation after a comprehensive review of all current alternative concepts to NGRI had been considered.

In the handling of the mentally ill and criminal, the public sentiment pendulum was swinging to the right; the public mood on criminal justice was punitive because of skyrocketing crime and the apparent inability of anyone to reverse the factors that controlled the trend. It was easy to target the mental illness area for blame: frightening ex-mental patients seen all over the streets,

224

occasional escaped mental patients involved in killings, hospital mistakes like Berwid and mass killers like Berkowitz who were chillingly and inevitably mentally ill no matter what anyone said. The public was not inclined to sift among these problems for the few patients who might be deserving of an insanity defense.

And the mental health establishment no longer wanted to be the whipping boy of public criticism. Fault was regularly found with how they treated barely treatable patients in the hospitals or in the "least restrictive alternatives," welfare hotels or adult homes. The department could be sued or harassed both for keeping people and for releasing people. In the context of inadequate funding, the department contained dangerous and/or criminally committed criminals in insecure facilities without adequate personnel and no longer wanted the responsibility. Personnel at Mental Health would have been glad to see the entire problem turned over to the Department of Corrections. Everyone, it seemed—the public, the politicians and the Department of Mental Hygiene—wanted the NGRI, the venerable symbol of benevolence, to die.

Originally, in the days when hanging was the invariable punishment for major crimes, the insanity law became a vehicle for leniency, for sparing a few defendants whose criminal intent was questionable. Even after the death penalty was voted out of existence, the law was retained. Theoretically, the need for its life-sparing protection was less since there was no death penalty, but it was in these latter years that the NGRI defense became most active. Now, as a part of the current punitive atmosphere and with the return of the death penalty as an imminent issue in New York State, there was clamor to get rid of the insanity defense.

Up to now I had always felt that prudent psychiatrists could have insured the proper use of the NGRI. I agreed with the view of Judge Bazelon, a respected jurist and authority, that the outcome of cases had rather less to do with the particular insanity formula used by any one jurisdiction and much more to do with the competence of the expert and the court. But by 1980, the willfulness factor was increasingly evident in the psychotic men I evaluated.

They might fit the NGRI but they were not exactly "good guys" because they had clearly aggressive if not psychopathic histories. Winning NGRI verdicts with hospital placement for such men had undoubtedly helped to erode public confidence in the criminal justice system and the field of psychiatry. In spite of the fact that many of my colleagues scrutinized and eliminated those cases where the willfulness factor was clear, I was apprehensive that psychiatry in general would be unable to provide the consistent and reasonable testimony that would safeguard the public from the misuse of the defense. Experts on release committees for hospitalized NGRI patients were too often finding that the patients had *never* been psychotic!

Maybe it was time to retire the NGRI. At the worst, the convicted men would be treated in prison and segregated—like Berkowitz—from the rest of the prison population if their condition required it. (Berkowitz has been transferred from Attica to a special segregated treatment facility at Clinton Prison.)

To the surprise of many—including me—the NGRI did not die. The New York State Law Revision Committee reported to the Governor on May 2, 1980, that they had voted to keep it intact. They explained that a few wrong calls should not doom the old institution and that moreover, with its removal, there would be inevitable problems in constitutionality. The demand for public safety had created the commission: their response to the public took the form of recommending that the old NGRI be teamed with new procedural safeguards against the release of mentally ill, dangerous patients.

In outlining their ideas, the commission explained the shortcomings of two other substitute plans that had been considered. One was the "bifurcated trial," which required two separate trial procedures, the first to clarify the issue of the defendant's guilt, the second to deal with his sanity. The flaw in the "bifurcated trial" was that it ran afoul of court-mandated due-process guarantees. If an individual is found guilty on the facts in the first part of the trial, it tends to presume guilt (sanity) on the second issue.

The commission had also ruled out the "guilty but mentally ill" verdict which had been widely discussed. This verdict, the

GMI, could be found if the defendant was guilty of the crime and mentally ill, but *not* legally insane at the time of the crime. (He was not sick enough to satisfy the standards for an NGRI defense.) Someone judged "guilty but mentally ill" would go to prison and if it became necessary, be treated there. Bills proposing the GMI had been authored by State Senator Padavan, the energetic chairman of the Senate Mental Health Committee, but legislation had never passed. The Law Revision Commission's point of view was that GMI was not significantly different from the current New York State law and its availability would confuse juries into thinking of it as a too-convenient middle ground between guilty and NGRI.

If the commission's findings clashed with the views of the conservative senator, they also offered a confusing package to Governor Carey. Carey had strongly favored the diminished capacity defense and now it was included only as a companion to the retained and "safeguarded" NGRI. It had not become the NGRI's successor.

A bill embodying the commission's recommendations would soon be presented to the legislature and I assumed that it would become law. As a member of the Law and Psychiatry Committee of the State Psychiatric Association, I took the opportunity to describe my misgivings. The committee asked that I submit my critique at the next meeting. A detailed memorandum (see Appendix B) accompanied my presentation at the joint meeting of the New York State Medical Society and the Psychiatric Association's Committee on Law and Psychiatry. That was on May 20, 1980.

In addressing the group, I agreed that the NGRI seemed to be here to stay and that the security against casual release of dangerous mental patients was a step in the right direction. But I hoped to make them aware that contriving this complicated new legal combination of diminished capacity and NGRI would open the door to more misuse. The increased defense opportunities for the mentally ill, over and above what was formerly provided (and abused) under NGRI would absolutely insure confusion. There were no controls in the bill and the misuse sure to follow would bring an inevitable public reaction. In the end no one

227

would be served, neither the defendants nor the professionals nor the system. I ended by saying that this law demanded its *own* provision to prevent overutilization and made a specific, practical recommendation of how it could be accomplished. I abstained from voting on the proposal as it stood.

The Law and Psychiatry Committee voted to endorse it.

But the bill that actually passed in the state legislature and was signed into law a few weeks later had absolutely no mention of the diminished capacity feature I had spoken against. Besides the political reasons for the decision to withdraw the provision from the bill, I was interested to hear from one DA's office that my memo had been helpful in arguments to exclude it.

At this writing, by my best estimate, there are six other state legislatures currently trying to modify the NGRI: Wisconsin, New Hampshire, Florida, California, Tennessee and Illinois. Three others, Michigan, Montana and Indiana, are going with the verdict of "guilty but insane." These states are making an effort to clarify the confusing business of who the "good guys" are and to tailor their NGRI formulas so that they can sift them from the others. The once considerable symbolic worth of the NGRI defense has been devalued and its humane standard seen by many as just another loophole in the law. A proper respect and credibility for the system can only come when defendants are convinced that there are no convenient technical gaps through which they can escape.

The really serious loophole is my old problem at Bellevue—defendants avoiding prosecution by being found incompetent. Much has improved at Bellevue: the courtroom and the prison ward are still there but the population of N,O-2 is half its former size and the men who wait in Bellevue's gloomy halls today are processed by a bigger staff in expanded offices. The burden of evaluation has been taken over by clinics in the courthouses and prisons. A special facility for observation and treatment of defendants and convicts has replaced the ugly old Mental Observation unit at Rikers. All these things are pluses, but the basic problem of malingerers persists. Out of thousands of yearly evaluations, at least half of the 1100 men currently sent to New York State hospitals on these criminal commitments each year have their charges terminated. So many of them have had prior arrests that it's fair to say that somebody is beating the rap! Criminal justice authorities were generally unaware of the problem of revolving-door "incompetent" defendants when I first wrote about determined malingerers to the Manhattan DA in 1968 (see Appendix A). Finally, in 1981, new legislation will revamp release procedures.

Criminally committed men must now be carefully evaluated before their release from the hospital. Financial and constitutional problems associated with preventing escapes and monitoring the patients' mental status on release will certainly arise. I have shared my opinion that the best way to avoid such problems is to start when patients are screened for commitment, not after they have reached the hospital. Methods must be found to ensure that the patients selected for commitment are first screened carefully for malingerers and those identified as such are firmly controlled to keep them from pressuring their way to hospital commitment. It's as important and practical to control opportunistic, criminally prone bug-outs today as it was when I served on Bellevue's prison ward.

Let's take a look at another problem altogether. Crime and violence in the United States are the acknowledged result of multiple socioeconomic factors, but sometimes those factors are not so obvious. In this book, one of my major concerns has been the media's role in the motivation of criminal behavior, particularly among the mentally vulnerable. Beginning in the sixties, I noticed that many people I evaluated professionally were definitely influenced by the media messages of those counterculture times, glorifying certain political and social attitudes and behavior. The anti-Establishment atmosphere prompted some to pacifism and life on a commune; others gave histories of instant political conversions resulting in belligerent political protests and bombs. Sometimes there was sudden criminality in someone without a record who had decided that criminal behavior *was* political protest!

Communications licensed other kinds of criminal behavior. They reinforced the idea that drug addicts had to commit crimes in order to support their habits. Long after experienced clinicians were recognizing that many so-called addicts were less hooked on drugs than on the criminal lifestyle of which drug abuse was merely one part, the media continued to describe them as sick and needing treatment. I observed an escalation in the degree of criminal conduct: men often went from burglaries to armed robberies with the rationalization that "the habit" made them do it.

At the same time, and more pertinent to a clinician, I observed that certain social and occupational misfits, self-indulgent and grandiose, were influenced to commit aggressive and antisocial acts by specific television example. These people, in a borderline mental state or completely out of touch with reality, might imitate exactly what they saw on television, from homicide to suicide. (Suicide was copied far more often.) They could all savor in advance what the media's treatment of their behavior would be and their quest for celebrity was the stuff of which assassinations are made. (Didn't the men who shot Pope John Paul and John Lennon admit that they had alternative celebrity targets in mind?)

When this book had been completed, I sought to confirm some of my clinical impressions. The major question was—and is—"Does media cause violence?" But my particular interest was television's motivating effect on a special audience—could it make psychotics become killers? Son of Sam was the worst example of this influence that I personally had seen.

I was not satisfied by the results of my reading on the subject and decided to ask the best-known experts for their views. Those I spoke to felt that there was a relationship between TV violence and viewer behavior. They described some startlingly direct connections—show a TV drama with a hostage-extortion theme in such widely separated places as California, Australia and Alaska and you can expect a real-life copy of the TV story in each locale after each show!

Americans, with a historical attitude that licenses us to react violently to emotional impetus, are susceptible to TV violence. Other cultures are less susceptible. The television networks are fond of citing the incredible violence on Japanese TV—it tops ours—pointing out that it is not reflected in Japan's crime rate. What the networks don't emphasize is that Japanese culture and

230

society place an extremely high value on control in emotional expression, while we do not! I am not suggesting that average American children, who see 13,000 killings on TV before they graduate from high school, are necessarily disposed to commit murder. Media violence must be modified by many other inhibiting or facilitating factors to explain our levels of crime and violence.

Research from one academic center deemphasizes real life modeling of aggressive social behavior against others (becoming a killer) as a consequence of exposure to media violence, suggesting instead that television's worst effects are on its viewers (worrying about being killed). It's contended that heavy viewers may begin to see reality as scary, especially if they belong to the groups most consistently victimized on television. Women and senior citizens, for example, can become anxious, trust few people, overestimate the existence of criminals and danger all about them—perhaps even develop a "victim set" that sends out psychological messages of fear, inviting plunder.

How does the television industry see its own responsibility? I interviewed some past and present chiefs of the broadcast standards departments of national networks. (Networks' designations for the departments may vary, but broadcast standards is the name that best describes their function.) In addition to their own staffs, networks employ or use the consultant services of psychologists, psychiatrists, educators and sociologists in an effort to determine what might be negatively received by their audiences. Enormous energy goes into reviewing programs (and commercials, too) for inappropriate sexual or violent themes, action and dialogue, as well as answering complaints or forestalling them by finding out in advance what various community power and special interest groups will tolerate before controversial material is televised. But they go only to this point. Beyond it, network managements and their lawyers cite the constitutional right of creative people to freedom of expression. At the same time, they suggest that the public does not have to view what it finds offensive and can always change the channel. In reply to studies correlating television violence with violence in the real world, they can point to other studies that contradict, or at least cloud the issue, and support their denial that American television audiences have become scared and passive. After eight congressional hearings, the controversy goes on.

The networks don't deny that some disturbed or otherwise inadequate people can be stimulated to commit antisocial or criminal acts. But they ask, "Why should TV, which serves such a large, diverse audience, change its programming to avoid negative influences on a small, unhealthy portion of the population?"

The answer, in plain English, is that the size of the vulnerable population is not really known and may be less important than the kinds of crime they can be influenced to commit. Son of Sam, one man, murdered six victims, injured seven others, and had plans to commit wholesale homicide with a submachine gun along the main street of a summer resort.

Certain mentally vulnerable viewers don't understand that the ordinary people shown on television are far from ordinary. They get the idea that TV-style job and social success should be theirs, even when their obvious (if unrecognized) personality handicaps make it improbable. Brooding on poverty or isolation, they fantasize taking retaliatory action to cure their discontent. They may still need some rationale and format to be bad—and television seems to have provided it. Without being aware of it, the viewer has witnessed a kind of distortion of moral behavior in stories that make violence seem acceptable.

The industry long ago recognized that there is less exposure to public criticism if they present stories in which violence is done by the good guys we call heroes. (Statistics show that today there are more superheroes doing bloody violence on television than villains.) This kind of character taking the law into his own hands is a common theme, usually avenging his honor or the death of a relative. And for over a decade, the movies have been presenting antiheroes and psychopaths in central roles: outlaws are now breezy heroes. The handsome, good-humored Paul Newman or Robert Redford type robs a bank, shoots up everyone in sight, outdrives the police and makes it to safety with his girl friend by his side. The message for anyone without a normal set of references to distinguish between real life and TV or movie fantasy is that the Establishment is arbitrarily stupid or cruel and that violence is okay because the good-guy heroes are doing it. It's not much effort for such a person, with his susceptible mentality, to turn himself into an "avenger" for a good cause. Through the centuries, disturbed people have self-indulgently, grandiosely allowed themselves to take a transparently personal vengeance in the guise of striking back at social or political inequity. Today—with all the causes to choose from, with all the weapons and explosives to disrupt a modern society—what opportunities for an "avenger"!

As pervasive as TV violence can be, the experts I polled did not think that violence alone was sufficient to produce psychotic killers, and particularly a multiple murderer like Son of Sam. For that, a variety of other factors must coincide.

The person who is "killer material" must have a disordered personality. When he has a notion to kill, he must be physically up to it and have access to weapons. His work or social situation must make it easy for him to plan the killings and do them; isolation, idleness, or perhaps the kind of undemanding job (or wife) that does not inhibit him in his disordered ideas.

Potential multiple killers can get their ideas from reading about others, and many are fans of celebrated murderers. They also have strange beliefs that act as built-in excuses for committing violence: command hallucinations or the delusion that they are under someone's absolute control (demonic or divine). These common ideas understandably have the effect of removing inhibitions. Another notion common to psychotic killers is that they are on a mission *to do good*. This frees them to act homicidally. What presidential (or papal) assassin did not insist that his cause was a good one?

In times past, psychotics had to contrive their rationalizations for themselves. But today, the unstable segment of the population for whom TV is reality is being sold a prepackaged message which confuses them about right and wrong. People who act on what they see ought not to be confused. The media's contribution to an act of criminal violence by repeated deliberate ambiguity is one more imponderable in the psychiatrist's dilemma—whether he can see someone as good or bad in deciding on an NGRI. Clearly the messages we are getting about what is moral behavior should be decoded before the situation grows worse.

A generation ago, the creation of the third national TV network led to a competition for viewers that resulted in a noticeably poorer quality of programming with more emphasis on sex and violence. Today's burgeoning cable TV and UHF stations—understaffed, uncensored by network standards—will create more competition and further worsen quality.

The networks tend to deny that anything has worsened, dismissing statistics on violent behavior as inconclusive and saying that all is well with the majority of viewers. With some justification, they complain that they are everybody's whipping boy and the mere mention of outside control brings protest about infringement of their First Amendment rights.

Each network now regulates itself, but only to the point of remaining competitive with others for the advertising dollar. There is obviously no commercial benefit for one to operate at the highest standards. In fact, if networks were pressured to step up pornography and violence to match pay TV, there would be a greater advantage to flexible standards. But the squeeze is on. With greater competition, there is on the other side a greater counterforce of protest. Not long after my first inquiries at the networks in 1980, evidence of public pressure could be seen. In the reaction to epidemic violent crime, a groundswell of activist protest against programming excesses had developed. One national group announced its aim of reducing TV violence by 75 percent (back to 1950s decade levels), hoping to do it by naming and organizing a boycott of those major advertisers sponsoring the most offensive shows. Today, the Moral Majority has evolved as a force to be reckoned with and even though many concerned citizens are mobilized against it, others of liberal persuasion are demanding everything from an imposed rating system on all TV presentations to straight censorship. It may not be enough this time around for the networks to promise less prime time violence and wait till things cool off. Instead, it could be advantageous for the networks to get together now in their own joint effort toward a genuine and sustaining improvement. Why not an internetwork planning and advisory group to appraise and set standards on all valid objectionable factors in programming, not just violence?

Individual broadcast standards departments have shown some sporadic initiative in attempts to be more than reactive and to promote certain types of quality programming. (ABC's documentaries on the lives of American Indians and the problems of homosexuals were described to me as good examples.) I did not establish, however, that they independently explored ways of identifying and countering adverse effects of general programming through the use of other messages. As a group they could agree to such a mission.

Some simple abuses are easy to spot and moderate. If there were complaints about TV's portrayal of police officers and if a review of prime time programming did indeed show that too many country sheriffs came on as noisy nitwits for too many seasons, then the group could make a recommendation to avoid such characterizations in the future.

The problem of identifying more subtle objectionable themes such as "vengeance" and "ambiguous heroes" which influence the vulnerable in the audience is more complicated. Composing specific inhibitory messages to defuse grandiosity and violence is problematic—but not impossible. Conventional TV melodrama can be used to show occasionally that the heroic characters acting out of self-centered beliefs are later revealed as sick. If the lone crusader is seen often enough at the program's end as a pathetic misfit on a head trip, that role as a vehicle for psychotics might diminish.

Aside from correcting objectionable themes, the group might even suggest ways in which communications could deliberately include helpful messages in addition to the public service spot announcements we now have. It would be in order to present a deliberately planned series of messages accurately describing psychiatric symptoms and conditions and how help may be obtained. This might compensate for the dramatic license regularly taken in the presentation of mental illness on soap operas. It might even dispel the too rosy representation of schizophrenia as a disease with a positive cure.

Obviously, using television for therapeutic messages can go only so far. I am speaking as a concerned psychiatrist in advocating changes and controls and don't pretend to an acquaintance with the practical considerations of such network coordination. But for the problems with which I have some familiarity, it seems a reasonable approach. And the time is now. If pay TV offers accelerated porn and violence and precipitates a more controlling federal regulatory body or other outside censoring agency, the commercial networks' own competitiveness and resistance on this score will have been responsible.

Regardless of who does the controlling, the number-one priority is danger to the public. From my point of view, the first best move to be made after a reduction in overall violence is a resolution to identify and limit the kinds of stories that tamper with the concept of good and bad for the sake of salable violence.

It may be that only a small segment of viewers is so influenced, but the fact that homicide victims are only a small part of the population has not yet served as an excuse for murderers. I'd like to see preventive measures started before too many more multiple killers and assassins force us to recognize them as media creatures, and before it's also recognized that they are a growing segment of our population.

Appendix A

September 27, 1968

Mr. Conboy, Assistant DA
155 Leonard Street
New York, N.Y. 10013

Dear Mr. Conboy:

I am sorry I have been unable to locate the more or less formal description of the "revolving door" patient that I made mention of. However, I hope this note will lend you some understanding of the problem.

Most of our patients are referred by the Criminal Court. Perhaps 20% are referred by the Supreme Court.

1. In the latter cases if evaluation leads to commitment under 662 C.C.P., the patient is usually sent to Matteawan State Hospital. Charges are not terminated and the man must face a return to the legal process when his condition is improved. It is noteworthy that this can be a stimulus to malingering in that a reduced plea may be more available to the defendant on major cases on the basis of his having been sent to Matteawan as incompetent. In effect, I am saying that it is definitely potentially profitable for a man who is facing trial on a major charge to feign mental disorder.

2. More frequent problems, however, are criminal repeaters who are very aware if convicted under 872 C.C.P. as a misdemeanant that the charges are generally terminated. We have seen cases in which these persons are sent to civil state hospitals from which they easily escape and go on to repeat crimes of violence before they are again apprehended. In some instances, these men have managed to be hospitalized prior to the time that an indictment was obtained, and thus avoided the prosecution which could otherwise be anticipated.

It is obvious that a man who is institution wise will make many efforts to be committed. Even if he is once found competent here, he can manipulate to be returned here time and again and by one or another act obtain commitment. The usual procedure for such individuals to use is to become unruly in the detention center, and act or pretend to act in what is thought a suicidal or aggressive manner. The particular tactics used differ with the individual defendant and situation. As often as we have tried, we have been unable to maintain certain unstable but competent persons in the detention milieu who manage to return to our facility so often we call them "revolving door" cases.

Sincerely,

/s/Martin I. Lubin, M.D.
Chief, Prison Ward

238

Appendix B

TO: Joint Meeting of NYS Medical Society Committee on
Mental Health — NYS Psychiatric Association Committee on Law and Psychiatry, May 30, 1980

FROM: Martin I. Lubin, M.D.

RE: Law Revision Commission Report on the Defense of
Insanity in NY State

The Commission Report on May 2, 1980, was presented to the Psychiatric Association at its Law and Psychiatry Committee Meeting
of May 20. In so far as I dissented from the general view to endorse the report, I am submitting the following written critique to
clarify my position and offer possible options. In particular, I
would discuss their two major recommendations.

    I.   Retention of the Insanity Defense

    II.   Introduction of a Codified Diminished Capacity Defense

I. We are all aware that, over the years, the real problem in the
mishandling of the mentally ill offender has been related to the
matter of competency and not to the matter of responsibility as reflected by the NGRI defense. This notwithstanding, the NGRI is
very visible and is a focus for public criticism. The public is right,

for example, to be offended by the four-fold increase in frequency of successful pleas when joined to the fact that substantial numbers of these individuals have had prior arrests. They are also right to be outraged by infrequent, but frightening incidents following casual release or elopement. They lump NGRIs with their belief that they are in danger and that the criminals are getting away with something.

The Law Revision Commission's proposed Act is responsive to what the public has identified as troublesome. As its acknowledged major recommendation, it outlines methods to control the dangerous individuals, after they have been found not responsible for their crimes and hospitalized. Indeed, this control factor may ensure a feeling of public safety and may actually act to decrease the total number of inappropriate NGRIs. This, of course, is laudable.

II. With the NGRI thus retained in a controlled form, their recommendation of a diminished capacity defense unfortunately brings to our attention the existence of a larger problem. We cannot avoid cognizance of our responsibility for a situation where there is frank statistical validation for large numbers of committed and NGRI patients having prior arrest records. We have criminalized the state hospital population even as the census has been markedly reduced. At the very least, it reveals an inadequate understanding by professionals in both law and psychiatry of those defendants the law was meant to assist—an inability to identify which defendants were mainly willful and which were inadvertent offenders. It is my opinion that the Commission's recommendation of "diminished capacity" as a now codified alternative defense will propel numerous psychiatric presentations to mitigate criminal intent. Such testimony is designed to assist defendants with "psychotic judgment" who may not quite fit the NGRI formula. Whereas this liberalization would be desirable in selected cases (especially since we now have a budget for mental health treatment once those defendants reach prisons), it will unfortunately create great confusion in its applications and open a door to further imprudent expert testimony from various behavioral disciplines. We have had no controls on naïve or self-serving attorneys and expert witnesses. In times past, inconsistent and sometimes absurd testimony has been observed by the public and has been painfully embarrassing to our specialty. Can we not assume that the same brand of poor judgment previously exhibited will be responsible for an inevitable increase in the number of inappropriate reduced pleas via the "diminished capacity" route? Will we then not be embarrassed on a grander scale?

240

The district attorneys complain about their budgets now. If they hire psychiatrists to respond to these new pleas, we may see more embarrassing and costly battles. If they don't, and I think this is just as probable, we may see them intimidated by defense experts and simply lay back and surrender reduced pleas to even those defendants with significant arrest records.

I cannot endorse the act as it is presented. I think the problem of confusion as to the utilization of diminished capacity in connection with criminal intent by both attorneys and psychiatrists will make for arbitrary elaboration.

Index

INDEX

INDEX

INDEX